"Using his gift for informed and inventive prose, and applying it to an unexplored topic, Paul Thompson has given us a unique view of masculinity in the lesbian-themed paperback fiction of the mid-20th Century."

Ann Bannon, author of the Laura Landon /
Beebo Brinker novels

"Opening a critically neglected and often maligned archive of popular lesbian paperbacks from the mid-20th century, Thompson's clear and accessible study fundamentally reshapes our understanding of American masculinity and sexuality."

Benjamin Bateman, author of *Queer
Disappearance in Modern and
Contemporary Fiction*

Masculinity in Lesbian "Pulp" Fiction

This book looks specifically and in depth, for the first time, at masculinity in cheap, lesbian-themed paperbacks of the two decades after WW2. It challenges established critical assumptions about the readership, and sets the masculinity imagined in these novels against the "masculinity crisis" of the era in which they were written.

The key issue of these novels is couplehood as much as sexuality, and the instability of masculinity leads to the instability of the couple. Thompson coins the term "heteroemulative" to describe the struggle that both heterosexual and homosexual couples have in conforming to heteronormativity.

As several of these novels have been republished and remain in print, they have taken on a new relevance to issues of sexuality and gender in the twenty-first century, and this study will attract readers within that area of interest. A valuable read for sociologists studying gender roles, and social historians of the cold war period in the United States. It is suitable for readers of all academic levels, from undergraduate, through postgraduate, to scholars and researchers, but also for a general readership.

Paul Thompson, PhD from University of St Andrew's, Scotland, is a former career civil servant who, on retirement, decided to become a scholar. Paul's research continues in lesbian-themed paperbacks, not only looking at the erasure of diversity and the overlap of trans narratives but also setting up an archive of the paperbacks in Special Collections at the Library of the University of St Andrews. Paul's most recent publication is a chapter outlining the philosophical influences on Sebald in *W.G. Sebald in Context*.

Routledge Research in Gender and Society

Epistolary Narratives of Love, Gender and Agonistic Politics
An Arendtian Approach
Maria Tamboukou

Re-Thinking Men:
Heroes, Villains and Victims (2e)
Anthony Synnott

My Body, My Choice, My Gun
Women and Firearms in the USA
Peter Squires

What is Sexualized Violence?
Intersectional Readings
Jana Schäfer

Queering Desire
Lesbians, Gender and Subjectivity
Edited by Róisín Ryan-Flood and Amy Tooth Murphy

Equality Dancesport
Gender and Sexual Identities Matter
Yen Nee Wong

Asexualities
Feminist and Queer Perspectives, Revised and Expanded Ten-Year Anniversary Edition
Edited by KJ Cerankowski and Megan Milks

Masculinity in Lesbian "Pulp" Fiction
Disappearing Heteronormativity?
Paul Thompson

For more information about this series, please visit: https://www.routledge.com/Routledge-Research-in-Gender-and-Society/book-series/SE0271

Masculinity in Lesbian "Pulp" Fiction
Disappearing Heteronormativity?

Paul Thompson

LONDON AND NEW YORK

First published 2024
by Routledge
4 Park Square, Milton Park, Abingdon, Oxon OX14 4RN

and by Routledge
605 Third Avenue, New York, NY 10158

Routledge is an imprint of the Taylor & Francis Group, an informa business

© 2024 Paul Thompson

The right of Paul Thompson to be identified as author of this work has been asserted in accordance with sections 77 and 78 of the Copyright, Designs and Patents Act 1988.

All rights reserved. No part of this book may be reprinted or reproduced or utilised in any form or by any electronic, mechanical, or other means, now known or hereafter invented, including photocopying and recording, or in any information storage or retrieval system, without permission in writing from the publishers.

Trademark notice: Product or corporate names may be trademarks or registered trademarks, and are used only for identification and explanation without intent to infringe.

British Library Cataloguing-in-Publication Data
A catalogue record for this book is available from the British Library

Library of Congress Cataloging-in-Publication Data
Names: Thompson, Paul, 1950- author. Title: Masculinity in lesbian "pulp" fiction : disappearing heteronormativity? / Paul Thompson. Description: Abingdon, Oxon ; New York, NY : Routledge, 2024. | Series: Routledge research in gender and society | Originally presented as author's thesis (doctoral)--University of St. Andrews, 2023. | Includes bibliographical references and index. Identifiers: LCCN 2024004486 (print) | LCCN 2024004487 (ebook) | ISBN 9781032727981 (hardback) | ISBN 9781032727998 (paperback) | ISBN 9781003422679 (ebook) Subjects: LCSH: Lesbians' writings, American--History and criticism. | Pulp literature, American--History and criticism. | American fiction--20th century--History and criticism. | Masculinity in literature. | Lesbians in literature. | LCGFT: Literary criticism. Classification: LCC PS153.L46 T48 2024 (print) | LCC PS153.L46 (ebook) | DDC 813/.5409353--dc23/eng/20240403 LC record available at https://lccn.loc.gov/2024004486LC ebook record available at https://lccn.loc.gov/2024004487

ISBN: 978-1-032-72798-1 (hbk)
ISBN: 978-1-032-72799-8 (pbk)
ISBN: 978-1-003-42267-9 (ebk)

DOI: 10.4324/9781003422679

Typeset in Sabon
by Deanta Global Publishing Services, Chennai, India

To Archibald Pelago,

whoever he is.

Contents

	About the author	*x*
	Foreword	*xi*
	Preface	*xv*
	Introduction: A mass literacy event: Introducing the cheap lesbian paperback	1
I	Male agency, and "the immense social power that accumulates around masculinity?"	35
II	Female masculinity: Bannon, beebo, and butchness	73
III	Female masculinity beyond Beebo	107
IV	"Everybody gets married."	134
V	Conclusion: Failure and another normality	174
	Index	*189*

About the author

Paul Thompson is a former career civil servant who, on retirement, decided to become a scholar. He gained a 1st class BA Honours degree in English Literature with the Open University before going on to achieve an MSc With Distinction in Literature and Modernity at the University of Edinburgh, presenting a dissertation which used phenomenology as a tool of criticism for the works of W.G. Sebald. Paul's most recent publication is a chapter outlining the philosophical influences on Sebald in *W.G. Sebald in Context*.

Rekindling an interest in the ephemeral literature of the twentieth century, Paul's PhD thesis at the University of St Andrews, on which this book is based, won the Samuel Rutherford Prize for the most distinguished thesis in the fields of English, Theology, Church History, and Scottish History. Paul's research continues in lesbian-themed paperbacks, not only looking at the erasure of diversity and the overlap of trans narratives, but also setting up an archive of the paperbacks in Special Collections at the Library of the University of St Andrews.

Foreword

In this sensitive and acutely observed study, Paul Thompson takes on the fraught topic of masculinity in the "golden age" of lesbian fiction. It can be fairly said that Thompson has ventured where others have feared to tread. He has little, if any, competition in analyzing the presentation of masculine characters in these novels, nor in comparing them to straight men considered to behave normally. Other analysts appear to have satisfied themselves with the stereotypical male behaviors, and have done little or nothing to look beyond those. But Thompson does a convincing job of showing how narrowly the complexities of the male readership were perceived in the time period when lesbian fiction was being produced in quantity—not to mention the limited qualities of the male characters themselves in these novels. And he takes a quite original approach with the characters, viewing them in the light of "heteronormativity."

What, in fact, was normal in the 1950s? What qualities could be reliably supposed to be shared by "normal men" and why does the reader find them mirrored in the lives of gay men? This time period comes close after the end of World War II, and the yearning for normalcy in human affairs was widespread. Furthermore, the drive to emulate what was conceived to be the ideal couplehood of young people in the years preceding the war affected not only straight couples, but can be clearly seen in gay and lesbian pairs, as well. In point of fact, lesbians had severely limited models to guide them into a homosexual relationship of their own. Rather than covering a range of options, gay women were trained up on just two: the Butch and the Femme. And they were expected to behave within their relationship as a heteronormal couple, with the butch acting as the "husband" and the femme as the "wife." But the unlucky men had an unforgiving model of what was presented as male normalcy. It was this model that they strove to imitate, whatever their natural sexuality. And, to be fair, efforts to define the standards for manly behavior were undependable at best. One finds shifting standards applied, depending on the book in hand.

Thompson rejects the long-established term "pulp" for these novels. It is, he correctly observes, a "gate-keeping" label. Retrospectively, of course, it was descriptive of the cheap paper used to print these books, a purely practical decision, given that they were to be marketed more like magazines than

xii *Foreword*

respectable hard-cover tomes. Most, it was thought, would be thrown out as soon as the reader finished with them. I was somewhat startled myself to start thinking of them in this way, since I was writing, like most aspiring novelists, earnestly and from the heart. The paperback houses of that era were the only ones who would let me into the august company of published authors.

But merely to be published, and by the grace of such an impudent agency, did not compel respect. The term "pulp" has contaminated every aspect of publishing with which it was associated. The provocative cover art, designed to lure a male readership, was cheap and then shoddy and then disreputable and finally, sleazy. Sleazy came to characterize not only the paper and the cover art, but the content. How could sex among the LGBTQ+ community be anything but? Not only did it violate notions of normalcy, it was frankly illegal. The gay identity itself was against the law. One's mere existence was an affront to the delicate sensibilities of those born within the bounds of perceived heterosexual norms. To prove the point, the danger of allowing the young to read, or even to see, such writing (it could not be called "Literature" although some of it was) was thought to lure them into a life of sin. Reading a pulp paperback would convert children otherwise headed for a life of comfortable sexuality in the tradition of their progenitors, into a life of crime instead. And there goes the grand tradition of heteronormativity – whatever it may have been.

Thompson points out that there was a false claim perpetuated by male readers: that masculinity, poorly defined though it is, is the exclusive domain of those born male. It is still a disputed identity in this era of gender fluidity, non-binary, cisgender, transexual, pansexual, intersexed, polyamorous fellow citizens. Women, too, must now negotiate these identities. It is hard to declare one's pronouns in an age that rejects labels.

In the grand tradition of doctoral candidates everywhere, who expand and refine the lexicon in their field, Thompson, too, undertakes to enlarge our understanding with words. He has thus expanded the trove of ideas in LGBTQ+ studies. Among others, he gives us "heteroemulative" to describe how all couples, no matter how or why they are constituted, must strive against nature to conform to heteronormative standards. And another worth consideration: "Alconormativity." Drunkenness he defines as a "clear, overriding normality" in the pulps. Of course, many of the authors were writing about young people in their late teens and early twenties, and they are, as a group, hell-bent on rule bending and experimentation. I wrote my share of hearty drinking scenes, and alas, Thompson is correct – although I never drank as much as my characters did. The novels I wrote would never have been written, had that not been the case. We did drink, however, for several reasons: to escape the definitions of us imposed by others; to escape from parental disapproval and rejection; from confronting our suspected non-normal sexuality head-on; in mimicry of adult behavior; and as a claim of independence before we were ready for it. In other words, we learned to drink

Foreword xiii

foolishly before learning to drink responsibly, and thus staked our claim to an adulthood we had not yet achieved.

On a personal note, how did these discerning insights escape analysis from the women who did the actual writing of these stories? Were we too close to them, to the characters, to the tenor of the times? There were only about a dozen of us working seriously in this genre, but that dozen comprised bright, committed, brave women, or they would never have mustered the brass to do the work. Where, then, was their courage when a frank and balanced analysis of the men in their stories would have shed much welcome light? I wrote about several men myself, and the one who engaged my interest and was the most approachable was surely the mentor of Beebo Brinker, Jack Mann. Perhaps I really believed that my word portrait of Jack brought him whole and intact to the reader. But did it? Would not a more specific rendering in an essay separate from the fiction have given him an enlightening presence? The so-called presentation of self so valuable in real-world introductions? Where were my sister authors in this virtuous task? Where was I?

In due course, the reign of the pulp paperbacks began to fade. When this change occurred, the focus shifted more to gay men from lesbian women, as movies and television began a cautious exploration. The men were overwhelmingly portrayed as pathetic, at first; then as angry and beyond society's control; then as violent. It was about a sixty-year wait before the men in these public media became neighbors, family men, fathers, wits and wags. But these observations take us beyond the scope of Thompson's excellent study.

So, in fact, the key issue throughout this fascinating analysis is one of couplehood, and how it is handled in the best record we have of the nascent LGBTQ+ community – the paperback novels of the 1950s and early 1960s. For these were the years before community was truly an accurate word for those who believed themselves to be, or possibly to be, or certainly interested in being, lovers of a same-sex partner. Community was yet to come, a gift of courage, insight, and action from the young who were to constitute that community.

These novels, disreputable though they were, carried the twin gifts of hope and knowledge, flawed but the best then available, and thus held their place for many readers. They could tell you more than the doctors, the churchmen, the therapists, and the adults of all stripes in your orbit. They told you the truth – some of it, anyway – and that was more than information, that was life-saving. And they found a great many readers, eagerly seeking their true identity and a way to make it viable in a hostile and frankly fearful society. Trivial and transitory as they seemed to mainstream readers at the time, the paperback novels offered instructions for life to gay men and lesbians. The instructions may have been limited and less illuminating than their eager readers hoped, but they were available everywhere. They were in print. They knew something and shared it at great risk. The supposed authorities in every field knew nothing, and shared it complacently, confident in their one ace: normal people don't do these things. No wonder the pulps found a place, an xiv *Foreword*

eager audience, and a life that lasted until the television, movies, and hardcover publishers screwed up their courage and took up the cudgels.

Thompson has added an important new perspective to the tales these books tell, the difficulties in rendering the men in these novels accurately, just as it was challenging to define the model of masculinity they were expected to follow. But few authors seemed secure in the knowledge of what that might be. And this led to much experimentation, exploration, and expansion of knowledge – a task still in progress today.

Paul Thompson has read so many of the lesbian paperback novels produced in the so-called "pulp era," and his writing shows a necessary familiarity with the assumptions and conventions of the genre. He thus has a solid knowledge base and much to teach us about the attitude of mainstream society toward the gay community. Even more fascinating, he shows us the received verities and biases of the gay community itself, and how its members struggled to conform where they had to, and to push for their own identity where they could. His research is a valuable enlargement of LGBTQ+ studies and will make a useful addition to every gay library.

Ann Bannon, Ph.D.
Stanford University, 1975
Author of the Laura Landon / Beebo Brinker novels
Associate Dean, College of Arts and Letters, Ret.
California State University, Sacramento

Preface

It may be unusual to write a book having not intended to in the first place, but in fact there is a certain amount of serendipity involved in how this book came to be. I have been an avid reader all my life, and since I was mocked, in my teens, by a schoolteacher, for expressing a liking for the 'Saint' novels of Leslie Charteris, I have stubbornly tried to fill in the ditch that has been dug between "popular" and "canonical" literature. My lifelong love of Shakespeare for example, kindled when I was ten and at an age when I couldn't hope to understand what was going on, has resolutely remained that of a groundling – one of the *polloi* for whom Shakespeare actually wrote. Notwithstanding this, somehow I ended up at university writing essays on Samuel Beckett, a dissertation and a journal article in which I used phenomenology as a tool of literary criticism for the works of W.G. Sebald, and a book chapter detailing the philosophical influences on Sebald. I never found the ditch untraversable and had always had a love for the cheap American paperbacks of the mid-twentieth century – I had a handful by Erle Stanley Gardner – without realising at the time how culturally important they had been. Even now some people must be shaking their heads at that idea.

Then at a time when I wondered what my next academic focus was going to be, a number of things seemed to happen at once. Some were trivial, like coming across an image online of the 1956 paperback edition of George Orwell's *Nineteen Eighty-Four*, its cover featuring the character Julia with a plunging neckline offsetting her "Anti-Sex League" badge. This chance encounter reintroduced "prolefeed" literature to my attention. Then I found out that Patricia Highsmith, whose storytelling I admired, had written a novel, under an assumed name, that had become a classic of "lesbian pulp." From there I discovered the novels of Ann Bannon, Valerie Taylor, Randy Salem, et al., and began to appreciate their position in queer history, and in particular in the history of post-war lesbian culture. Looking at critical sources, I became convinced that writing that had taken this sub-genre seriously had, whilst being valuable as far as it went, had been both scattershot and theory-led. There was an opening for a book-length study, and one that looked at the corpus from a different angle. For a start, although the novels were about women, there were many prominent male characters, sometimes driving the narrative along, sometimes as a conventional foil to the women

xvi *Preface*

at the heart of the narrative. What, I wondered, did these male characters say about the masculinity of the day, and how did their masculinity strike the novelists who created them? Then, the importance of Ann Bannon's celebrated character Beebo Brinker, Randy Salem's Christopher Hamilton, and other women whose presentation and behaviour could be counted as masculine – did their presence argue against masculinity being solely the possession of men? Would the answers to these questions have any relevance to the way gender is looked at in the twenty-first century? These were among the critical questions I asked myself as I began my research.

It is in the nature of research that one sometimes finds oneself led to make a necessary right-angled turn, and so I found myself looking at many other aspects of gender and sexuality, at the concept of the couple, at the concept of butch-femme relationships, at characters who were not content to fit into those neat stereotypes, and at the whole issue of gender and the strain on heteronormativity during the two decades after World War II. The more the work went on, the more difficult it got to find adequate definitions for such concepts as masculinity. The texts I was studying, whether any among them passed muster for literary quality or not, gave me surprise after surprise, and some of the *idées fixes* that existed about these novels began to seem inadequate. One of the surprises was that I enjoyed reading them, even though some of them made me raise an eyebrow or roll my eyes. I could easily imagine myself walking down a street in an American city, spotting a rack of cheap novels on a newsstand, and buying one to read as I rode the subway home. Whenever I gave a talk about these novels, I would call a couple of people from the audience and let them slip a book into their jacket pocket or handbag because that would put them a little in touch with the physicality of these small, slim volumes, and they would appreciate them more as cultural objects, not simply something containing text. I found myself arguing that literature, or indeed culture as a whole, is indeed like a pick-and-mix store, and nothing is forbidden from the selection. I would read aloud from Frank O'Hara's poem "The Day Lady Died" to show how one person found nothing strange about mixing hamburgers, milkshakes, Jazz, and Strega liqueur with Ghanaian poetry, Verlaine, and Brendan Behan. Or, in my case, mixing study at the august University of St Andrews with the cheap, throwaway cultural ephemera of 1950s America. I also found myself having to look at aspects of American sociology, in order to make sense of the place that cheap novels occupied, and in particular the cheap novels that told stories of love and sex between women. Within the novels I even found grey areas where gay and transgender overlapped, and importantly I found that, although a boundary between the two was never sharp, neither erased the other.

There were some barriers to this research. It was both good news and bad news to find a community of avid collectors of mid-twentieth-century paperbacks. Good news because the online community of such collectors provided me with a lot of background information that is missing from academic books and articles; from that community I pick out collectors such as

Todd Mason and Gary Farber for acknowledgement – they are cited in this book. The bad news is that as paperbacks of that era are now highly collectable, their rarity has forced the price up. No longer can they be picked up in thrift shops and garage sales. Books such as Claire Morgan's *The Price of Salt* and Fred Haley's *Satan was a Lesbian* now command three-figure prices. Some books from this era have been republished, but most have not. Even where they have, the originals still command a high price. In sourcing originals, I had enormous, valuable help from Lisa Vecoli, former archivist at the University of Minnesota and herself a collector, who was even kind enough to lug a box of books for me from the United States to Scotland, when she came here on a golfing trip. I amassed a modest collection, all of which is being turned over, little by little as I finish studying each book, to Special Collections at the Library of the University of St Andrews – the intention is to set up an archive which, though it may not ever rival some of the academic and public collections in North America, may well be the first such collection of mid-twentieth-century lesbian-themed novels on this side of the Atlantic. The books I have managed to bring together will probably have come much further, in "air miles," than their publishers might have thought possible.

On the way to becoming a book, my research manifested itself as a PhD thesis which won the Samuel Rutherford Prize at St Andrews in 2023. I must thank several academic colleagues, friends, and acquaintances whose presence while I was researching proved to be vital. Dr Zoë Carroll of the Open University was the person who encouraged me in the discipline of research in the first place. Dr Benjamin Bateman of the University of Edinburgh nudged my research in a particular direction. My colleague and friend Dr Katerina García-Walsh, with whom I collaborated on a number of projects while we were both at the University of St Andrews, offered me criticism and advice that often made me see things from a different angle. Dr James Purdon of the University of St Andrews provided a valuable and steadying oversight during my research, and guidance about the process of getting published. Dr William Zachs, Director of the Blackie House Library and Museum in Edinburgh, by a subtle osmosis of which maybe even he was unaware, encouraged me to look at book collecting as both an academic discipline and a delight. Beyond these there have been so many friends, too many to list, from and beyond the universities with which I have studied – if anybody is reading this who knows or knew me, then chances are you will at some time have said more than an encouraging word, so consider yourself thanked.

Of course I owe a great deal of gratitude to my family, to Stephanie Thompson and Ruth Thompson, for their patience during a time when they would have been forgiven for feeling relegated to second place in my life. Their support for and pride in what I was doing have been priceless.

I have always been of the opinion that it is no use wondering about something when one could ask, and I never hesitated to pester professionals, academics, or writers when I thought they might have greater knowledge about something, which, when put together with existing knowledge, would make

xviii   *Preface*

a picture clearer and more detailed. I always hoped that I was asking something that hadn't been asked before, and that they would have the patience to bear with me and answer. I did exchange a couple of emails with Marijane Meaker, whom readers of lesbian-themed paperbacks will know as Vin Packer, and I wish we could have had a greater correspondence that I could thank her for. However, she is no longer with us, and a link with that era has gone with her departure. I can certainly thank Jennifer M. Lynch, Archivist at the U.S. Postal Service, for her help with information about official procedures of examining and seizing mail in the 1950s. The best known and best loved author of lesbian paperbacks' "golden age" is, of course, Ann Bannon. Ann deserves my special thanks, for putting up with my emails over the past few years, for giving me the benefit of her recollections, and for doing so with extreme courtesy and kindness. Without her, this book would be a lot poorer. It has been an honour.

Paul Thompson
Perth, Scotland

Introduction

A mass literacy event: Introducing the cheap lesbian paperback

Tonight, the Better America Forum brings to your attention the monumental problem confronting your children today – the ever-growing threat and menace of the cheap pulps found on all newsstands [...][1]

Background to an investigative project: Why this field of research?

In 2006 Barbara Grier in the introduction to the Arsenal Pulp Press edition of Valerie Taylor's *Whisper Their Love*, wrote:

What can possibly be gained by reprinting yet another novel that is clearly a historical artifact, one with a view of lesbianism that can best be described as archaic? Especially now, when collection after collection of lesbian-created erotica is easily available, when lesbian families dominate our literature, when lesbians write about all kinds of lesbian characters freely and openly in every literary genre, a time when our political writings go beyond mere homosexuality, to consider questions about the very fabric of gender itself.[2]

Yet republished it was – a quarter of a century after such novels were considered "boring and badly written," and generated anger amongst lesbian readers of that time[3] – as were others from a select canon garnered from the cheap paperback industry of the nineteen-forties, fifties, and sixties, many of which are still available in modern imprints,[4] while their original editions

---

1 Frank Tashlin, "Artists and Models," (Paramount, 1955).
2 Introduction to Valerie Taylor, *Whisper Their Love*, Little Sister's Classics, (Arsenal Pulp Press, 2006). 20.
3 Andrea Loewenstein, "Sad stories: a reflection on the fiction of Ann Bannon," *Gay Community News* (24th May 1980), tinyurl.com/LoewensteinBannon. Unnumbered.
4 Brian McHale refers to this recycling of a "low" genre as "high," as the "elevation of the cadet branch," attributing the phrase to Russian Formalist Yury Tynyanov. Brian McHale, "Genre Fiction," in *Routledge Encyclopedia of Narrative Theory*, ed. David Herman, Manfred Jahn, and Marie-Laure Ryan (Routledge, 2007). 199. The translation of Tynyanov I have refers to

DOI: 10.4324/9781003422679-1

2 Introduction

change hands between collectors for hundreds of pounds or dollars. At much the same time as Grier wrote the above, Yvonne Keller noted that "Lesbian pulps have so far mostly been ignored in the emerging field of lesbian/gay/ queer studies,"[5] and said that "[n]o book-length academic studies have been done."[6] If there is a single impetus behind this volume, then it is that statement by Keller. She goes on to list the work – mainly journal articles, chapters in edited collections, etc. – that actually had been done at the time of her writing, as well as the various republished novels. She mentions Christopher Nealon's *Foundlings* which, although book-length, does not deal exclusively with lesbian-themed fiction.[7] The only work of substantial length that has been done since then, up to the preparation of this book for publication, appears to have been three Doctoral theses and one Master's dissertation, all but one concentrating on the work of Ann Bannon. Melissa Sky's 2006 thesis examined the "bitextual" nature of Bannon's novels from the point of view of her "need to speak simultaneously to the desires of two sexually-differentiated audiences."[8] In 2008, S. Lou Stratton produced a thesis based on a study of the lesbian periodical *The Ladder*, in particular readers' discussions of lesbian-themed novels.[9] Malia McCarrick's 2010 thesis looked at the five Bannon novels "known as the Beebo Brinker series," and asked whether the portrayal of lesbian identity formation in them followed what science would later prove to be the stages most women actually go through when developing a lesbian identity.[10] As far as I can discover at the time of preparing this book, none of these theses has yet been developed into a monograph. Allyson Miller's 2009 dissertation is a much shorter study, covering Bannon's *I am a Woman*, and though it is headed "Postwar Masculine Identity [...]" its theme is narratology, and it deals specifically with focalisation within the text and

---

it as the "canonisation of the younger genres," attributing the phrase to Viktor Shklovsky, without reference; in this volume, I deal with books that have become "a fact of literature" by this process. Yuri Tynyanov, "The Literary Fact," in *Modern Genre Theory*, ed. David Duff (Routledge, 2000). 33, 41.

5 Yvonne Keller, "Ab/normal Looking: Voyeurism and surveillance in lesbian pulp novels and US Cold War Culture," *Feminist Media Studies* 5, no. 2 (2005). 178.

6 Keller, "Ab/normal Looking: Voyeurism and surveillance in lesbian pulp novels and US Cold War Culture." 191n1.

7 Keller, "Ab/normal Looking: Voyeurism and surveillance in lesbian pulp novels and US Cold War Culture." 192n1 cont. Ann Bannon, perhaps the best known author of the period, was very complimentary of Nealon's work, calling him "a fine young scholar." Personal email, 30th September 2018.

8 Melissa Sky, "Twilight Tales: Ann Bannon's Lesbian Pulp Series 'The Beebo Brinker Chronicles'" (PhD Thesis, McMaster University, 2006). iii.

9 S. Lou Stratton, "More Than Throw-Away Fiction: Investigating Lesbian Pulp Fiction through the Lens of a Lesbian Textual Community" (PhD Thesis, University of Birmingham, 2008).

10 Malia (Mary) L. McCarrick, "The Influence of Lesbian Identity Development on Lesbian Literature Through a Study of Character Experience in Ann Bannon's Beebo Brinker Series: A Creative Dissertation with Contextual Essay" (PhD Union Institute & University, 2010). i.

Introduction 3

how that enables male readers to "try on" alternate identities.[11] Beyond these there is a chapter in a 2011 thesis by Elizabeth M. Matelski, which deals with both the post-war butch-femme bar scene and the depiction of women in lesbian-themed novels,[12] but little else.

Text and time before theory. Theory where it is due

This book is an exploratory exercise and therefore its methodology throughout will be to pay close attention to the texts, and to refer to critical theories when they can help to illuminate what is found there. Apart from McCarrick's and Miller's work, referred to above, two things have characterised the study of these novels up to now: firstly, it has taken them out of their historic, cultural, and social context,[13] and secondly it has focused solely on female characters, has assumed a female readership, and has adopted the points of view of feminist, lesbian, or queer criticism, all of which are valid and vital critical positions. Melina Alice Moore, writing in 2019 specifically about Ann Bannon's character Beebo Brinker, says:

> The critical lens of queer theory, with its emphasis on unsettling the notion of stable gender identity, necessitates a reading that either erases Beebo's masculinity or interprets her cross-gender identification as an outmoded expression of homosexuality in relation to more fluidly defined characters. What would it mean to read Beebo's insistent masculine identification as an articulation of embodied experience, rather than an unfortunate relic of days and politics past?[14]

Moore goes on to make a telling argument for claiming the four novels that feature Beebo as "an integral part of the history of trans storytelling."[15] This interpretation may well be reinforced by Ann Bannon's recollection that

---

11 Allyson Miller, "Postwar Masculine Identity in Ann Bannon's *I am a Woman*" (MA University of Missouri-Columbia, 2009). v.

12 Elizabeth M. Matelski, "The Colour(s) of Perfection: The Feminine Body, Beauty Ideals, and Identity in Postwar America, 1945-1970" (Doctor of Philosophy Loyola U, 2011). 195-231.

13 I note that Tynyanov says: "The researcher who studies a work of literature out of context is in no way setting it beyond the reach of historical projections, he is merely approaching it with the wretched, imperfect historical apparatus of a contemporary from another age." Tynyanov, "The Literary Fact." 34.

14 Melina Alice Moore, "'A Boy Inside It': Beebo Brinker and the Transmasculine Narratives of Ann Bannon's Lesbian Pulp," *GLQ: A Journal of Lesbian and Gay Studies* 25, no. 4 (2019). 571. It is worth noting that the understanding of "trans" has moved – and is still moving – beyond the issue of hormonal and surgical transition ("transmedicalism"). *Trans**, the recent book by Jack Halberstam, is a relevant source for this issue. Jack Halberstam, *Trans** (U of California P, 2018).

15 Moore, "'A Boy Inside It': Beebo Brinker and the Transmasculine Narratives of Ann Bannon's Lesbian Pulp." 571.

4   *Introduction*

amongst the readers who sent letters to her, via her publisher, there were "also trans people, some of whom sent photos. They demonstrated considerable courage back in the 50s and 60s, when it was risky to confirm a gay identity, but downright dangerous to reveal rarer forms of queerness."[16] As far as I am aware, that in itself is a new piece of information in transgender history; I do not foreground it in this book, but I note it in the final chapter as an area of study that should be developed in the future.[17]

Interesting and persuasive as Moore's article is, it deals with one character from one author and, despite the interest shown by transgender readers, interprets that character as the author did not originally intend.[18] I deal with several novels from the sub-genre of cheap, lesbian-themed paperbacks. I do not pre-suppose a particular theoretical orthodoxy, but rather acknowledge the unsettled and unsettling nature of queer theory.[19] I find queer theory useful inasmuch as it sees sexuality and gender as social and cultural phenomena, tending to break down traditional assumptions about them and about heteronormativity.[20] As this book looks at the way sexuality and gender were portrayed in fiction created during a period in American history when social change and increased affluence impacted with political and sexual conservatism, its conclusions will inevitably involve a degree of contradiction and indeterminacy; hence the question mark that follows the word "heteronormativity" in the subtitle. Sexuality, as shown in these novels, is set firmly in the world of the sexual binary.[21] I acknowledge that there is a current controversy between views which prioritise the experience of gender on the

16 Personal email, 28th December 2020.

17 Beebo Brinker's "transmasculinity" is touched upon in Chapter II of this book.

18 Personal email, 28th October 2017. Bannon's intention does *not* invalidate Moore's interpretation, however.

19 As Stuart Hall says: "Theory is always a detour on the way to something more important." Stuart Hall, "Old and New Identities, Old and New Ethnicities," in *Culture, Globalization and the World-System: Contemporary Conditions for the Representation of Identity*, ed. Anthony D. King (Macmillan, 1991). 42.

20 In particular I would cite Halberstam, along with Eve Kosofsky Sedgwick, Judith Butler, and Gayle Rubin for their acknowledgement of the difficulty of defining masculinity (see Chapter II). Also I acknowledge Susan Stryker for her work on cheap paperbacks such as those under study in this book.

21 According to Moore, there were "dozens" of "pulp novels" that cashed in on the publicity generated by Christine Jorgensen, the United States's first high-profile transgender person. These novels were "salacious (and inaccurate)," and included Cyril Kornbluth's *Half*, which conflated transgender with intersex. Moore notes, citing Susan Stryker, that according to *Editor and Publisher*, "over a million words were printed about Jorgensen in 1953 – more than about any other person and enough to fill around fifteen books." It is likely that the bulk of these words were in newspaper articles, however, not books *per se*; the "dozens" of paperback novels on transgender are far outweighed in quantity by the hundreds on a lesbian theme, and I have so far noted no obvious overlap in the latter. Moore's assertion that narratives of transgender women and transfeminine subjects were "prominent in the paperback industry that Bannon knew at midcentury" is a slight exaggeration. Moore, "'A Boy Inside It': Beebo Brinker and the Transmasculine Narratives of Ann Bannon's Lesbian Pulp." 571,

Introduction 5

one hand, and those which prioritise observed sex at birth on the other; I have found it necessary to refer to such diverse and comparatively contemporary critics, from either side of that controversy, as Jack Halberstam (*The Queer Art of Failure* and *Trans**) and Sheila Jeffreys (*Unpacking Queer Politics*), wherever appropriate, as well as to commentators of an earlier generation such as Joan Nestle ("Butch-Fem Relationships: Sexual Courage in the 1950s," "The Fem Question," *A Restricted Country*, "The Will to Remember") and Audre Lorde (*Zami: A New Spelling of my Name*).

The innovative approach of this book is to readmit a selection of lesbian-themed paperbacks into the commercial and social milieu from which republication and academic study has isolated them, thereby reintroducing the typical readership, which was both female and male. This is akin to the approach of new historicism as a literary theory, which observes intellectual history through literature, and literature through its social and historical context. However, again my project does not assume any theoretical orthodoxy, nor does it pre-suppose that the relevance of the texts ended with the culture in which they were first published, but rather my project acknowledges new historicism as one of the contents of its critical toolbox. As Colm Tóibín says, "Any novel has to be read in the context of its date of publication [...] but a novel is a living document, people are reading it now."[22] Additionally, the starting point will be the male characters. I must state plainly that I do not claim that these novels are "about them" – that would be a perverse viewpoint – however, as the purpose of this book is to examine masculinity, it is appropriate to start with the prominent characters who, according to societal expectations, are most supposed to display it. It is important to stress, however, that although this book places the novels in their historical and social context, which includes the contemporaneous attitudes to and assumptions about masculinity, it can only study how masculinity is imagined in those novels. Amy Villarejo makes a point about participation in the butch-femme lifestyle of the nineteen-forties and fifties, which can be legitimately extended to the creation of fiction, and can be seen as a caution against taking the text of any sub-genre of paperback romance as history: "the participation in subcultural leisure activities [...]" let alone using them as a setting for fiction, "does not guarantee a politics, much less [...] awareness of the competing determinations of political subjectivity"[23] – I assume that by "politics" Villarejo means a micro- or identity-specific politics rather than national party-politics and statecraft. The direct relevance of imagining masculinity in fiction and imagining masculinity within a society and a culture, will be seen

---

594n3. Susan Stryker, *Queer Pulp: Perverted Passions from the Golden Age of the Paperback* (Chronicle Books, 2001). 73.

22 Colm Tóibín, Merve Emre, and Daniel Mulhall, "Ulysses," interview by Chris Power, *Open Book*, 16th January 2022.

23 Amy Villarejo, *Lesbian Rule: Cultural Criticism and the Value of Desire* (Duke UP, 2003). 188.

6 *Introduction*

further on in this introduction, where I deal with the readership, and also in the chapter on male characters.

The historic context: challenging the notion of lesbian "pulp"

In putting these books back into their historic context, the first task is to contest the word "pulp." This is not a matter of bibliographical pedantry; it is an essential part of understanding that context. The continued use of "pulp" in critical writing is lazy, apologetic, and dismissive. That term, applied to mass-market paperback fiction has proliferated, even to the extent that *Pulp Fiction* became the name of a popular movie, titled due to its deliberately unsophisticated characters and shlock violence.[24] It has also become a matter of hipness and commercialism,[25] and a matter of almost wry jokiness amongst its modern readers, with their twenty-first century attitudes to sexuality and gender identity. Thus the literature has become distanced from how it was received in its time, which potentially devalues it for modern readers and critics. Disregard for a historical item – and a flippant misnomer is evidence of such a disregard – causes a paucity of contextual knowledge and an eventual erroneous appraisal. That is why this book starts from this particular point of correction, and goes on to challenge several critical assumptions about the genre.

After the heyday of the cheaply produced, cheaply sold, lesbian-themed paperback, it was regarded with a mixture of fascination and condescension, and the term "pulp" typified that attitude. Kate Millet's autobiographical *Flying*, published in 1974, portrays her asking herself "What was I then, some pulp Sappho?" and describing the "library of cheap paperback lesbian affairs" that she collected in secret and burned.[26] Fran Koski and Maida Tilchen picked up on Millett's self-description for the title of their 1975 article and described the genre as "dyke books" and "lesbian pulp novels."[27] In 1983, Jeff Weinstein, writing in *Village Voice*, referred to "potboiler" novels with their "reader's expectation of simplistic, unlikely plot and routinely passionate characters" as "pulp lit."[28] In 1992, Joke Hermes referred to the "pulp" genre as "lesbian trash."[29] The stigma of "pulp" became established, institutional, and the term stuck. In her foreword to the 2002 republication of her novel *Odd Girl Out*, Ann Bannon refers to her publisher, Gold Medal Books, as "a major publisher of pulp novels,"[30] repeating the term in the

---

24 Quentin Tarantino, "Pulp Fiction," (Mirarmax, 1994).
25 I deal with this a little in Chapter IV.
26 Kate Millett, *Flying* (Ballantine Books, 1975). 202.
27 Fran Koski and Maida Tilchen, "Some Pulp Sappho," *Margins: A Review of Little Magazines & Small Press Books*, no. 23 (1975).
28 Jeff Weinstein, "In Praise of Pulp," *Voice Literary Supplement* (1983). 8.
29 Joke Hermes, "Sexuality in Lesbian Romance Fiction," *Feminist Review*, no. 42 (1992). 49.
30 Ann Bannon, *Odd Girl Out* (Cleis, 2001). vii.

Introduction 7

forewords to her other novels.[31] But these seem, on the face of it, to be retrospective definitions. The OED gives examples of "pulp" going back to 1906 but does not refine the meanings implicit in each example.[32] Bannon, writing in 2001, refers to a different dictionary entry:

> Webster's defines "pulp" as "tawdry or sensational writing." In other words, sleaze. It never entered my head that I was writing sleaze; I was writing romantic stories of women in love. But it certainly entered the heads of the editors and publishers of the original pulps, and in a far from negative sense. Their job was to promote, market, and sell the books, and sleaze had a huge appeal.[33]

The definition in Webster's ties the term to literary style and quality, or lack thereof, from which Bannon would naturally prefer to distance herself, as would many of her contemporaries, but the word itself implies a physical quality, and Bannon goes on to say that the "[…] physical material of the books was so fragile that it hardly survived a single reading. The glue dried and cracked, the pages fell out, the paper yellowed after mere months, and the ink ate right through it anyway."[34] Paula Rabinowitz's excellent book on mid-twentieth-century paperbacks of all genres, *American Pulp*, repeats the view of the physical properties: "They were, of course, meant to pass away: the paper of poor quality, the bindings barely holding the pages, the covers prone to puckers, rips, and tears."[35]

However, two important comments to all the above must be given, which contradict all that has been said about these paperbacks. First, that although they were produced comparatively cheaply, many books of that era still exist, and some of them in very good condition. Second, and most importantly, they were not known as "pulps" during their era, for the simple reason that something else was. The quotation from Frank Tashlin's film "Artists and Models", with which I headed this Introduction, actually continues: "[…] the cheap pulps found on all newsstands masquerading under the titles of comic books."[36] Whilst Ann Bannon is adamant that this quotation shows that the term "pulp" was applied to any disreputable publication in her day,[37] other sources contend that the term is specific. The equation of "pulp" with "comic

---

31 "I was writing paperback pulp fiction." Ann Bannon, *I am a Woman* (Cleis, 2002). "These *were* the pulps, after all!" vi. Ann Bannon, *Journey to a Woman* (Cleis, 2003). ix..

32 "The Oxford English Dictionary 2nd edn. online," (2021), tinyurl.com/OEDictry. s.v. "Pulp."

33 Bannon, *Odd Girl Out*. ix.

34 Bannon, *I am a Woman*. vi.

35 Paula Rabinowitz, *American Pulp: How Paperbacks Brought Modernism to Main Street* (Princeton UP, 2014). xii.

36 Tashlin, "Artists and Models."

37 Personal email from Ann Bannon, 8th July 2023.

8   *Introduction*

book" can be found in the proceedings of the Gathings Committee, which sat in late 1952 and early 1953:

> Mr. BLACK. Well, again, you don't know where comics begin and end. There are no more pulps. Pulps have rapidly been taken over by the comic field, pulp so-called. I don't know whether you recall, but there used to be magazines that we in the trade called pulps, westerns, love, mystery; they are fast disappearing. There are very few left, and the comic format is taking its place. You now have love comics; you have western comics. So you don't know where a comic begins and a pulp ends, and vice versa.[38]

The "MR. BLACK" referred to is Samuel Black, who was at the time the Vice President of the Atlantic Coast Independent Distributors Association. Nowhere in the well-documented proceedings of the Gathings Committee are novels conflated with comic books, magazines, or pulps.[39] Marijane Meaker, author of the landmark paperback *Spring Fire* as Vin Packer, which will feature in this book, made it clear that "'pulp', to me, were those wonderful pulp magazines that paid a penny a word;"[40] and Valerie Taylor, whose *Whisper Their Love* also will feature in this book, protested about the stigmatisation of paperback writing, "if Paula Christian's work and mine are pulps, why not Gale Wilhelm and Djuna Barnes?"[41] Taylor recognised that "pulp" was a gatekeeping term that separated popular literature from canonical, and damned a medium of delivery no matter what the literary merit of an individual work might be. That the novels were comparatively cheaply produced is not in dispute, nor is the fact that they were ephemeral items, more often than not thrown away; but the supposition in 1970 that one could still dig up discarded novels along the banks of the Erie Canal, which are "lined with tossed-out paperbacks pulped, that is, remaindered with their front covers ripped off, and dumped when they had not sold during the recession of 1953,"[42] testifies that the paper they were made of is

---

38 Ezekiel C. Gathings and others, *Investigation of Literature allegedly containing Objectionable Material: Hearings before the Select Committee on Current Pornographic Materials* (U.S. Government, 1952). 52.

39 Today, neither does the Popular Culture Association do so. unattributed, *Pulp Studies*, Popular Culture Association (2021), tinyurl.com/pcaacapulp.

40 Meaker, in: unattributed, *Fresh Air: Writer Marijane Meaker*, podcast audio2003.

41 Interviewed in Eric Garber, "Those Wonderful Lesbian Pulps: A Roundtable Discussion," *The San Francisco Bay Area Gay & Lesbian Historical Society Newsletter* 4, no. 4 (1989). 1. As it happens, Wilhelm's two novels on a lesbian theme were both republished as cheap paperbacks during this era; Djuna Barnes's *Nightwood* was published in softcover in 1961 by New Directions, an independent publishing house. Taylor makes a strong point about serious writing with a lesbian theme.

42 Rabinowitz, *American Pulp: How Paperbacks Brought Modernism to Main Street*. 65. Rabinowitz is citing Clarence Petersen, *The Bantam Story: Twenty-five years of Paperback Publishing* (Bantam, 1970). 17.

Introduction 9

much less fragile than its reputation suggests. Rabinowitz is wrong to refer to the books having been "pulped," however. That specifically means what it says – that the paper has been reprocessed as pulp to make more paper. The disposal of unsold books by the removal of the cover is known as "stripping," not pulping; and throwing away the body of the book as trash, whilst returning the cover to the publisher was an integral part of claiming credit on unsold books. It was never financially viable to incur carriage costs and take the books back into stock or to transport them to a pulping mill. Stripping is not uncommon even now.[43]

Cognoscenti from amongst the collectors of ephemeral literature are often much better providers of information than many academic and republishing sources. Asking a group of them where "pulp novels" could be bought in the nineteen-fifties, resulted in answers such as "if someone asked this question in, say, 1952 […] everyone would have blinked in confusion, and pointed out that the pulps were over here, and the paperbacks are over there and what do you mean 'pulp novels'? Did you mean pulps, or novels?"[44] Other comments, quoted below bring us closer to understanding what a "pulp" actually is.

> Books weren't pulps. Only magazines. Pulps existed from 1896 […] through the late 1950s, by which time remaining fiction magazines had converted to digest formats or slicks, and paperback books (not published on pulp) took over the newsstand fiction market for the most part.[45]
>
> Seriously, there's no debating. If something was printed on pulp paper and thus was a pulp. Either it was or wasn't. It's not subjective at all, nor thematic. It's literally chemical […] Pulp paper is dark and cheap and absorbent and [the pulps] had untrimmed edges. It's impossible to mistake actual pulps from magazines or books printed on higher-quality […] paper, with trimmed edges. Pulps also age like crazy even days after being first printed, when exposed to sunlight and/or air.[46]

---

43 Thomas L. Bonn, "The Paperback: Image and Object," in *International Book Publishing: An Encyclopedia*, ed. Philip G. Altbach and Edith S. Hoshino (Routledge, 1995). 265. See also: Josie Leavitt, "Why Must We Continue to Strip Covers?," *Publishers Weekly: ShelfTalker*, 2011, tinyurl.com/CoverStrip. And: Albert N. Greco, *The Economics of the Publishing and Information Industries: The Search for Yield in a Disintermediated World* (Routledge, 2014). 204. There have been lawsuits brought against retailers who sell coverless books, see for example: unattributed, "Defendants Settle in N.Y. Stripped Paperback Suits," *Publishers Weekly* 233 (29th April 1988). 13.

44 Gary Farber, a collector, commenting on a thread about "pulp novels," in the Facebook group "Vintage Paperback and Pulp Forum," on 30th July 2018. tinyurl.com/PulpDefine. Throughout these block quotes, punctuation is as seen. Bracketed suspension marks, as usual, indicate where I have omitted text.

45 Gary Farber again, in the same thread.

46 Gary Farber, same thread.

10   *Introduction*

Roland Barthes's description of a cheap paper product, destined for "refuse: either the drawer or the wastebasket [...] it flourishes for a moment then ages [...] Attacked by light, by humidity, it fades, weakens, vanishes; there is nothing left to do but throw it away,"[47] seems to fit the true pulp rather than the novel. It is therefore the misnomer that has come down to us, and meanwhile the original definition, as ephemeral as the untrimmed original, is as good as lost. Relatively cheap and subject somewhat to yellowing though the paper may be in the novels under research, the print survives, and the pages are neatly trimmed – Rabinowitz admits that paper "despite Barthes's necrotic image of it, is slow to disintegrate."[48] Unless making a direct quotation, therefore, or for sheer brevity, I will avoid using the word "pulp" to describe the novels under study.

In considering now the history of these paperbacks – how they came to be produced and marketed in the first place – a better definition will emerge. A Facebook comment from a collector mentions Fawcett Gold Medal, Pocket Books, and New American Library;[49] all of these three publishing houses had an important place in the cheap paperbacks' timeline. Yvonne Keller notes that the mood of the United States in the 1950s was "on one level confident and optimistic, on another anxious and afraid," citing McCarthyism as one cause of the latter.[50] The "hostile era of McCarthyism" is mentioned often in commentaries, notably by Ann Bannon,[51] Christopher Nealon,[52] and Paula Rabinowitz.[53] This emphasis on the fear and anxiety, while it stresses the courage of pro-lesbian[54] authors and female purchasers, ignores the economic situation and the buoyancy of the mood it produced. Doris Kearns Goodwin reminds us that the United States came out of the Second World War in better economic shape than it went in, speaking of an "economic surge" during the war and expansion after it,[55] which was only interrupted by occasional and relatively short-lived slumps such as happened in 1953. Personal income

---

47 Roland Barthes, *Camera Lucida: Reflections on Photography*, trans. Richard Howard (Hill & Wang, 1981). 93.

48 Rabinowitz, *American Pulp: How Paperbacks Brought Modernism to Main Street*. 65.

49 Todd Mason in the Facebook group "Vintage Paperback and Pulp Forum," on 30th July 2018. tinyurl.com/PulpDefine.

50 Keller, "Ab/normal Looking: Voyeurism and surveillance in lesbian pulp novels and US Cold War Culture." 180. Keller cites Wini Breines, *Young, White, and Miserable: Growing Up Female in the Fifties* (Beacon, 1992). 8.

51 Bannon, *Odd Girl Out*. v.

52 Christopher Nealon, "Invert-History: The Ambivalence of Lesbian Pulp Fiction," *New Literary History* 31, no. 4 (2000). 745.

53 Rabinowitz makes a point of quoting Nealon's article mentioned in the note immediately above.

54 A term credited to Yvonne Keller. Yvonne Keller, "Pulp Politics: Strategies of Vision in Pro-Lesbian Pulp Novels 1955-1965," in *The Queer Sixties*, ed. Patricia Juliana Smith (Routledge, 1999). 1.

55 Doris Kearns Goodwin, "The Way We Won; America's Economic Breakthrough During World War II," *The American Prospect* (Fall 1992). 66.

Introduction 11

had risen, the middle class was growing, and businesses took advantage of this optimism and relative affluence to expand. The first significant mass-marketed paperback books in America were produced from 1939 by Pocket Books and sold for twenty-five cents. These thrived during the war, due to shortage of materials for books of hardback quality. Also, the war saw the phenomenon of "the mass production of paperbound books at low cost for distribution to soldiers and sailors overseas," totalling 122,951,031 volumes and covering 1,324 individual titles – including established works of fiction of all genres, and non-fiction – at a cost of less than seven cents per volume,[56] and surely tough enough, despite their cheapness, to survive conditions of active service. Amongst the Directors of Editions for The Armed Services Inc. were Robert de Graff of Pocket Books, and Richard L. Simon of Simon and Schuster who was one of the founders of Pocket Books.[57] The knowledge of how cheaply books could be produced, and how avidly they could be read, was carried forward into the post-war years.

In 1948, paperback producer Penguin Books of the UK set off its American subsidiary, which became New American Library, which from its inception, according to Rabinowitz, "took pride not only in its discerning literary taste but also its progressive attitude toward sexual and racial minorities."[58] What Rabinowitz implies here is that NAL opened the way for more liberal attitudes than are generally supposed to be the cultural norm in the post-war era. Very soon after the foundation of New American Library, the company entered into a distribution deal that would affect the paperback trade significantly; writing for the website Bookscans, which is dedicated to showcasing paperback cover art, commentator Bruce Black says:

> In 1949, Fawcett Publications, which was an independent distributor, made an historic agreement with *New American Library* to distribute *Signet* and *Mentor* books at the same locations it sold its magazines and comic books. One of the stipulations of the deal was that Fawcett could not compete with *NAL* by publishing their own paperback reprints. Roscoe Fawcett [...] desperately wanted to enter the paperback market. But how could he do so without breaking the *NAL* agreement?

---

56 John Jamieson, *Editions for the Armed Services, Inc.: A History Together with the Complete List of 1324 Books Published for American Armed Forces Overseas* (Editions for the Armed Services, Inc., 1948). tinyurl.com/EditionsArmed . 3. According to Jamieson, the "Armed Services Editions" involved a number of Army and Navy agencies, the US War Production Board, some seventy publishing firms, and more than a dozen printing houses, composition firms, and paper suppliers. Of the 1,324 titles, only ninety-nine were re-issued titles from earlier in the series.

57 Jamieson, *Editions for the Armed Services, Inc.: A History Together with the Complete List of 1324 Books Published for American Armed Forces Overseas*. i.

58 Rabinowitz, *American Pulp: How Paperbacks Brought Modernism to Main Street*. 36.

12 *Introduction*

The answer was the Paperback Original (PBO): that is, they wouldn't compete with "paperback reprints;" they would produce titles that had never before been released. This was not the first time PBOs had been printed, but it would be the first time that a paperback publishing house would release ONLY original works; a significant precedence in the annals of U.S. literary history.[59]

It was this agreement between New American Library and Fawcett Publications which, more than anything else, placed books for sale elsewhere than bookshops. It was also crucial in encouraging the practice of writing novels quickly and prolifically,[60] thus ensuring that a turnover of new titles was placed in the path of a commuting and travelling population. A good book that "could be had for the same cost as a pack of cigarettes and bought in the same shops,"[61] attracted a passing trade. Paula Rabinowitz describes them being found in bus and train stations, soda fountains and candy stores, drugstores and newspaper kiosks, aimed at a mobile population of working men and women commuting by public transport to work in midsize cities, or crisscrossing the country as travelling salesmen or leisured vacationers.[62]

The availability of these books on the routes taken by thousands of people every day reveals, by implication, how they were read. They were read casually, in the main, on subway trains and buses, in the park whilst eating sandwiches or at the lunch counter over a coffee and a hamburger in the middle of the day. They were read from cover to cover in order to pass the time and provide escape from office or workshop life – it would have been pointless simply to flick through them to look for titillating passages, few and far-between, buried in the narrative. Also, the range of books offered in paperback was even wider than Rabinowitz implies. Signatories to the minority report of the Gathings Committee listed "some of the important titles which have been made available at low prices to the public at large by publishers of pocket-sized volumes."[63] These included books by Louisa May Alcott, Dwight D. Eisenhower, A.E. Housman, Elizabeth Barrett Browning, W. Somerset Maugham, G.K. Chesterton, Robert Louis Stevenson, George Eliot, and Rudyard Kipling. According to Rabinowitz, "pulp" publishing actually brought modernism to a wider readership in mid-twentieth century America; her featuring illustrations of the covers of books by Christopher Isherwood, D.H. Lawrence, Henry James, George Orwell, and Truman Capote evidence

---

59 "Bookscans: Gold Medal," 2020, tinyurl.com/FawcettGM. Author's emphasis.
60 This is not in itself a tendency initiated by cheap paperbacks. Erle Stanley Gardner, for example, produced books for Morrow consistently between 1933 and 1970.
61 Rabinowitz, *American Pulp: How Paperbacks Brought Modernism to Main Street*. 246.
62 Rabinowitz, *American Pulp: How Paperbacks Brought Modernism to Main Street*. 33.
63 Ezekiel C. Gathings and others, *Report of the Select Committee on Current Pornographic Materials* (U.S. Government, 1952). 126.

Introduction   13

that breadth. Her mother's nightstand regularly held paperbacks by a wide range of authors from Harrison E. Salisbury to Boris Pasternak.[64]

The boom in paperbacks, both reprints and original works, was therefore one of the most significant mass literacy events of the twentieth century. The necessity to "pile them high and sell them cheap"[65] meant that they had to be instantly attractive. They were displayed, face forward,[66] on stands, and their covers had to draw the eye and give an instant impression of what was inside. Publishers such as Fawcett found it economically viable to employ recognised commercial artists to design their covers, but the codes that were devised to dominate the cover art, or that seemed to grow organically, were simple. A six-gun, a rearing pony, and a Stetson hat – sometimes the Stetson on its own – advertised an adventure in the American "Wild West" of the nineteenth century. A trench coat and a fedora, a crumpled suit and a loosened tie, or a lined face, a cigarette, and a whisky glass, betokened the world of the spy or the private eye. A steel helmet and a rifle offered a story from the Second World War, or from the conflict in Korea. Because of the transient nature of the novels that were written to go direct to paperback and were seldom republished, the seemingly obvious dichotomy between cover and text blurs. These books, which could be slipped into a pocket or a handbag, were integrated cultural objects, cultural texts that reveal something about the mobile, fast-moving society in which they existed.

The fact that they could be slipped into a pocket indicates a preferable name to "pulp." The report of the Gathings Committee mentions that:

> There are many companies engaged in publishing books known as "pocket-size books," a designation which has been generally adopted to avoid use of the term "pocket book" to describe such books. Pocket Books being a registered trade name owned by Pocket Books, Inc., a Marshall Field enterprise.[67]

That distinction notwithstanding, even the drafters of the Committee's reports often lapsed into using the shorter form, tending to make Pocket Books Inc. the hoover or biro of the paperback boom.[68] Thus "pocket-size book" or "pocket book" were the terms used and heard for the general category, where "pulp" was not – the term "pocket book" even making it into

---

64 Rabinowitz, *American Pulp: How Paperbacks Brought Modernism to Main Street.* xi.
65 I have no exact reference for this familiar phrase; it is attributed to Jack Cohen, founder of Tesco stores.
66 As opposed to having the spine facing outward, as is common in bookshops.
67 Gathings and others, *Report of the Select Committee on Current Pornographic Materials.* 18.
68 For example, the drafters of the minority report alternated between each usage. On a single page there could be four instances of "pocket-sized" and three of "pocket books;" see Gathings and others, *Report of the Select Committee on Current Pornographic Materials.* 125.

14 Introduction

the pages of the literary journal *The Antioch Review*[69] – and "paperback original" was coined to cover the particular subcategory of newly composed novels. In a diary entry for April 16, 1952, novelist Patricia Highsmith used the term "The Pocket Books" to describe paperbacks, adding that their publishers were "currently outbidding the general Hollywood buyers, and claiming to reach a hitherto unexploited audience – unexploited is the word – of the middlebrow, who yet wants "realism.""[70]

The semiotic codes of lesbian paperback cover art

Highsmith wrote that diary entry on the day she heard that the paperback rights of her second novel, *The Price of Salt*, a lesbian love story recently published under the pseudonym of Claire Morgan by Coward-McCann, had been sold to Bantam Books.[71] Novels on a lesbian theme were, in many ways, just like any other paperback sub-genre. They needed a cover with instant recognition. Amy Villarejo suggests that the foremost function of a cover is to lure the potential reader at the point of sale, the moment of transaction between retailer and consumer.[72] Rather than a lure, however, the cover is a definite hook that captures the customer before the point of sale, in a place of rapid footfall or a deliberate stopping-place such as a general store. For the potential customer, the slimmest of indications was enough:

> The books were displayed with the other books, with mysteries and westerns and everything, and you had to dig for them. The only way you could identify them was by the pictures on the cover. So if there was a picture of two women I'd say, "Oh yeah, this has to be one!" Grab! That's great![73]

The cover illustration of *The Price of Salt* prominently features two women. The artwork, by commercial artist Barye Phillips, introduced many of what became familiar visual tropes. The narrative of the novel concerns a love

---

69 James Rorty, "The Harassed Pocket-Book Publishers," *The Antioch Review* 15, no. 4 (1955). 411 *et seq.*

70 Patricia Highsmith, *Patricia Highsmith: Her Diaries and Notebooks*, ed. Anna von Planta (Weidenfeld & Nicholson, 2021). 558.

71 Inside the Bantam edition is a note containing the sentence, "The low-priced Bantam edition is made possible by the large sale and effective promotion of the original edition, published by Coward-McCann, Inc." Claire Morgan, *The Price of Salt* (Bantam, 1953). 249.

72 Amy Villarejo, "Forbidden Love: Pulp as Lesbian History," in *Outtakes*, ed. Ellis Hanson (Duke University Press, 1999). 321.

73 Stephanie Ozard, in Aerlyn Weissman and Lynne Fernie, "Forbidden Love: The Unashamed Stories of Lesbian Lives," (National Film Board of Canada, 1993). Ann Bannon also noted that the books were found "[a]mong the cowboy tales, the cops-and-robbers, and the science fiction [...]" in a preface to Ann Aldrich, *We Walk Alone* (The Feminist Press, 2006). Unnumbered page.

Introduction 15

affair between Therese, who works in a department store, and Carol, a wealthy patron of the store. These two principals are in the foreground of the cover and are both depicted as conventionally feminine. This is typically the case, whether or not either character in the text can be considered masculine or "butch." A caveat to add at this stage is that butch characteristics in the world outside fiction were not always signalled by presentation but were sometimes more a matter of character. A witness of the era said:

> You can't tell butch-fem by people's dress. You couldn't even really tell in the '50s. I knew women with long hair, fem clothes, and found out they were butches. Actually I knew one who wore men's clothes, haircuts and ties, who was a fem.[74]

In a typical cover illustration, the junior or submissive partner is always depicted as feminine; she sits or reclines in the foreground, while the senior or dominant partner is standing.[75] In the cover illustration for *The Price of Salt*, Carol's dominance is also signalled by her clothing being darker. She rests a possessive hand lightly on Therese's shoulder. The gaze adopted by each principal is typical; the dominant partner looks directly at the other principal, whilst the latter's gaze is outward, but not direct at the viewer. Hair colour is often significant. The seated figure will typically be blonde, whilst the standing figure's hair will be darker. This is not so for *The Price of Salt*, but another visual trope – the comparative shortness of the dominant woman's hairstyle – is hinted at by Carol's hair being gathered at her nape.[76] The cigarette is another indicator of dominance, even with a phallic suggestion according to the pop-Freudianism of the era. Although the presence of a piece of furniture such as a bed, a divan, or a sofa suggests an interior, the background is often left vague and ambiguous. Sometimes there will be a peripheral male figure, the third and marginal member of a "love triangle" who, in the narrative, may or may not win the junior principal from the senior.

---

74 "Reggie," quoted in Elizabeth Lapovsky Kennedy and Madeline D. Davis, *Boots of Leather, Slippers of Gold: The History of a Lesbian Community* (Penguin, 1993). 192.

75 It is no easy task to come up with a cover-all description for the two principals in these novels. "Senior" and "junior" imply an age difference as well as a status, and in some cases either is appropriate. "Dominant" and "submissive," though fairly descriptive, are terms often applied to a specific lifestyle. "Butch" and "femme" might be appropriate in some cases, but by no means in all. Robert Silverberg, writing as L.T. Woodward MD in a work of faux sexology, refers to "lover" and "beloved," but these terms are supplied by one of the supposed "subjects" of Woodward's "study." L. T. Woodward, *Twilight Women* (Lancer, 1963). 39.

76 By coincidence, Highsmith constructed the plot for the novel on the day on which she, in a temporary job at Bloomingdale's department store in New York, sold a doll to the wealthy Mrs. E.R. Senn. She became obsessed by Kathleen Senn, to the extent of walking down her street in New Jersey, where she saw "a pale aqua automobile" driven by "a woman with dark glasses and *short blonde hair*." Highsmith, *Patricia Highsmith: Her Diaries and Notebooks*. 490, my emphasis.

16 *Introduction*

There is such an indistinct, male figure in the middle ground of the cover of *The Price of Salt*, standing for Carol's husband; it is a fairly typical example, and another such can be found on Don Morro's *The Virgin*.[77] On Helen Morgan's *Killer Dyke* a similar figure wears a crumpled suit and a fedora, signalling a cross-genre novel, such as were fairly common, with a private-eye theme.[78] Where male figures are more prominent, they stand and regard the lesbian principals. Their conventional masculinity is signalled by their clean-cut, broad-shouldered look – they may be half-naked or in swimming trunks,[79] in a tight t-shirt that does not hide a muscular frame,[80] in a white shirt with turned-back sleeves,[81] or in a conservative suit.[82] Occasionally these very simple semiotics will be varied, as in Gerald Kramer's *Penthouse Party*, where the male figure is an *éminence grise*, handsome in middle age, lounging in a planter's chair.[83] The basic semiotics of dominance are repeated into the 1960s, with slight variations, on the covers of novels such as Adam Coulter's *Lesbian Captive*,[84] Agnete Holk's *Strange Friends*,[85] and A.P. Williams's *Tutor from Lesbos*.[86] Some covers became more risqué and, to cut costs, designed by less talented artists – Clancy Markham's *Wild, Way Out and Wanton*,[87] A.M. Willis's *Butch Fever*[88] – particularly for those novels published by smaller presses who had taken advantage of the trend. In some cases, the figures were elongated and fetishistic, for example on the covers of Edward Marshall's *Madame Butch*[89] and Peter Willow's *Odd Neighbors*.[90] Very rarely did the covers show a female principal with a masculine presentation; the exceptional butch figures on Lora Sela's *I am a Lesbian*[91] and Harrison Kent's *Tropic of Lesbos*[92] are slight and boyish.

---

77 Don Morro, *The Virgin* (Beacon, 1955). This cover artwork, together with those mentioned below and throughout this book, can be found on websites such as pulpcovers.com, book-scans.com, and strangesisters.com, or sometimes simply from an image search on a search engine. They are well worth finding to be looked at alongside the descriptions in this book.

78 Helen Morgan, *Killer Dyke* (Exotik, 1964).

79 Carolyn Weston, *Tormented* (Berkley, 1956). Barry Devlin, *Forbidden Pleasures* (Berkley, 1953).

80 Artemis Smith, *This Bed We Made* (Monarch, 1961).

81 David Key, *Strange Sisters* (Bee Line, 1967). Willi Peters, *Lesbian Twins* (Vega, 1962). Rex Weldon, *Love Me Wild* (Brandon House, 1965).

82 Fletcher Flora, *Desperate Asylum* (Lion Library, 1955). Fletcher Flora, *Strange Sisters* (Lion, 1954). Frank G. Harris, *Mike Addison* (Saber, 1963).

83 Gerald Kramer, *Penthouse Party* (Midwood, 1965).

84 Adam Coulter, *Lesbian Captive* (Brandon, 1964).

85 Agnete Holk, *Strange Friends* (Pyramid, 1963).

86 A.P. Williams, *Tutor from Lesbos* (Beacon Signal Sixty, 1964).

87 Clancy Markham, *Wild, Way Out and Wanton* (Royal Line, 1965).

88 A.M. Willis, *Butch Fever* (Private Edition, 1965).

89 Edward Marshall, *Madame Butch* (After Hours, 1966).

90 Peter Willow, *Odd Neighbors* (Wee Hours, 1967).

91 Lora Sela, *I am a Lesbian* (Saber, 1959).

92 Harrison Kent, *Tropic of Lesbos* (Private Edition, 1966).

Introduction 17

Gathings, Granahan, and the US Postal service: Pressure on "the freedom to act unwisely?"[93]

The cheap paperbacks, with their obvious cover-art semiotics as described above, flourished for the best part of two decades, and emerged from what is considered a time of political and sexual repression. Their popular image, certainly with regard to the 1950s sets them in "the hostile era of McCarthyism,"[94] the "atmosphere of the [...] trials" making it frightening and difficult for most women to take a lesbian-themed paperback off the drugstore rack and pay for it at the counter.[95] Paula Rabinowitz quotes Christopher Nealon, to the effect that even to write such novels "in the McCarthy era" took courage.[96] Indeed, Senator Joseph McCarthy did scorn intellectuals as "pink," implying treason to country and gender.[97] It does not cast any general doubt on that courage, however, to state that McCarthy was far from universally popular even in his own Republican Party, and was given a position of which Republican Senator Robert A. Taft could say, "We've got McCarthy where he can't do any harm."[98] McCarthy is often mentioned in the same breath as the House Committee on Un-American Activities, although obviously as he was Senator and not a member of Congress he had nothing to do with that body; the supposed sinecure in which he was placed was in fact the Permanent Subcommittee on Investigations on Government Operations. Issues relating to the publication and sale of books were not in the remit of this Subcommittee. It was from that position that he chaired the hearings with which he is associated. However, when the papers of those hearings were made public in 2003, Senators Susan Collins and Carl Levin said, in their preface, that McCarthy's "freewheeling style caused both the Senate and the Subcommittee to revise the rules governing future investigations and prompted the courts to act to protect the Constitutional rights of witnesses at Congressional hearings."[99] He was condemned by the Senate in 1954 and died in 1957. Although he was an outspoken and prominent figure

---

93 Dan Lacy, "Should the Book Publishing Industry Set Up a Self-Policing Program?," *The American Scholar* 29, no. 3 (1960). 448.

94 Foreword to Bannon, *Odd Girl Out*. v.

95 Christopher Nealon, *Foundlings: Lesbian and Gay Historical Emotion before Stonewall* (Duke University Press, 2001). 148. Nealon mentions Roberta Yusba as the source for this; however, the two short articles by her that I have been able to locate nowhere contain those precise words.

96 Rabinowitz, *American Pulp: How Paperbacks Brought Modernism to Main Street*. 349n.12. And Nealon, "Invert-History: The Ambivalence of Lesbian Pulp Fiction." 745.

97 James Gilbert, *Men in the Middle: Searching for Masculinity in the 1950s* (U of Chicago P, 2005). 189.

98 Richard M. Fried, *Nightmare in Red: The McCarthy Era in Perspective* (Oxford UP, 1991). 134.

99 Preface to Joseph McCarthy and others, *Executive Sessions of the Senate Permanent Subcommittee on Investigations of the Committee on Government Operations, 1953-1954* (U.S. Government, 2003).

18   *Introduction*

for about three years, his personal contemporaneous presence cannot have had quite the scale influence as is supposed by later critics, on the publication and sale of cheap, lesbian-themed, paperback books, which continued to flourish.[100] Nevertheless, he has undoubtedly lent his name posthumously and in an exaggerated manner to an era, to such an extent that the commentators cited *supra* make a point of mentioning him.[101] I do not suggest for one moment that life suddenly became easy for dissenters in politics, gender, or sexuality after McCarthy's condemnation – it didn't; the persecution continued, along with the national paranoia about communism and its supposed link to sexual non-conformity. I do however maintain that in many ways the envelope of that dissent was being pushed, despite the hard times, and maybe being pushed more than many people realise. This book will go some way to show how lesbian-themed paperbacks played a part in that.

Two other U.S. Government bodies were concerned directly with the distribution of publications, however. These were the Select Committee on Current Pornographic Materials, which held hearings in 1952, and The Subcommittee on Postal Operations of the Committee on Post Office and Civil Service, which held hearings in 1959. When the former came to order under the chairmanship of Congressman Ezekiel Chandler Gathings in late 1952, and drafted its report on the last day of that year, it had considered not only the question of pornographic materials in general, but had singled out a list of seven books. These are listed in the report thus:

The Tormented
Women's Barracks
Spring Fire
Unmoral
Forbidden
Artists' Model
The Wayward Bus[102]

---

100 In 1953 the Senator did attempt to initiate a "slashing attack" on State Department libraries outside the United States and threatened to extend that to domestic libraries. However, the attack was blunted by the joint efforts of the American Book Publishers Council's and the American Library Association's 'Declaration on the Freedom to Read'. Dan Lacy and Robert W. Frase, "The American Book Publishers Council," in *The Enduring Book: Print Culture in Postwar America*, ed. David Paul Nord, Joan Shelley Rubin, and Michael Schudson, A History of the Book in America (U of North Carolina P, 2009). 197-198.

101 For added historical context, in 1955 Allen Ginsberg gave a public recital of his poem 'Howl', which was later cleared of obscenity; in 1956 the same poet published the poem 'In the Baggage Room at Greyhound', which contained the declaration, "I am a communist." Allen Ginsberg, *Howl and other poems*, The Pocket Poets, (City Lights Books, 1959). 47.

102 Gathings and others, *Report of the Select Committee on Current Pornographic Materials*. 16.

Introduction 19

No mention was made, specifically in that list, of the authors' names. Two of those are, of course, very familiar to those who know about lesbian-themed mass-market paperbacks of the 1950s – *Women's Barracks* is by Tereska Torrès, and *Spring Fire* is by Vin Packer.[103] The latter will feature prominently in this book. *The Wayward Bus* is the novel by John Steinbeck, second on the *New York Times* best seller list in March and April of 1947.[104] *Unmoral* is a 1933 title by Jack Woodford, repackaged and published during the late 1940s by 'The Jack Woodford Press', which had been specially set up to market his erotica – this can be ascertained from a brief mention of the publishing house buried in another part of the committee's deliberations.[105] *Artists' Model* is most likely a novel of that name by Norman Bligh, a prolific author of the period. *The Tormented* is identified further down the page from the bare list as being by Theodore Pratt,[106] to highlight an opinion by a prominent psychiatrist about the book.[107]

The point is that at the moment of listing these, the Gathings Committee took no cognisance of the authorship, nor the literary merit, nor the work involved in writing them, nor the name of the publishing house that produced them beyond noting that "[m]ost of the publishers engaged in this sordid competition operate in the field of cheap prints selling from 10 to 75 cents."[108] It took no cognisance of the fact that this short list contained books that might have been either potboilers or works by one of the most highly-regarded writers of the twentieth century. To the Committee they were things. They were nothing more than objects that allegedly held pornographic content, in furtherance of "demoralization for profit."[109] Later in the committee's deliberation, the subject of authorship would come up, specifically in the case of *Women's Barracks*, though the question as it was raised was more about whether the book was autobiographical or diarial and therefore not a fictional enterprise designed specifically to contain material of a kind the committee defined as "sordid."[110] The committee did take cognisance of the fact that a Judge in a County Court in Ottawa, Canada,

---

103 Throughout this book I will use the author's pen name, unless there is good reason to mention the person behind it. Vin Packer is, of course, a pen name of the prolific Marijane Meaker.
104 Gathings and others, *Report of the Select Committee on Current Pornographic Materials*. 124.
105 Gathings and others, *Investigation of Literature allegedly containing Objectionable Material: Hearings before the Select Committee on Current Pornographic Materials*. 254.
106 Gathings and others, *Report of the Select Committee on Current Pornographic Materials*. 16.
107 Gathings and others, *Report of the Select Committee on Current Pornographic Materials*. 17.
108 Ibid.
109 Ibid.
110 Gathings and others, *Report of the Select Committee on Current Pornographic Materials*. 37.

20   *Introduction*

had concluded that *Women's Barracks* was obscene,[111] in a judgment handed down on the 22nd of November 1952.[112] A spirited if rather disingenuous defence of *Women's Barracks* was made by Ralph Foster Daigh, editorial director and vice president of Fawcett Publications Inc., under whose 'Gold Medal' imprint both *Women's Barracks* and *Spring Fire* appeared. Daigh declared that

> It cannot be argued that soft-cover books are works of art, or classics. Frankly, there is no gigantic market for the so-called classics, although they are sold in large numbers in soft covers. However, the fact that a novel may be classified as a mystery, a suspense story, a love story, a western, a historical novel should not connote that these stories are unworthy or bad. That would suggest that anyone not devoted exclusively to reading the classics is a low person [...] Fawcett Publications has no more desire to print indecent literature than does any other respectable book publisher [...] [113]

Daigh's complete statement reads well as a declaration of faith in the reading public's capability to self-censor and the publishing industry's right – duty indeed – to provide reading material at an affordable price. It seems to be a clarion call of liberalism in the face of the fogeyism of the Gathings Committee. The reason I called Daigh's defence disingenuous, however, is because Fawcett Publications was in business to make money, and no matter how much of a mission statement Daigh had made to the committee, his first concern must always have been the bottom line. He must have been well aware that sex sells. Although the Gathings Committee seems to have construed "pornography" to include "the greater part of all paper-back books sold everywhere at newsstands and drug counters,"[114] it turned out to be ineffective. Little more than two years after the publication of the Committee's reports, Eric Larrabee stated:

> The Gathings Committee seems genuinely not to have desired censorship; it merely desired censorship to be unnecessary. It would rather the whole equivocal business of obscenity were somebody else's problem. Aware that the Post Office is one of the few effective censors left, it asked to have lifted the last pretense of due process from the

---

111 Gathings and others, *Report of the Select Committee on Current Pornographic Materials*. 40.

112 unattributed, "Firm Fined On Obscene Books Charge: Judge Finds Novel To Be 'Lewd, Filthy'," *Winnipeg Free Press*, 24th November 1952. 9.

113 Gathings and others, *Investigation of Literature allegedly containing Objectionable Material: Hearings before the Select Committee on Current Pornographic Materials*. 33-34.

114 Edward de Grazia, "Obscenity and the Mail: A Study of Administrative Restraint," *Law and Contemporary Problems* 20, no. 4 (1955). 616.

Introduction 21

star-chamber methods by which an opinionated postal inspector can put a publisher out of business. Aware that no definition of obscenity is satisfactory, it tried to evade the word by diffusing it into a cloud of indefiniteness, recommending that the publishing business eliminate on its own initiative not only the conceivably obscene, but "that proportion of its output which may be classified as 'borderline' or 'objectionable'" – in other words, stop haggling about specific books and throw them all out wherever there is the slightest question.[115]

The US Post Office is the most often-cited influence on the narrative structure of lesbian-themed paperbacks. For the 2004 Cleis republication of *Spring Fire*, Vin Packer wrote an introduction in novelesque style, containing a dialogue between herself and Dick Carroll, a Fawcett Gold Medal editor at the time that Daigh was editorial director and vice president of Fawcett Publications Inc., handling "paperback originals ... [t]he idea that good books could appear in paper without having to be in hardcover first."[116] Carroll suggested a plot development that would circumvent the Comstock laws, which governed sending "censurable [sic] material" through the mail.[117] Packer quotes Carroll as saying "If one book is considered censurable, the whole shipment is sent back to the publisher. If your book appears to proselytize for homosexuality, all the books sent with it to distributors are returned."[118] What Dick Carroll actually did, however, by insisting that Packer should not give her lesbian characters a happy ending, was create a successful narrative formula which others copied.[119] After all, *Spring Fire* was one of the best-selling books of 1952. Ann Bannon's *Odd Girl Out* applied the formula almost exactly, if with a slightly more timid ending, five years later. Paula Christian received the same advice from her literary agent, Joe Elder of Scott Meredith, showing that knowledge of the successful formula had migrated to reputable literary agencies.[120] In fact the successful template adheres to an earlier narrative archetype, the fairy tale, in which, according to Andrea Dworkin, "There are two definitions of woman. There is the good woman. She is a victim. There is the bad woman. She must be destroyed. The

---

115 Eric Larrabee, "The Cultural Context of Sex Censorship," *Law and Contemporary Problems* 20, no. 4 (1955). 678.
116 Vin Packer, *Spring Fire* (Cleis, 2004). vi.
117 Packer, *Spring Fire*. vi.
118 Packer, *Spring Fire*. vi. Carroll was "a sharp fellow from Hollywood, new to paperback publishing." Aldrich, *We Walk Alone*. x.
119 Nevertheless, in a 1989 interview Packer said "Nobody [at Fawcett] told me what to write." Eric Garber, "Those wonderful lesbian pulps, part 2," *San Francisco Bay Area Gay and Lesbian Historical Society Newsletter* 5, no. 1 (1989). 7.
120 In Garber, "Those Wonderful Lesbian Pulps: A Roundtable Discussion." 4.

22 Introduction

good woman must be possessed. The bad woman must be killed or punished. Both must be nullified."[121]

The US Post Office did have considerable independent authority, exercising a "system of precensorship"[122] in preventing distribution, which was criticised as "prior restraint" in 1954.[123] In 1955, outspoken lawyer Edward de Grazia said that "the functions of "prosecutor" and "judge" *merge*" in the person of the Solicitor for the United States Post Office Department.[124] A legal precedent had been established whereby allegedly obscene mail had to be carried and delivered unless and until such time as the Department had determined, "upon fair notice and full hearing," that it was obscene, and that merely to seize mail pending such a hearing was unlawful; the Department ignored that and proceeded "as though *Walker v. Popenoe* were but a bad dream, continuing to seize all mail conceived by it to be obscene – without prior notice and hearing."[125] In practice, the Post Office could effect a "stop-order"[126] on carrying all the mail for a particular publisher or distributor, again despite legal precedent. De Grazia reported:

> The Associate Solicitor for the Post Office Department recently was asked: "If you were to find that the Chevrolet Division of the General Motors Corporation had posted an obscene book, could you, as you construe your existing powers, issue an order to stop all mail sent to the Chevrolet Division?" The Associate Solicitor for the Post Office Department answered, "Yes."[127]

As part of the research leading to this book, I corresponded with Jennifer M. Lynch, Archivist at the U.S. Post Office; she could find neither copies of orders directing Postmasters to stop a specific publisher from mailing items ("stop-orders"), nor any notice relating to Fawcett, nor any record of a hearing related to Fawcett.[128] Absence of evidence is not evidence of absence, but it implies that the pressure on Fawcett Gold Medal, at least, may not

---

121 Andrea Dworkin, *Our Blood: Prophecies and Discourses on Sexual Politics* (The Women's Press, 1982). 55. I mention the "possession" of the "good" woman later in this study, when I bring in the "Big Handsome Hero" cited by Bradley and Damon.

122 Rorty, "The Harassed Pocket-Book Publishers." 417.

123 unattributed, "Censorship of Obscene Literature by Informal Governmental Action," *The University of Chicago Law Review* 22, no. 1 (1954). 216-217 *et seq.*

124 de Grazia, "Obscenity and the Mail: A Study of Administrative Restraint." 609

125 de Grazia, "Obscenity and the Mail: A Study of Administrative Restraint." 610.

126 de Grazia, "Obscenity and the Mail: A Study of Administrative Restraint." 613. Such an order was based on the Department's understanding of section 259 and 259a of title 39, United States Code, under which "the Postmaster General may issue orders stopping the mail of persons in connection with [...] sale of obscene materials." unattributed, *Annual Report of the Postmaster General* (United States Post Office Department, 1955). 38.

127 de Grazia, "Obscenity and the Mail: A Study of Administrative Restraint." 613-614.

128 Personal email, 26th December 2018.

Introduction 23

have been as severe as Dick Carroll supposed. Indeed, Dan Lacy, Managing Director of the American Book Publishers Council, said in 1959 that he was only aware of two findings of "non-mailability" against a member of that Council, one of which was set aside by a federal court and the other reversed by the Post Office itself.[129]

Postal employees did not have a set routine for inspecting items deposited for mailing; if they had "reason to suspect" that items were either unmailable or not eligible for mailing under the rules for a particular class of mail, they were obliged to verify their mailability.[130] How such suspicion may have arisen is not further detailed anywhere. In 1956, The Postmaster General was pleased to announce that Post Office procedure had been expanded to grant hearings "not only in cases of revocation of a second-class entry, but also where the Department proposed to deny an application for entry."[131] The announcement had a self-congratulatory air, as though the Department itself had come up with the idea. Self-congratulation ran through the Postmaster General's Annual Reports, in which selected statistics were prominently mentioned: "Arrests for the mailing of pornographic matter established a new record;"[132] "Arrests during the year totaled 389 [...] a 23.5 percent increase over the record year 1959;"[133] "Arrests for the mailing of obscene matter continued at an unprecedented pace, totaling 457 for the year;"[134] "[...] 503 convictions, the highest number ever recorded in a fiscal year [...]"[135] Despite these proud claims, reports still complained about "an avalanche of salacious material" in the mails.[136]

The Postmaster General seemed to recognise that, despite the powers of the Post Office, taking the risk of distributing via the mail was considered increasingly viable. Testifying in 1959 before the Subcommittee on Postal Operations of the Committee on Post Office and Civil Service, chaired by Representative Kathryn E. Granahan, Arthur E. Summerfield, then Postmaster General spoke of a "multimillion dollar mail-order traffic in obscenity," and

---

129 Fawcett might not have been a member of the Council at the time of Gathings, but it certainly became one. From 1963, at which time books by Packer &c. would still have been in print, they make a point of saying so on their title pages.

130 Jennifer M. Lynch, personal email 6th December 2018.

131 unattributed, *Annual Report of the Postmaster General* (United States Post Office Department, 1957). 87.

132 unattributed, *Annual Report of the Postmaster General* (United States Post Office Department, 1958). 88.

133 unattributed, *Annual Report of the Postmaster General* (United States Post Office Department, 1960). 103.

134 unattributed, *Annual Report of the Postmaster General* (United States Post Office Department, 1961). 96.

135 unattributed, *Annual Report of the Postmaster General* (United States Post Office Department, 1962). 109.

136 unattributed, *Annual Report of the Postmaster General*. 88.

24 *Introduction*

said that "\$500 million is realized annually in mail-order pornography."[137] He had no doubt what and who was to blame – the cheapness of production, and the attitude of the liberal, metropolitan establishment:

> There appear to be two basic reasons for the increasing volume of filth in the mails. First, the tremendous profits realized from a relatively small capital investment; and second, the very broad definition of obscenity handed down by certain courts, including those in certain metropolitan areas, notably Los Angeles and New York, where most of the mail-order business in obscenity and pornography originates.[138]

Though the Granahan Committee's remit was mainly in material other than books, Dan Lacy made a statement to them that the Phi Beta Kappa Society felt worth printing in *The American Scholar*, in which he defended the existence of the cheap paperback:

> But of course among the hundreds of book publishers, large and small, in the United States, both within the Council and without, books will continue to be published to which many will object. Nearly 150,000 different books will be published in this country in the 1960s. Some of them will be cheap and tawdry. Many of them will be tasteless and sensational. Some of them will be luridly covered. This is part of the price of freedom, just as sensational crime and sex headlines and photographs in some newspapers are part of the price of an unregulated newspaper press. All freedom is the freedom to act unwisely, and hence all freedom bears a price.[139]

It was within that freedom to act, wisely or unwisely, that cheap paperbacks continued to thrive, despite official pressure. It is worth noting that by the end of the 1950s, publishers such as Midwood, Beacon, Brandon House, Saber/Fabian, and Monarch had printed order slips in the rear paratext pages, encouraging readers to order further titles by mail, using the very medium of carriage that Dick Carroll had warned about.[140]

---

137 Kathryn E. Granahan and others, Obscene Matter sent through the Mail: Hearing before the Subcommittee on Postal Operations of the Committee on Post Office and Civil Service, House of Representatives, (U.S. Government, 1959). 4.

138 Granahan and others, Short Obscene Matter sent through the Mail: Hearing before the Subcommittee on Postal Operations of the Committee on Post Office and Civil Service, House of Representatives. 4.

139 Lacy, "Should the Book Publishing Industry Set Up a Self-Policing Program?." 446, 448.

140 At one point, however, Fabian Books did suspend their mail slip, pending a legal case, and directed their readers to send letters of support to the publisher's lawyers. Sela, *I am a Lesbian*. Rear paratext. I have found mail-order coupons of a similar type in UK editions, for example Edwina Mark, *My Sister, My Beloved* (Corgi, 1972).

"One-handed?" – "underground?": Who read these books and how did they read them?

The received wisdom about who read lesbian-themed genre fiction in the 1950s and 1960s is that the readership was split into two groups: the majority were men[141] with a voyeuristic interest in lesbians, and the minority were closeted or emerging lesbians. Of the majority group, Barbara Grier wrote scathingly in 2006 about male authors "writers writing for "one-handed" male readers who saw the lesbian theme as the stuff of classic heterosexual male masturbation fantasies," and about the "voyeuristic demands" of the readership.[142] To Roberta Yusba, the books were simply "designed to fulfil straight men's sexual fantasies."[143] Fran Koski and Maida Tilchen suspected that "some basically fine novels of lesbian love have been routinely injected with voyeuristic sex scenes for saleability" by male editors.[144] Valerie Taylor spoke of men's "erotic daydreaming,"[145] Marion Zimmer Bradley of the "drooling male" and the "one-handed reader,"[146] and Paula Christian of "the truck driver mentality" and men who wanted to know "what we did in bed."[147] Vin Packer admitted that, of course, some of her readers were men, hoping for a "pornographic buzz."[148] This dichotomy between the stereotypical "drooling male" and the closeted female has gained academic status, certainly in Melissa Sky's 2006 thesis, which deals with the bitextual nature of Ann Bannon's writing; Sky uses the words "pornography/pornographic" and "voyeur" liberally. Yvonne Keller juxtaposed "homophobia and voyeurism" in a near-paradox.[149] By contrast, the women readers showed they had "guts just to buy those books and confront the smirk on the face of the clerk at the cash register,"[150] and courage "to purchase explicitly lesbian pulp novels in

---

141 It is worth noting that even the popular name of the paperbacks – "pocket books" – can be considered gendered, as it refers to a feature of masculine clothing. They were never called "purse books."

142 In the Introduction to Taylor, *Whisper Their Love*. 11.

143 Roberta Yusba, "Twilight Tales: Lesbian Pulps 1950-1960," *On Our Backs*, no. Summer 1985. 30.

144 Koski and Tilchen, "Some Pulp Sappho." 42. Earlier in the same paragraph as this quote, Koski and Tilchen put the word *male* into italics, in case anyone should miss their point.

145 Garber, "Those Wonderful Lesbian Pulps: A Roundtable Discussion." 1.

146 Garber, "Those Wonderful Lesbian Pulps: A Roundtable Discussion." 4.

147 I find the phrase "truck driver mentality" to be rather classist. Christian attributes these phrases to her publisher. Garber, "Those Wonderful Lesbian Pulps: A Roundtable Discussion." 5.

148 Packer, *Spring Fire*. ix.

149 Keller, "Pulp Politics: Strategies of Vision in Pro-Lesbian Pulp Novels 1955-1965." 20.

150 Bannon, *Odd Girl Out*. viii.

26 Introduction

the days before the lesbian and gay liberation movement,"[151] and "to walk a gauntlet of fear up to the cash register."[152]

I do not wish to diminish anyone's courage nor the social and cultural pressures of the era, but this highlighting tends to establish a female default of timidity, which is another unhelpful stereotype. Purchasers of these paperbacks were not always shy, some would gleefully "grab" books with two women on the cover.[153] To many counter clerks it must have been a matter of indifference who bought what, under the principles that *pecunia non olet* and "everybody's money was good."[154] Equally stereotypical, but much more disparaging, is the language used about male readers, as quoted above. Again I do not wish to diminish the idea that these novels were mostly written with a largely male readership in mind – that supposition is, after all, one of the bases of this book – and had an instant hook for a readership on the move as they approached the newsstand. The fascination with lesbians is not easy to account for. In a lightweight article on pornography in 2016 – in the absence of any more serious study of the issue – Olga Khazan quotes neuroscientist Ogi Ogas as saying: "Sexual fantasy obeys its own set of rules that have nothing to do with propriety, common sense, or even the physical laws of the universe."[155] Ogas, however, goes on to make up the rule that men's fascination for seeing two women engaged in lovemaking is a simple matter of "doubling up" the visual stimulus of seeing one woman.[156] That not only contradicts his statement about sexual fantasy obeying its own set of rules, it is also plainly illogical; to "double up" the stimulus of the sight of one woman it is only necessary to see two women – they do not have to be engaged in any activity at all. Khazan's article is based on a data dump from the popular porn site "Pornhub," and she admits that the results are far from scientific; but she also maintains that the fascination with lesbians is not solely a male phenomenon: "In a *Marie Claire* survey of mainly female respondents, lesbian porn was the second most popular option [...]"[157] Whilst Khazan's find-

---

151 Nealon, *Foundlings: Lesbian and Gay Historical Emotion before Stonewall.* 141.

152 Katherine V. Forrest, ed., *Lesbian Pulp Fiction: The Sexually Intrepid World of Lesbian Paperback Novels 1950-1965* (Cleis, 2005). ix.

153 Stephanie Ozard, as quoted previously. Weissman and Fernie, "Forbidden Love: The Unashamed Stories of Lesbian Lives."

154 I am quoting directly from Keely Moll's assessment of the customer policy of the former Vanport Hotel in Vancouver, which had a bar popular with lesbians in this era, rather than specifically about book-buying. However, the principal is similar. Weissman and Fernie, "Forbidden Love: The Unashamed Stories of Lesbian Lives."

155 Olga Khazan, "Health: Why Straight Men Gaze at Gay Women: The psychology behind the male sexual desire for lesbians," *The Atlantic online* (28th March 2016), tinyurl.com/OlgaKhazan. Unnumbered.

156 Khazan, "Health: Why Straight Men Gaze at Gay Women: The psychology behind the male sexual desire for lesbians." Unnumbered.

157 Khazan, "Health: Why Straight Men Gaze at Gay Women: The psychology behind the male sexual desire for lesbians." Unnumbered.

Introduction 27

ings are from more than a half a century after the cheap paperback boom, and from a changed culture, her observations open the speculation that the female readership of lesbian-themed paperbacks may also have been wider than commentators suppose.

The width and attitude of the readership is further established by looking at the correspondence received by the authors. It may be hyperbole to say that men bought these books "by the millions,"[158] because there are no reliable data. Having been read, they were tossed into trash cans and forgotten.[159] Patricia Highsmith's diary contains a brief entry in 1953 to the effect that every day she got "a letter from someone regarding *The Price of Salt*,"[160] without further note about the correspondent's gender. Quite a lot of Ann Bannon's mail came from male readers, but most of them were gay or bisexual.[161] She also received mail and photos from transgender readers, as already stated.[162] According to Marijane Meaker, letters to her as Ann Aldrich were mainly from young women; "Mail that came from males was sparse and most often included boasts of sex prowess, the "all you need is a good man" response. A few females enclosed very explicit naked poses of themselves."[163] Stephanie Foote, in her Afterword to Aldrich's re-issued *We Walk Alone*, reiterates the bitextual assumption:

> Firstly, it's important to see that Ann Aldrich wrote to and within a generalized, even stereotyped straight culture, trying to interest readers in the question of homosexuality [...] Second, it's important to see that Aldrich was writing to and within a gay culture just beginning to organise politically and socially.[164]

However, the picture that is now emerging is more varied and more complex than that. The majority readership who snapped up these books from the newsstands is largely invisible. Whatever diabazophilia[165] motivated someone's initial purchase and continued reading, facetious generalisations about voyeuristic, one-handed masturbation fantasies of drooling males simply will not do. It is difficult not to sound facetious in reply, but I doubt if anyone who used or uses any of these phrases has actually tried to read

---

158 Ann Bannon, "The High Bar with Warren Etheredge: Interview with Ann Bannon," interview by Warren Etheredge, 2012, tinyurl.com/BannonEdge.
159 Bannon, *Odd Girl Out*. ix.
160 Highsmith, *Patricia Highsmith: Her Diaries and Notebooks*. 614.
161 Personal email, 28th May 2019.
162 Personal email, 29th December 2020.
163 Aldrich, *We Walk Alone*. xi.
164 And thus to push the envelope. Stephanie Foote, "Afterword to *We Walk Alone*, by Ann Aldrich," (The Feminist Press, 2006). 161.
165 "Diabazophilia" is my coining, to be the equivalent in terms of the written word to "scopophilia." It is not to be confused with "diavazophilia," which appears to be derived from modern Greek, and simply means the love of reading.

28   *Introduction*

a pocket-sized paperback without employing both hands, using the thumb of the hand holding it to turn the pages. Furthermore, someone who has a propensity to masturbate will do so irrespective of direct stimulus, and will certainly not do it where most of these books must have been read – on the bus or subway, at the lunch counter, or on a park bench. Neither are these books the only source of erotic stimulus available in the 1950s; although the 1960s are thought of as a time of increasing permissiveness, the 1950s was the era of Bettie Page, of pin-up and glamour magazines galore, and of course of the "avalanche of salacious material" in the mails,[166] besides which the sparse titillating passages in paperbacks seem almost tame. The invisibility of their readership points to what has already been proposed in this introduction, that they were read casually. "I was writing ephemeral literature for a casual audience," said Ann Bannon. "That was what was being asked of me, and what I tried to do."[167] Apart from the subject matter, there must be little to differentiate the readership from the consumers of any of the cheap genre fictions available at the time.

Formulaic or progressive? The novels in this book and their narratologies

Merja Makinen's work on feminist popular fiction affords some insight into genre fiction in general. "People enjoy genre fiction," she says, "it sells by the truckload."[168] In a passage that may be easily applied to the grabbing and reading of cheap paperbacks daily from the racks of newsstands, she says:

> The fact that popular genre readers consume vast amounts of their chosen genres is often taken as a sign of their complete lack of discernment, and therefore evidence of the text-dominated reading position. In fact it is often quite the opposite: the reading of large numbers of works of one genre allows the ordinary, non-academic reader a level of authority because of their overview of their subject. They come to hold a body of knowledge about the genre that informs their judgments about any particular text, however personal that judgment might be for their own uses.[169]

Frederic Jameson summed this up by calling genres "literary institutions" that are "social contracts between a writer and a specific public,"[170] and Peter H. Mann defined "popular formulaic fiction" as "fiction that is read for pleasure, as a form of escapism [...] the popular novel is there simply to entertain and

---

166 unattributed, *Annual Report of the Postmaster General*. (1958). 88.
167 Bannon, *Journey to a Woman*. v.
168 Merja Makinen, *Feminist Popular Fiction* (Palgrave, 2001). 10.
169 Makinen, *Feminist Popular Fiction*. 13-14.
170 Frederic Jameson, *The Political Unconscious* (Methuen, 1981). 106.

Introduction 29

to divert; if it fails to do this then it fails in its main function."[171] Mann's and Jameson's opinions might lead us to expect a rigidity of narrative formulae, and indeed there is plenty of indication that the winning formula established by Vin Packer's *Spring Fire* encouraged many copyists. But Makinen contradicts this assumption by maintaining that "no popular genre can be called 'inherently conservative' because they are all such loose, baggy chameleons," and that it is the genre canon that is conservative;[172] "Each genre is more than, and other than, its canonical construction."[173] Her statement to the effect that all genres "become conservative as they build up conventions"[174] seems to be borne out by the declaration in the second edition of *The Lesbian in Literature* that the editors had deleted "almost all "Trash" entries, thus removing over three thousand books from the bibliography,"[175] and by the republishing of selected novels in the late twentieth and early twenty-first centuries by such houses such as Naiad, the Feminist Press, and Cleis. Again, Makinen contradicts, by speaking about "the transformability of formula fiction."[176]

In looking at masculinity and heteronormativity, the following chapters of this book will draw on a range of texts, some of which are found in these later canons, and some not. In Chapter I, which deals with male characters, their agency, and their struggles with masculinity in an era of crisis, the first novel studied is Lora Sela's *I am a Lesbian*. Despite being the novel with the least literary merit – branded "T" for "Trash" in *The Lesbian in Literature* – it is the one which breaches the formula most clearly, having an overtly and even unrealistically "happy ending" for the principal lesbian couple.[177] The next novel is Vin Packer's seminal *Spring Fire*, which established the formula that *I am a Lesbian* breaks. Ann Bannon's *I am a Woman*, unlike her *Odd Girl Out*, does not follow that formula. Its importance in Chapter I is the way it features the complex character of Merrill Landon, the protagonist's father, whom we follow to his more peripheral role in Bannon's *Journey to a Woman*. This novel, which sees the end of the narrative timeline of Bannon's corpus, has an ending that is if not happy then at least optimistic.

---

171 Peter H. Mann, "The Romantic Novel and its Readers," *Journal of Popular Culture*, no. 5 (1981). 10.
172 Makinen, *Feminist Popular Fiction*. 1. Interesting that she echoes Henry James's description of works by Thackeray, Dumas, and Tolstoy as "loose baggy monsters." Henry James, *The Tragic Muse*, vol. 1 (Charles Scribner's Sons, 1936). x.
173 Makinen, *Feminist Popular Fiction*. 2.
174 Makinen, *Feminist Popular Fiction*. 1.
175 Gene Damon, Jan Watson, and Robin Jordan, *The Lesbian in Literature: a bibliography*, 2nd ed. (The Ladder, 1975). 4.
176 Makinen, *Feminist Popular Fiction*. 7.
177 Perhaps that is why, despite the editors' disdain for it, it could still be found in *The Lesbian in Literature*'s 3rd edition. Barbara Grier, *The Lesbian in Literature*, 3rd ed. (The Naiad Press, 1981). 138.

30 *Introduction*

Chapter II introduces "female masculinity," which is as elusive a concept as the equivalent with which the male characters struggled – an attempt to define "masculinity" is not made in this book up until this point. The section focuses on Ann Bannon's famous butch lesbian character Beebo Brinker and her place in the twentieth century midway, in terms of date of publication, between Stephen Gordon[178] and Jess Goldberg,[179] looking at her style, behaviour, and physicality in the light of what was considered masculine. Beebo features in four of Ann Bannon's novels, *I am a Woman*, *Women in the Shadows*, *Journey to a Woman*, and *Beebo Brinker*. None of those adheres to the expected formula, unless one counts the happy marriage of convenience between a male and female at the end of *Women in the Shadows*; however, the issue of convenience makes this an ironic nod to the formula. *Beebo Brinker* is a prequel, and the upbeat ending could well be taken as dramatic irony.

Chapter III is announced as "Female masculinity beyond Beebo" and is concerned with novels outside Bannon's corpus, such as Valerie Taylor's *Whisper Their Love*, to a lesser extent E.S. Seeley's *Sorority Sin* and Joan Ellis's *Girls Dormitory* [sic] as comparators, and also Claire Morgan's *The Price of Salt*. Taylor's novel is often treated as pro-lesbian, probably due to the quality of her writing and to the fact that she was a left-wing lesbian activist, but in fact it has a formulaic ending where the young, female protagonist finds romance with a young man. Seeley's novel is from the reservoir of lesbian-themed paperbacks written by men, and adheres to the expected formula, whilst Ellis's has only peripheral lesbian content. All of these touch on relationships where a young woman meets an older woman in a socially dominant position, but only Morgan's hints at optimism for the relationship. The chapter deals at length with Randy Salem's *Chris* and with its unconventionality; it has an ending in which the protagonist loses a lover to a male character, but there is a wryness to the latter's win that takes it a step away from the formulaic, and the protagonist advances in self-knowledge and integrity.

Chapter IV looks at the pro-lesbian literature of the era, particularly Ann Bannon's corpus, and examines the assertion that their project is "to present homosexuality as an acceptable identity – and, more than that, as an acceptable *life*."[180] The couple, however, whether straight or gay, emerges if not as the deliberate project, then as the effective one. The starting point of the

---

178 Protagonist of Radclyffe Hall's *The Well of Loneliness*. It is becoming more common these days to refer to Stephen Gordon as a trans man and use "he" pronouns; see for example Zoë Playdon, *The Hidden Case of Ewan Forbes: The Transgender Trial that Threatened to Upend the British Establishment* (Bloomsbury, 2021). 13-14. This is an entirely legitimate interpretation. For the purposes of this project, however, and in keeping with the episteme, I align Stephen's birth identity with Beebo Brinker's.

179 Protagonist of Leslie Feinberg's *Stone Butch Blues*.

180 Nealon, "Invert-History: The Ambivalence of Lesbian Pulp Fiction." 757.

Introduction   31

chapter, as regards text, is Bannon's *The Marriage*, which puts the notion of heterosexual couplehood under severe stress. Stress is reiterated in the façade of a Hollywood marriage (in Bannon's *Beebo Brinker*), in marriages of convenience between a gay man and a lesbian (notably Jack and Laura Mann, in Bannon's corpus), and in a ménage of two lesbians (notably in Randy Salem's *Chris*).

In the final chapter of the book – Chapter V – I note that in order to produce tension in the novels' narratives, masculinity as popularly understood is seen to fail in all characters, irrespective of their sex. Moreover, heteronormativity, rather than being a measure of statistical distribution of something natural, is seen as a state that has to be striven for. In this respect my conclusions do veer towards the general instability of gender. I put forward the use and abuse of alcohol as being the normative cultural influence in these novels, before closing with pointers to further research.

Bibliography

Aldrich, Ann. *We Walk Alone*. The Feminist Press, 2006.
Bannon, Ann. "The High Bar with Warren Etheredge: Interview with Ann Bannon." By Warren Etheredge. 2012. tinyurl.com/BannonEdge.
———. *I am a Woman*. Cleis, 2002.
———. *Journey to a Woman*. Cleis, 2003.
———. *Odd Girl Out*. Cleis, 2001.
Barthes, Roland. *Camera Lucida: Reflections on Photography*. Translated by Richard Howard. Hill & Wang, 1981.
"Bookscans: Gold Medal." 2020, tinyurl.com/FawcettGM.
Bonn, Thomas L. "The Paperback: Image and Object." In *International Book Publishing: An Encyclopedia*, edited by Philip G. Altbach and Edith S. Hoshino, 262–70. Routledge, 1995.
Breines, Wini. *Young, White, and Miserable: Growing up Female in the Fifties*. Beacon, 1992.
Coulter, Adam. *Lesbian Captive*. Brandon, 1964.
Damon, Gene, Jan Watson, and Robin Jordan. *The Lesbian in Literature: A Bibliography*. 2nd ed. The Ladder, 1975.
de Grazia, Edward. "Obscenity and the Mail: A Study of Administrative Restraint." *Law and Contemporary Problems* 20, no. 4 (1955): 608–20.
Devlin, Barry. *Forbidden Pleasures*. Berkley, 1953.
Dworkin, Andrea. *Our Blood: Prophecies and Discourses on Sexual Politics*. The Women's Press, 1982.
Flora, Fletcher. *Desperate Asylum*. Lion Library, 1955.
———. *Strange Sisters*. Lion, 1954.
Foote, Stephanie. "Afterword to *We Walk Alone*, by Ann Aldrich." 157–83: The Feminist Press, 2006.
Forrest, Katherine V., ed. *Lesbian Pulp Fiction: The Sexually Intrepid World of Lesbian Paperback Novels 1950–1965*. Cleis, 2005.
Fried, Richard M. *Nightmare in Red: The Mccarthy Era in Perspective*. Oxford University Press, 1991.
Garber, Eric. "Those Wonderful Lesbian Pulps, Part 2." *San Francisco Bay Area Gay and Lesbian Historical Society Newsletter* 5, no. 1 (1989): 7–8.

32 Introduction

———. "Those Wonderful Lesbian Pulps: A Roundtable Discussion." *The San Francisco Bay Area Gay & Lesbian Historical Society Newsletter* 4, no. 4 (1989): 1, 4–5.

Gathings, Ezekiel C., and others. *Investigation of Literature Allegedly Containing Objectionable Material: Hearings before the Select Committee on Current Pornographic Materials.* U.S. Government, 1952.

———. *Report of the Select Committee on Current Pornographic Materials.* U.S. Government, 1952.

Gilbert, James. *Men in the Middle: Searching for Masculinity in the 1950s.* University of Chicago Press, 2005.

Ginsberg, Allen. *Howl and Other Poems.* The Pocket Poets. City Lights Books, 1959.

Goodwin, Doris Kearns. "The Way We Won; America's Economic Breakthrough During World War Ii." *The American Prospect* (Fall 1992): 66.

Granahan, Kathryn E., and others. *Obscene Matter Sent through the Mail: Hearing before the Subcommittee on Postal Operations of the Committee on Post Office and Civil Service, House of Representatives.* U.S. Government, 1959.

Greco, Albert N. *The Economics of the Publishing and Information Industries: The Search for Yield in a Disintermediated World.* Routledge, 2014.

Grier, Barbara. *The Lesbian in Literature.* 3rd ed.: The Naiad Press, 1981.

Halberstam, Jack. *Trans*.* University of California Press, 2018.

Hall, Stuart. "Old and New Identities, Old and New Ethnicities." In *Culture, Globalization and the World-System: Contemporary Conditions for the Representation of Identity*, edited by Anthony D. King, 41–68. Macmillan, 1991.

Harris, Frank G. *Mike Addison.* Saber, 1963.

Hermes, Joke. "Sexuality in Lesbian Romance Fiction." *Feminist Review*, no. 42 (1992): 49–66.

Highsmith, Patricia. *Patricia Highsmith: Her Diaries and Notebooks.* Edited by Anna von Planta. Weidenfeld & Nicholson, 2021.

Holk, Agnete. *Strange Friends.* Pyramid, 1963.

James, Henry. *The Tragic Muse*, Vol. 1. Charles Scribner's Sons, 1936.

Jameson, Frederic. *The Political Unconscious.* Methuen, 1981.

Jamieson, John. *Editions for the Armed Services, Inc.: A History Together with the Complete List of 1324 Books Published for American Armed Forces Overseas.* Editions for the Armed Services, Inc., 1948. tinyurl.com/EditionsArmed

Keller, Yvonne. "Ab/Normal Looking: Voyeurism and Surveillance in Lesbian Pulp Novels and Us Cold War Culture." *Feminist Media Studies* 5, no. 2 (2005): 177–95.

———. "Pulp Politics: Strategies of Vision in Pro-Lesbian Pulp Novels 1955–1965." In *The Queer Sixties*, edited by Patricia Juliana Smith, 1–25. Routledge, 1999.

Kennedy, Elizabeth Lapovsky, and Madeline D. Davis. *Boots of Leather, Slippers of Gold: The History of a Lesbian Community.* Penguin, 1993.

Kent, Harrison. *Tropic of Lesbos.* Private Edition, 1966.

Key, David. *Strange Sisters.* Bee Line, 1967.

Khazan, Olga. "Health: Why Straight Men Gaze at Gay Women: The Psychology Behind the Male Sexual Desire for Lesbians." *The Atlantic online* (28 March 2016). tinyurl.com/OlgaKhazan.

Koski, Fran, and Maida Tilchen. "Some Pulp Sappho." *Margins: A Review of Little Magazines & Small Press Books*, no. 23 (1975): 41–45.

Kramer, Gerald. *Penthouse Party.* Midwood, 1965.

Lacy, Dan. "Should the Book Publishing Industry Set up a Self-Policing Program?" *The American Scholar* 29, no. 3 (1960): 407, 38, 40, 42, 44, 46, 48.

Lacy, Dan, and Robert W. Frase. "The American Book Publishers Council." In *The Enduring Book: Print Culture in Postwar America*, edited by David Paul Nord, Joan Shelley Rubin, and Michael Schudson. A History of the Book in America, 195–209. University of North Carolina Press, 2009.

Larrabee, Eric. "The Cultural Context of Sex Censorship." *Law and Contemporary Problems* 20, no. 4 (1955): 672–88.

Leavitt, Josie. "Why Must We Continue to Strip Covers?" *Publishers Weekly: ShelfTalker*, 2011. tinyurl.com/CoverStrip.

Loewenstein, Andrea. "Sad Stories: A Reflection on the Fiction of Ann Bannon." *Gay Community News* (24 May 1980): unnumbered. tinyurl.com/LoewensteinBannon.

Makinen, Merja. *Feminist Popular Fiction*. Palgrave, 2001.

Mann, Peter H. "The Romantic Novel and Its Readers." *Journal of Popular Culture* 15, no. 1 (1981): 9–18.

Mark, Edwina. *My Sister, My Beloved*. Corgi, 1972.

Markham, Clancy. *Wild, Way out and Wanton*. Royal Line, 1965.

Marshall, Edward. *Madame Butch*. After Hours, 1966.

Matelski, Elizabeth M. "The Colour(S) of Perfection: The Feminine Body, Beauty Ideals, and Identity in Postwar America, 1945–1970." Doctor of Philosophy, Loyola University, 2011.

McCarrick, Malia (Mary) L. "The Influence of Lesbian Identity Development on Lesbian Literature through a Study of Character Experience in Ann Bannon's Beebo Brinker Series: A Creative Dissertation with Contextual Essay." PhD, Union Institute & University, 2010.

McCarthy, Joseph, and others. *Executive Sessions of the Senate Permanent Subcommittee on Investigations of the Committee on Government Operations, 1953–1954*. U.S. Government, 2003.

McHale, Brian. "Genre Fiction." In *Routledge Encyclopedia of Narrative Theory*, edited by David Herman, Manfred Jahn and Marie-Laure Ryan, 199. Routledge, 2007.

Miller, Allyson. "Postwar Masculine Identity in Ann Bannon's *I am a Woman*." University of Missouri-Columbia, 2009.

Millett, Kate. *Flying*. Ballantine Books, 1975.

Moore, Melina Alice. ""A Boy inside It": Beebo Brinker and the Transmasculine Narratives of Ann Bannon's Lesbian Pulp." *GLQ: A Journal of Lesbian and Gay Studies* 25, no. 4 (2019): 569–98.

Morgan, Claire. *The Price of Salt*. Bantam, 1953.

Morgan, Helen. *Killer Dyke*. Exotik, 1964.

Morro, Don. *The Virgin*. Beacon, 1955.

Nealon, Christopher. *Foundlings: Lesbian and Gay Historical Emotion before Stonewall*. Duke University Press, 2001.

———. "Invert-History: The Ambivalence of Lesbian Pulp Fiction." *New Literary History* 31, no. 4 (2000): 745–64.

. "The Oxford English Dictionary 2nd Edn. Online." 2021. tinyurl.com/OEDictry.

Packer, Vin. *Spring Fire*. Cleis, 2004.

Peters, Willi. *Lesbian Twins*. Vega, 1962.

Petersen, Clarence. *The Bantam Story: Twenty-Five Years of Paperback Publishing*. Bantam, 1970.

Playdon, Zoë. *The Hidden Case of Ewan Forbes: The Transgender Trial That Threatened to Upend the British Establishment*. Bloomsbury, 2021.

Rabinowitz, Paula. *American Pulp: How Paperbacks Brought Modernism to Main Street*. Princeton University Press, 2014.

Rorty, James. "The Harassed Pocket-Book Publishers." *The Antioch Review* 15, no. 4 (1955): 411–27.

34 *Introduction*

Sela, Lora. *I am a Lesbian*. Saber, 1959.

Sky, Melissa. "Twilight Tales: Ann Bannon's Lesbian Pulp Series 'the Beebo Brinker Chronicles'." PhD Thesis, McMaster University, 2006.

Smith, Artemis. *This Bed We Made*. Monarch, 1961.

Stratton, S. Lou. "More Than Throw-Away Fiction: Investigating Lesbian Pulp Fiction through the Lens of a Lesbian Textual Community." PhD Thesis, University of Birmingham, 2008.

Stryker, Susan. *Queer Pulp: Perverted Passions from the Golden Age of the Paperback*. Chronicle Books, 2001.

Tarantino, Quentin. "Pulp Fiction." Mirarmax, 1994.

Tashlin, Frank. "Artists and Models." Paramount, 1955.

Taylor, Valerie. *Whisper Their Love*. Little Sister's Classics. Arsenal Pulp Press, 2006.

Tóibín, Colm, Merve Emre, and Daniel Mulhall. "Ulysses." By Chris Power. *Open Book*. BBC Radio4. 16 January 2022.

Tynyanov, Yuri. "The Literary Fact." Translated by Anna Shukman. In *Modern Genre Theory*, edited by David Duff, 29–49. Routledge, 2000.

unattributed. *Annual Report of the Postmaster General* (United States Post Office Department, 1960).

———. *Annual Report of the Postmaster General* (United States Post Office Department, 1961).

———. *Annual Report of the Postmaster General* (United States Post Office Department, 1955).

———. *Annual Report of the Postmaster General* (United States Post Office Department, 1957).

———. *Annual Report of the Postmaster General* (United States Post Office Department, 1958).

———. *Annual Report of the Postmaster General* (United States Post Office Department, 1962).

———. "Censorship of Obscene Literature by Informal Governmental Action." *The University of Chicago Law Review* 22, no. 1 (1954): 216–33.

———. "Defendants Settle in N.Y. Stripped Paperback Suits." *Publishers Weekly* 233 (29 April 1988): 13+.

———. "Firm Fined on Obscene Books Charge: Judge Finds Novel to Be 'Lewd, Filthy'." *Winnipeg Free Press*, 24 November 1952, 9.

———. *Fresh Air: Writer Marijane Meaker*. Podcast audio2003.

———. *Pulp Studies*. Popular Culture Association, 2021. tinyurl.com/pcaacapulp.

Villarejo, Amy. "Forbidden Love: Pulp as Lesbian History." In *Outtakes*, edited by Ellis Hanson, 316–45. Duke University Press, 1999.

———. *Lesbian Rule: Cultural Criticism and the Value of Desire*. Duke University Press, 2003.

Weinstein, Jeff. "In Praise of Pulp." *Voice Literary Supplement*October 1983): 8–9.

Weissman, Aerlyn, and Lynne Fernie. "Forbidden Love: The Unashamed Stories of Lesbian Lives." National Film Board of Canada, 1993.

Weldon, Rex. *Love Me Wild*. Brandon House, 1965.

Weston, Carolyn. *Tormented*. Berkley, 1956.

Williams, A.P. *Tutor from Lesbos*. Beacon Signal Sixty, 1964.

Willis, A.M. *Butch Fever*. Private Edition, 1965.

Willow, Peter. *Odd Neighbors*. Wee Hours, 1967.

Woodward, L.T. *Twilight Women*. Lancer, 1963.

Yusba, Roberta. "Twilight Tales: Lesbian Pulps 1950–1960." *On Our Backs*, no. Summer 1985: 30–31, 43.

I Male agency, and "the immense social power that accumulates around masculinity?"

I'm strictly a female female
And my future I hope will be
In the home of a brave and free male
Who'll enjoy being a guy, having a girl like me[1]

The masculine power that moves a narrative?

The quoted part of the title of this chapter, taken from Jack Halberstam's book *Female Masculinity*,[2] is simply a phrase that occurs within that text, along with many others that speak of the power that accrues to the binary male and that attaches the epithet "masculinity" to it. It is not the only occurrence of the word "power" in the book. Halberstam speaks, for example, of "the complex social structures that wed masculinity to maleness and to power and domination,"[3] and "the static loop that makes maleness plus power into the formula for abuse."[4] In this chapter, I will examine two main aspects of the melding of maleness and masculinity within the texts of the novels. One is the aptitude, or ineptitude, with which male characters appear to wear or to wield masculinity; the other is the way that male power manifests in these novels, at a structural level, as agency, i.e., when male characters shape the events of the narratives. On the face of it, these two aspects appear to pull against each other – how can an inept man have agency? – but in fact this is often not the case. Under the sub-heading **Male characters: the stereotype in isolation**, I foreground two male characters from Lora Sela's novel *I am a Lesbian* for both their agency in the narrative and the challenge to masculinity, or masculinities, that they embody. The next section, **The homosocial environment: frat men and sorority girls**, deals with the novels that place young masculinity in a social context and relates young men's behaviour to

---

1 Richard Rodgers and Oscar Hammerstein, "I Enjoy Being A Girl," (1958).
2 The phrase in the book appears without a question mark. Jack Halberstam, *Female Masculinity* (Duke University Press, 1998). 269.
3 Halberstam, *Female Masculinity*. 2.
4 Halberstam, *Female Masculinity*. 276.

DOI: 10.4324/9781003422679-2

36 *Male agency*

the "masculinity crisis"[5] of the 1950s, and the peer pressure of dating habits of the same era. Attitudes to non-consensual and assumed-consensual sex in the texts are compared to those demonstrated by Ayn Rand, in her defence of *The Fountainhead*. **Generational isolation: the absent father** deals with the influence of fathers, based on money and status, remote from their daughters' life in college. This section introduces Ann Bannon's Merrill Landon, one of the most important male characters in her corpus and in the texts under study, in his role as an absent figure in *Odd Girl Out*. The next section, **The shock of the paternal presence: Merrill Landon's agency**, may seem at first to be an apologia for the character who emerges fully in Bannon's *I am a Woman*. However, the superficial and stereotypical reading of Landon as nothing more than a brutal and uncaring father, merely there in Laura's *Bildung* to be broken free from, is inadequate for a study of masculinity in these novels. His character has far more depth and far more agency than that, and will be given the close attention it warrants. In particular, I will go into considerable textual detail about the confrontation between Laura and Merrill in his hotel room, and Laura's quasi-Freudian claims that he forced her sexuality on her. In the section **Redemption for the absentee father?** I look at the character of Merrill Landon beyond *I am a Woman*, and in particular his absentee agency in *Journey to a Woman*, and ask whether by the time Ann Bannon came to write the prequel *Beebo Brinker* she had become reconciled to father-figures in general. The overall conclusion of this chapter, however, will be that in the chosen texts, masculinity has failed as a comfortable and identifiable characteristic of men and has been left open to adoption by women, as will be considered in Chapter II.

Male characters: the stereotype in isolation

Looking back in 2018 on what she perceived to be the sociology of the 1950s, Ann Bannon said of her own ability to write male characters:

> The very model of a stereotypical straight male at the time was a serious turn-off. Too many of them were trying to be Alpha Males, virtually all of them expected to be admired, catered to, and pursued by silly women, and there were floods of testosterone animating their speech and behavior. I'm not unsympathetic—it was a tough ideal to live up for the young men of the time, but they felt driven to act out their mastery over the environment, and certainly over women. They were relentlessly competitive. Making all this worse for me was my perdurable naivete. Even in my twenties, I had a great deal to learn about human

---

5 James Gilbert, *Men in the Middle: Searching for Masculinity in the 1950s* (U of Chicago P, 2005). 16.

Male agency   37

behavior. So when I did try to write about straight guys, I resorted to what now sounds, many decades later, like a bad movie typecasting.[6]

This points to the existence in the 1950s of a binary cultural attitude which polarised the sexes, and considering that the authors dealt with in this book are mainly female, one difficulty with looking at the male characters in this literary niche is the possibility that they are less fully drawn than are their female counterparts. The "tough ideal" that Bannon speaks of existed because the 1950s were unusual across a wide area of American culture, as James Gilbert puts it, for their "relentless and self-conscious preoccupation with masculinity,"[7] where men strove to enjoy being the Rodgers and Hammerstein "brave and free male"[8] from the quotation at the top of this chapter, with its allusion to the Americanness of "The Star-Spangled Banner." In the novels written by men – the "virile adventures" as Yvonne Keller called them[9] – whether under their own name or a male or female pseudonym and with an assumed male readership, there was as much stereotyping. Marion Zimmer Bradley[10] and Gene Damon referred dismissively to the prevalence in the male-authored novels of "[...] some Big Handsome Hero who eventually converts the girls to 'normality' with some secret formula of caresses,"[11] as the authors strove to provide male readers with a character they could identify with. Bradley and Damon referred to such books as a "short course in voyeurism" or "scv" for short, and thus starting this analysis of male characters with Lora Sela's *I am a Lesbian* is a double disadvantage, as they dismissed the book with "[t]his isn't even scv, since the writers of sexy trash usually know something about sex or trash or both. Read it and snicker."[12] This is despite the fact that the author was a woman and

---

6 Personal email, 28th May 2019.
7 Gilbert, *Men in the Middle: Searching for Masculinity in the 1950s.* 2. Gilbert does concede that the 1950s were not unique in this respect but were particularly marked for their sense of "male panic" and "masculinity crisis." 2, 16.
8 Rodgers and Hammerstein, "I Enjoy Being A Girl."
9 Yvonne Keller, "Pulp Politics: Strategies of Vision in Pro-Lesbian Pulp Novels 1955–1965," in *The Queer Sixties*, ed. Patricia Juliana Smith (Routledge, 1999). 2.
10 Though Bradley's posthumous reputation is irredeemably tarnished, she is an important source of information about fiction with this theme.
11 Marion Zimmer Bradley and Gene Damon, *Checklist 1960: A Complete, Cumulative Checklist of Lesbian, Variant, and Homosexual Fiction, in English, or Available in English Translation, with Supplements of Related Material, for the Use of Collectors, Students, and Librarians* (Self-published by Marion Zimmer Bradley, 1960). Unpaginated.
12 Bradley and Damon, *Checklist 1960: A Complete, Cumulative Checklist of Lesbian, Variant, and Homosexual Fiction, in English, or Available in English Translation, with Supplements of Related Material, for the Use of Collectors, Students, and Librarians.* Bradley and Damon also damn a book written under Hales's real name, *Such is My Beloved* (Berkley, 1958), thus: "Sad, sad, sad story of the psychoanalysis of a young lesbian such as was never seen on sea or land. Harmless and nitwitted … read it and weep, or giggle."

38 Male agency

there was no stereotypical "hero" figure for them to point at.[13] Saber Books, the publisher of *I am a Lesbian*, put on a front of social campaigning. Sela's novel was promoted thus: "Lesbians are a part of our society and they will very likely remain so [...] real lesbians whose hearts are as warm and deserving of understanding as any other segment of human life."[14] The paratext on the final, unnumbered leaves of the novel contains a note about Saber's victory in the court case, brought by "the Government," concerning the alleged obscenity of three of their novels, and an appeal for letters expressing opinions as to whether Saber publications should be available to "the average, normal person."[15] The same paratext contains a promotional paragraph for the magazine *Sex and Censorship*, which purports to examine "the wide gap between our sexual code and our conflicting social behavior."[16]

Saber's campaigning was, however, rather disingenuous. A one-page article in *The Ladder*, shortly after the novel was published, quoted extracts from a letter Sela had sent to them. *The Ladder* notes that the book is "designed to appeal to the reader looking for a thrill," but then quotes Sela as saying:

> I agreed to give the publisher overt sex scenes IF he would allow me to get my own propaganda over – to gain understanding and tolerance for Lesbians [...] To reach the persons who choose a novel for its sex content you cannot plug for understanding without also stressing sex scenes.[17]

The Ladder concluded that the problem of reaching the "mass audience" – presumably those readers seeking a vicarious thrill – was "a serious one for the homophile" in the late 1950s, and that perhaps *I am a Lesbian* was one answer to the problem.[18] A physical examination of the novel shows it to be a very slim paperback by the standards of the era, containing only one hundred and twenty-four pages of story text, amounting to about thirty-seven thousand words. At a cover price of thirty-five cents, this seems meagre even by 1950s standards. The slimness of the book may be reflected in the fact that the female protagonist is almost entirely passive, devoid of agency. Apart

---

13 Lora Sela is the pseudonym of Carol Hales (acknowledged in *Checklist*). It is easy enough to see that the real forename and surname have been shorn of their initial letters and then reversed.

14 Lora Sela, *I am a Lesbian* (Saber, 1959). Rear cover blurb.

15 Sela, *I am a Lesbian*. Rear paratext – NB I have had access to two printings of this novel, one prior to and one after the court case (but otherwise not differentiated by displayed date), each with a different rear paratext. The court case was originally brought in respect of eleven books, according to Saber, but the Government dropped its case against eight of them. There is no indication that any of the books concerned were lesbian-themed or had any lesbian plot elements.

16 Sela, *I am a Lesbian*. Rear paratext.

17 unattributed, "I am a Lesbian," Review, *The Ladder* (January 1959). 17. Capitalisation and underlining as per original.

18 unattributed, "I am a Lesbian." 17.

from one brief intervention by a young butch lesbian, agency throughout rests in the hands of two male characters, each of which is one-dimensional. If either offers any challenges to the idea of masculinity, they do so first of all by way of their very flatness as characters.

Bob Kemp, who dominates the first four-fifths of the novel, is handsome, or would be, were it not for his scowl.[19] Early in the novel, the author catalogues Bob's childhood and teenage molestations of the protagonist, Melba.[20] In adulthood, he becomes vindictive towards her but still wants to "make" her, "make" being an obsolescent slang term meaning to have sex with someone.[21] Rebuffed, he wastes no opportunity to hurt or torment Melba and her lover Jan, doing everything from foisting his company on them when they were hoping for privacy,[22] to attempting to run them down in his car and taunting them that any court case brought against him would give him an opportunity to reveal their covert relationship.[23] There is nothing written into his character that is not pure vindictiveness, which Jan explains with the words "When a male who doesn't, who won't even try to understand women like us – hates us [...] then he misses no opportunity to hurt us."[24] His vindictiveness comes to a head when he rapes Melba, under threat of strangulation,[25] crowing "I've made a female of you!"[26] The rape results in pregnancy. Melba is pressed by Bob's parents to marry him, and when she refuses, he simply outs her.[27] The slimness of the novel means that the pace does not flag and, as is the case with melodrama, narrative pace is more important than characterisation,[28] although that does not excuse the lack of the latter. Melba's baby is stillborn;[29] Jan having been tricked by Melba's family into abandoning her, Melba settles for marriage to kindly, gentle, older Granger Macy, which proves to be calm but sexually and emotionally unfulfilling.[30]

It takes some considerable narrative time for Granger to realise that something is wrong with the marriage. Melba can't bring herself to be "cruel" to

---

19 Sela, *I am a Lesbian.* 84.
20 Sela, *I am a Lesbian.* 13–18.
21 Sela, *I am a Lesbian.* 29.
22 Sela, *I am a Lesbian.* 43–45.
23 Sela, *I am a Lesbian.* 54–55.
24 Sela, *I am a Lesbian.* 28.
25 Sela, *I am a Lesbian.* 59–60. It would be impossible to find out whether such a violent rape was one of the "overt sex scenes" for which Sela was asked.
26 Sela, *I am a Lesbian.* 61.
27 Sela, *I am a Lesbian.* 64.
28 Joke Hermes, " "Sexuality in Lesbian Romance Fiction," *Feminist Review*, no. 42 (1992). 62. "Melodrama" is a word used by many critics, especially Christopher Nealon in his article "Invert-History: The Ambivalence of Lesbian Pulp Fiction," to refer to the works of Ann Bannon. In my opinion, Lora Sela's *I am a Lesbian* is far more deserving of the term.
29 Sela, *I am a Lesbian.* 76.
30 Sela, *I am a Lesbian.* 79 et seq.

40 *Male agency*

him and confess her sexuality,[31] and he takes her sobs to be a sign of passion.[32] When he eventually learns from Melba that she can't love a man the way she loves Jan, he takes over agency in the novel. He promises: "Little Melba, I'm going to try and help you live a normal life [...] I mean the kind that is *normal for you.*"[33] The italics are as printed. "Normal" is used here with little regard to its statistical meaning, but more to signify what Granger considers to be natural for Melba; this is slightly more in keeping with the twentieth-century conflation of normality and health.[34] Granger promises to be a friend to Melba,[35] spares no effort to find Jan,[36] eventually granting Melba a quiet divorce and convincing Melba's family to accept her lesbian relationship.[37] It is the thinness of this resolution which prompts Bradley and Damon to damn the book: "all that God wants of her, according to the author, is for her to be a Happy Well-Adjusted Noble Lesbian."[38] Yet a challenge to the male characters remains. Bob, having had his comeuppance when laid out by a single punch from Mac, the peripheral butch character, and delivered home by her in his own car, watches the total if clumsily expressed triumph of a lesbian relationship. Granger, having shown a total lack of perspicacity about his wife and having quietly given up his marriage to someone he genuinely loves, cedes his place to "a masculine lesbian" between whom and the femininity of Melba "nature strikes a balance."[39] In Sela's melodrama, not even the gentlest of males can do other than fail the challenge offered to traditionally triumphant masculinity, although it is masculinity said to be vested in a woman that does triumph.[40]

This novel, with its optimistic resolution for the lovers, appeared only one year after Ann Bannon had published her first novel, *Odd Girl Out*, which, to an extent, followed the "unhappy ending" template on which Fawcett

---

31 Sela, *I am a Lesbian.* 80.

32 Sela, *I am a Lesbian.* 82.

33 Sela, *I am a Lesbian.* 116.

34 This is dealt with in detail in the first chapter of Karma Lochrie's *Heterosyncrasies*, quoted elsewhere in this book. It is notable that the word "normal" appears several times in quotation marks in *I am a Lesbian*. At one point Melba finds it almost impossible to say, and Granger vows to "strike it from [his] vocabulary." Sela, *I am a Lesbian.* 91. I am aware that simply substituting "natural" for "normal" can be seen as introducing an essentialist argument, but that is precisely what I see here in the text.

35 Sela, *I am a Lesbian.* 118.

36 Sela, *I am a Lesbian.* 122.

37 Sela, *I am a Lesbian.* 125.

38 Bradley and Damon, *Checklist 1960: A Complete, Cumulative Checklist of Lesbian, Variant, and Homosexual Fiction, in English, or Available in English Translation, with Supplements of Related Material, for the Use of Collectors, Students, and Librarians.*

39 Sela, *I am a Lesbian.* 10.

40 As I have previously noted, this is a particularly diluted triumph, as Jan has very little agency in the novel. Beyond Melba's eventual confession to Granger, the agency involved in this triumph is that of Granger's willing capitulation.

Male agency   41

editor Dick Carroll insisted,[41]and one year before her more upbeat *I am a Woman*.[42] It shows that other publishers, even those with venal motives, were prepared to push the envelope in the contest between the sexual code and social behaviour. It also shows that not all pro-lesbian authors and pro-lesbian texts are necessarily considered, by the gatekeepers of later publishing houses such as Naiad and Cleis, to be of a literary quality sufficient to elevate them to canonical status within their publishing niche, and consequently they have been largely ignored in academic studies so far.[43]

The homosocial environment: frat men and sorority girls

Both Bob Kemp and Granger Macy may be considered aberrant characters. Bob is a singleton example of an extreme, aggressive masculinity, and Granger of an unaggressive one. Both are assertive in their own way; Granger takes the lead in sex, and has agency in the narrative, so he is certainly not passive. Their aberration lies in the way that they are isolated socially, so perhaps the aberrance is attributable to the paucity of Sela's narrative. There is no apparent background for their characters, no social context in which they stand. Bob's viciousness and Granger's kindness evidence a kind of essentialist thinking in the author. One has to look elsewhere in this literary niche for masculinity in a distinct social context. Seven years before *I am a Lesbian* was published, Vin Packer's *Spring Fire* presented a microcosm in which aggressive masculinity was the social norm – the college fraternity in its relation to a corresponding sorority. The two principal female characters in both novels entered adulthood with a history of suffering a certain amount of childhood molestation. Melba's was at the hand of Bob. By way of background to a distinct period in her life, Mitch's experience might have been considered infantile play: "She thought of Billy Erikson – the day in

---

41 Vin Packer, *Spring Fire* (Cleis, 2004). vi. Vin Packer met Ann Bannon, was an influence on her, and introduced her to Dick Carroll, who was still in post at Fawcett Gold Medal. *Odd Girl Out* does share some plot similarities with *Spring Fire* but is lighter in tone. Dick Carroll also persuaded Bannon to shorten her manuscript and focus on two college girls, thereby enhancing the similarities. See Bannon, *Odd Girl Out*. viii. The lighter tone of *Odd Girl Out*, in which the two principals part, each to a new life, may have been the result of Carroll's realisation that it was time for a change. Bannon said, "Somehow, Dick Carroll had recognised something I didn't know until years later was important. And that was that these two women did not have to self-destruct [...]" Kate Brandt, *Happy Endings: Lesbian Writers Talk About Their Lives and Work* (Naiad, 1993). 77.

42 It is worth noting in passing that the first paperback of any repute in which there was an optimistic ending was the reprint of Claire Morgan's *The Price of Salt* in 1953. Its hardback edition appeared the same year as Vin Packer's *Spring Fire*, the first novel to the Carroll template. Both sold well, both attracted letters from readers, only one became the formula for "easy winners" in the sub-genre.

43 The name Lora Sela, for example, returns no result in Google Scholar, apart from one mention in *Checklist*.

42 *Male agency*

the bushes when he had showed it to her. The snake, she had called it to herself. The snake that men have."[44] The repercussions, however, carry forward into her impression of "men," as it is their sex that has the menacing "snake," both an obvious phallic symbol and a reminder of the instigator of human unhappiness in Genesis chapter 3.[45] For Leda, molestation was at the hands of one of her mother's boyfriends, in her mother's presence,[46] compounded by the psychological pressure of hearing her mother's compulsive promiscuity through the dividing wall between their rooms.[47] But whereas the abuse Melba suffers in adulthood is a continuation of the abuse she suffered in childhood, Mitch enters this distinct period, away from her childhood home, in a college sorority. The corresponding college fraternity depicted in *Spring Fire* is a male homosocial environment, but one which has a pre-defined social interaction with the female homosocial sorority, and which actively interpenetrates college life whilst remaining somehow aloof. Fraternity "men" are:

> [...] suave, confident young men whose loafered feet stretched out in the aisles, and whose bold guffaws echoed after the prof's jokes. They had names like Grey Gregg and Big Tom D. and Rabbit Man and they sat in clumps together. There was something different about them [...] something that was not neutral but cold and hot as they willed in their way with others.[48]

Their fraternity songs are genuine examples from campuses of the time and take on a menacing tone, especially this one, which occurs almost immediately after a rape scene:

> We are the great big, wow! Hairy-chested men, wow
> Hairy-chested men! Wow! Hairy-chested men!
> We are the great big, wow! Hairy-chested men!
> We can do an-nee-thing! Wow![49]

---

44 Packer, *Spring Fire*. 16.
45 I make no apology for using the hackneyed term "phallic symbol" here, given the prevalence of pop-Freudianism in paperbacks and in the popular imagination of the time. An internet search for "pop-Freudianism" in the 1950s brings up countless references in journal articles, for example David Baker's on rock rebels in film. David Baker, "Rock Rebels and Delinquents: the Emergence of the Rock Rebel in 1950s 'Youth Problem' Films," *Continuum* vol.19, no. 1 (2005). 45.
46 Packer, *Spring Fire*. 36.
47 Packer, *Spring Fire*. 37.
48 Packer, *Spring Fire*. 42.
49 Packer, *Spring Fire*. 56. The tune is "The Old Gray Mare."

Songs such as "Roll me over, Yankee Soldier" boast of sexual adventures and conquests.[50] Another song emphasises the fraternity's sense of exceptionalism, and conveys a warning to female students:

> He's a goddamn independent,
> He's a G.D.I.
> Ignore! Ignore! Ignore the bas-tard!
> Ditch the guy,
> The G.D.I.[51]

An independent – someone not accepted into a fraternity – with his awkwardness, plain loose fitting clothes, and conspicuous absence of frat pin[52] is not considered an acceptable date or partner for a sorority girl.[53] Sorority songs, by contrast, repeat lines like "Love you, I love you / Come be a Tri Ep girl"[54] and "Tri Epsilon is a sisterhood / Of love that lasts forever."[55] The repetition of "love" is not simply a contrast with the banal copulatory nature of the frat songs, but is also ironic given the emotional and sexual relationship that grows between the main characters Mitch and Leda. The fraternity's membership process is a rejective one, depending on vetting and a period of probation, recalling what Foucault called "the exclusions that we practice" in what is thought to be the gathering of like to like,[56] evidenced by the contempt shown for the independent student. But its insistence, seen throughout *Spring Fire*, not only on its formal and unspoken rules but on a culture of behaviour and a collective self-belief in aggressive heterosexuality, is a function of the internal normativity of an established group; Foucault again:

> The norm brings with it a principle of both qualification and correction. The norm's function is not to exclude and reject. Rather, it is always linked to a positive technique of intervention and transformation, to a sort of normative project.[57]

---

50 Packer, *Spring Fire*. 29.
51 Packer, *Spring Fire*. 40.
52 Packer, *Spring Fire*. 41–42.
53 In *Spring Fire* reference is always made to frat "men" and sorority "girls."
54 Packer, *Spring Fire*. 10.
55 Packer, *Spring Fire*. 87.
56 Michel Foucault, "What is an Author?," in *The Foucault Reader: An introduction to Foucault's thought*, ed. Paul Rabinow (Penguin, 1991). 110. NB. I have drawn a general principle here from something Foucault has applied solely to the way we decide what is an author.
57 Michel Foucault, *Abnormal: lectures at the College de France, 1974–1975*, trans. Graham Burchell, ed. Valerio Marchetti and Antonella Salomoni (Verso, 2016). 50. This does not contradict the previous principle; rather it states that the "like" within a taxonomy is more of an internal product than a pre-requisite.

44   *Male agency*

Attempting to think outside this particular box would demonstrate "the limitation of our own [taxonomy], the stark impossibility of thinking *that*."[58] Of course the sorority functions in a parallel or complementary manner, as can be seen throughout *Spring Fire*, but that is not the issue in this section, except inasmuch as they both enforce and reinforce a strictly binary culture along sex category and heterosexual lines. Thus, the college culture as a whole can be classified as a "regime"[59] designed to turn a young woman into what her father might call "a real lady"[60] on the assembly line of what Valerie Taylor described as "the Female Factory."[61] The appropriation of women by men, and the latter's assumed superiority, is summed up in the college vocabulary; in the words of a sorority song, "Tri Epsilon is a friendly house where every girl's a queen [...] All the frat men love her."[62] In all cases, throughout the book, it is frat "men" but sorority "girls," stressing the latter's junior position, expressed in terms of age or maturity. A fraternity has the authority to blacklist a sorority, in fact one influential frat man can apparently damn a single female student and her sorority with the words "she's the last Tri Ep to come to this house," for it to be so.[63]

That arbitrary pronouncement occurs in a chain of events which starts with a practical joke taking advantage of someone's sexual curiosity, develops into an angry confrontation between two characters, and becomes an attempted rape in a bathroom which is only thwarted by the victim breaking a vase over her attacker's head.[64] The damnation of a whole sorority in retaliation marks the attacker's sense of entitlement to force sex upon someone, and to punish her refusal by a retaliation against all her colleagues. In her article "The Perils of the Back Seat," Lisa Lindquist Dorr deals with sexual relationships between young men and young women in the 1950s.[65] Dorr points out that the prevalent culture amongst that age group at that time was a new phenomenon – "By 1950, going steady had become the dominant form of dating"[66]

---

58 Michel Foucault, *The Order of things*, trans. not named (Verso, 1994). xv.
59 Monique Wittig, *The Straight Mind and other essays* (Beacon, 1992). xii: "I describe heterosexuality not as an institution but as a political regime which rests on the submission and appropriation of women."
60 Packer, *Spring Fire*. 16.
61 Valerie Taylor, *Whisper Their Love*, Little Sister's Classics, (Arsenal Pulp Press, 2006). 27.
62 Packer, *Spring Fire*. 27.
63 Packer, *Spring Fire*. 34.
64 Packer, *Spring Fire*. 31–33. The practical joke concerns a cardboard figure of a man, naked except for a fig leaf; if the fig leaf is lifted up and alarm bell sounds throughout the house.
65 Lisa Lindquist Dorr, "The Perils of the Back Seat: Date Rape, Race and Gender in 1950s America," *Gender & History* vol.20, no. 1 (2008). 43n2. Dorr's focus on white youth, including high school and college students, sits well with my selection of novels such as *Spring Fire*, *Odd Girl Out*, and *Whisper Their Love*. Her article deals specifically with "white teens" because the "erasure of diversity from mainstream popular culture" meant her source material was racially limited.
66 Dorr, "The Perils of the Back Seat: Date Rape, Race and Gender in 1950s America." 29.

Male agency 45

– and that numerous magazines aimed at mothers were publishing articles raising concern about this.[67] Going steady, under peer pressure, represented the desire for conformity and security among teenagers.[68] On campus, strictly monogamous dating was formalised by "pinning," the custom of a frat man giving his fraternity pin to his steady girl to wear.[69] However, steady dating was not the only aspect of the sexual culture amongst young persons in the 1950s that Dorr draws attention to. From an article by Jane Whitbread in a 1959 issue of *Mademoiselle* magazine, Dorr quotes:

> 'A man should know more and lead the woman [in sexual relations]', one Ivy League freshman reported. Invoking the double standard, he went on, 'I want my wife to be all mine – undamaged by premarital relations with anyone else. But I have to learn about sex for my own good. I will have to take advantage of every opportunity I get with girls who are the type you go out with for sex'.[70]

This attitude sprang from a culture in which, though it seems strange in retrospect, many people worried that there were no longer clear-cut differences between men and women.[71] This perception gave rise to a behavioural backlash in which:

> [...] sexual experimentation and conquest before marriage allowed boys 'to grow and mature and test themselves, not only sexually but as men'. The media reinforced this version of masculine dominance. Extramarital sexual relations – even coercive ones – served as a way to reinforce male identity, despite widespread focus on monogamy within marriage. Sexual aggression in search of conquest was men's 'one sure proof of masculinity', in a society in which men's 'roles are indistinguishable from women's'.[72]

---

67 Dorr, "The Perils of the Back Seat: Date Rape, Race and Gender in 1950s America." 44n6.
68 Dorr, "The Perils of the Back Seat: Date Rape, Race and Gender in 1950s America." 29.
69 Packer, *Spring Fire*. 6. "Maybell Van Casey [...] was pinned to a Delta Pi who played baseball."
70 Dorr, "The Perils of the Back Seat: Date Rape, Race and Gender in 1950s America." 35. See: Jane Whitbread, "A Report on Current Attitudes to Chastity," *Mademoiselle*, no. 49 (1959). 39.
71 Dorr, "The Perils of the Back Seat: Date Rape, Race and Gender in 1950s America." 30.
72 Dorr, "The Perils of the Back Seat: Date Rape, Race and Gender in 1950s America." 31. Again see Whitbread, 39. Susan Love Brown dates the cultural acceptance of coercive sexual relations and male sexual aggression back a generation to the "Hollywood mores" and fiction of the 1930s and 1940s that "glamorized male dominance and rape as a sign of masculinity." Susan Love Brown, "Ayn Rand and Rape," *The Journal of Ayn Rand Studies* vol.15, no. 1 (2015). 4.

46 Male agency

This feeling that men's roles are indistinguishable from women's was one expression of the "masculinity crisis" and "male panic" – the former being the observation that assumptions about masculinity and expected male behaviour are being undercut by social and psychological change, the latter being the rebellion by men against perceived feminisation – noted by James Gilbert.[73] American psychiatrist Irene Josselyn said, some time in or before 1958, "We are drifting toward a social structure made up of he-women and she-men."[74] A response to this perception of feminisation, and to the accusation that intellect was somehow effeminate, was that the new middle-class man of the 1950s adopted – or tried to – the cultural swagger of the working-class.[75] The homosocial concentration of the fraternity house in *Spring Fire* is somewhere where the swagger flourishes, where the frat men can be seen melding the aspirational, patrician, Ivy League image of feet in loafers stretched casually out,[76] with the culture of hard drinking and sexual aggression stereotypically associated with the working-class. In fact, these frat men can be seen as a confused amalgam of several competing masculinities, as their time at college was a preface of freedom – a time to let one's hair down – before graduating to the socially-aspired-to career, house, and "companionate family"[77] of what Spectorsky called the "Exurbanite."[78] It was also a time in academia, a supposedly intellectual milieu, during a decade when intellectuals defended the masculinity of learning and high culture, and the virile and hard-edged character of modernism.[79] It was from within this milieu, which sought to meld several competing, perceptions of masculinity, that the Ivy League freshman mentioned before made his remark about want-

---

73 Gilbert, *Men in the Middle: Searching for Masculinity in the 1950s*. 16 and 3.
74 Gilbert, *Men in the Middle: Searching for Masculinity in the 1950s*. 62. Gilbert does not provide a reference for this quotation, and it has proved impossible to track down a definitive source for it. Melissa Stenmetz's 2014 thesis traces it no further than an essay by J Robert Moskin. Melissa A Steinmetz, "National Insecurity in the Nuclear Age: Cold War Manhood and the Gendered Discourse of U.S. Survival, 1945-1960" (Doctor of Philosophy Kent State, 2014). 236. J. Robert Moskin, "Why Do Women Dominate Him?," in *The Decline of the American Male* (Random House, 1958). 24.
75 Gilbert, *Men in the Middle: Searching for Masculinity in the 1950s*. 25.
76 Packer, *Spring Fire*. 42.
77 Gilbert, *Men in the Middle: Searching for Masculinity in the 1950s*. 16. Gilbert actually uses this term to express what was seen at the time to be undercutting older concepts of masculinity and contributing to the masculinity crisis of the 1950s.
78 Auguste Comte Spectorsky, *The Exurbanites* (Lippincott, 1954). The dust jacket of the hardback has a cartoon illustration of a line of clone-like men with trilby, suit, and briefcase, filing out of a leafy suburb. The later mass-market paperback version shows a man, his body and arms pointing one way and his head and legs the other, dashing between suburb (represented by the branch of a tree at one margin of the cover) and town (represented by a street light and the suggestion of an office block at the other). The reader is left in no doubt that Spectorsky is a prophet of the "male panic" I referred to earlier, seeing the 1950s man as a negation of the perception of the rugged individualism of the bygone frontier age.
79 Gilbert, *Men in the Middle: Searching for Masculinity in the 1950s*. 189.

Male agency 47

ing a presumably suburban wife undamaged by premarital relations with anyone else, whilst taking advantage of every opportunity he got with the type of girls who you "go out with for sex."[80] That is the culture, full of the tensions of a masculinity crisis, in which Bud Roberts is determined to "make" Susan Mitchell.

Bud, described ironically as "a commanding personality" by Mitch's platonic friend, an unconventional frat man who goes by the nickname of Lucifer, arrives late for a date with her, his excuse being his having sought "the right kind of flower" to present to her.[81] This feigned gallantry is to persuade her to forgive him for the tussle in which she had defended herself with a vase[82] and to gild his subsequent sexual assault as what Ayn Rand might have disingenuously called "rape with an engraved invitation."[83] In dancing with Bud, flattering him, squeezing his arm affectionately, and allowing him to spike her drinks, Mitch participates in the sorority's ritual of submitting to someone from a high-status fraternity, and to familial expectations too – "Now she was the lady her father wanted her to be and this was the ball and Bud Roberts was a gentleman."[84] It was not as though she had not seen these expectations challenged and bucked before:

> "… and so I told him," a short girl with jewel-studded rims on her large-framed glasses was saying, "that as far as I was concerned, he was the blindest date I'd ever had."
>
> "Robin!" Marybell Van Casey looked horrified. "He was an Omega Phi. They're a big fraternity, sweetie, and a Tri Ep can't afford to run around insulting their pledges. You be careful."
>
> "Well, I don't care. I hate those oafs that maul you around as though you were a punching bag. I just won't take it."
>
> There was a tense silence. Marybell looked across the table significantly at Kitten Clark. Robin was due for a conference with the social chairman.[85]

---

80 Dorr, "The Perils of the Back Seat: Date Rape, Race and Gender in 1950s America." 35. Dorr is quoting from Whitbread, "A Report on Current Attitudes to Chastity." 39.

81 Packer, *Spring Fire*. 50. Lucifer's unconventionality extends to his fraternity house which "ditched the rule book a long time ago," and which accepted him as a member despite his being of mixed ethnic heritage – see p.86 – thus showing that fraternities were not entirely a rule-bound cultural monolith. Packer is inserting a small element here against the trend of what Dorr referred to: the "erasure of diversity from mainstream popular culture." Dorr, "The Perils of the Back Seat: Date Rape, Race and Gender in 1950s America." 43n2.

82 Packer, *Spring Fire*. 32.

83 Quoted in Barbara Branden, "Ayn Rand: The reluctant feminist," in *Feminist Interpretations of Ayn Rand*, ed. Mimi Reisel Gladstein and Chris Matthew Sciabarra (Pennsylvania State UP, 1999). 37.

84 Packer, *Spring Fire*. 51–52.

85 Packer, *Spring Fire*. 23–24. Robin and Lucifer are the two iconoclasts in the novel, but in this instance, despite Robin's independence of spirit, sorority rules and fraternity status trump

48 *Male agency*

In the sorority's basement kitchen Bud forces himself on Mitch. She says no three times, but he ignores her, strikes her, and places his hand over her mouth, saying "Shut up [...] you wanted this, Miss Virgin."[86] It is an ugly scene, long in narrative time but short in discourse, dismissed with "For a long time she was down in the mire of pitch black [...] Then it was over [...]"[87] Nowhere does Packer call it "rape," but it most certainly is. It is characterised by brutality and sexual immaturity – Bud tells Mitch to "take a hot bath and keep your mouth shut," on hearing of which, Leda exclaims "A hell of a lot a man knows."[88] The episode bears comparison with the more famous rape in Rand's *The Fountainhead*.[89] Certainly Bud Roberts cannot be equated to Howard Roark, Rand's quasi-Nietzschean *Übermensch*, as the former is Packer's more realistic portrayal of a young man of the era and the latter is Rand's philosophical construct. In each case, one participant hands the other the metaphorical engraved invitation, and neither episode contains the word "rape." For all the popular appeal of *Spring Fire*, Packer was never called on to defend her scene, while Rand was, for making an individualistic hero out of someone who would carry out such a brutal act. Rand did use the word "rape" in the many statements she made, saying at one time "she had asked for it, and he knew that she wanted it."[90] Susan Love Brown points out that Rand's defence uses language that replicates "the phrases frequently used by men to deny rape."[91] That language, in the mouth of Bud Roberts, stands out.

Rand gives Roark no conscience, symbolically absolving him for all his behaviour by acquitting him of a single crime in a court of law, and setting him finally on top of his monumental building as though on top of the world, waving to his victim – now his wife – below; Packer, by contrast, puts self-doubt into Bud's mind and shows him for the small figure he is. Back in the fraternity house after the rape, he confesses to his friends, "It was the first time I ever got such a creepy feeling. Now, I've fooled around a lot. Plenty.

---

sexual assault. Robin earns a demerit for her defiance, and storms out declaring "Hooray for the team spirit we all got! Three big cheers for our team spirit!" Packer, *Spring Fire*. 25.

86 Packer, *Spring Fire*. 54.

87 Ibid.

88 Packer, *Spring Fire*. 55, 56.

89 This was not only a novel, but also a Warner Brothers movie, scripted by Rand herself. King Vidor, "The Fountainhead," (Warner Bros, 1949). This movie would be fairly fresh in the consciousness of consumers of popular culture, at the time *Spring Fire* was published. Although it was not a great box office success it boosted sales of Rand's novel, exposing more readers to the rape episode; the movie episode was bowdlerised in obedience to the Hays Code, but the publicity poster depicted co-stars Gary Cooper and Patricia Neal, with the former forcefully embracing the latter. A cheap paperback edition of *The Fountainhead* was released in 1952 by Signet.

90 Quoted in Michael S. Berliner, ed., *Letters of Ayn Rand* (Dutton, 1995). 282.

91 Brown, "Ayn Rand and Rape." 8.

Male agency 49

But I never got such a creepy feeling."[92] He is unable to square what he has done, and what he has experienced in doing it, with the sexual mores of the fraternity to which he is accustomed and in which he is practised, and he has no vocabulary with which to express how he feels:

> "Listen," Roberts yelled. "Listen. I'm telling you it wasn't like that! You don't know what the hell I'm telling you. I'm so goddamn drunk I don't know what I'm telling you either. But this girl – she was like my dog at home after I kick him when I don't mean to but I lose my temper. Ever kick your dog and see his eyes? She was like that. I never –"[93]

The words Packer gives him here leave it unclear whether he is feeling sorry for Mitch, sorry for his actions, or sorry for himself. His lack of self-control is absolutely clear; saying "I don't mean to" may be a confession of that lack, but it may equally be a coded way of blaming his victim. Whichever is the case, his fraternity colleagues do not understand what he is saying, and his outburst results in an argument that only physical restraint stops from developing into a drunken fight. Bud's colleague Jake forces Bud to his knees and is softened by his abjection. "G'night, Clive, Bud," he says, "I'm going to bed. Get some sleep, men!"[94] Clive's reaction is telling: "When he said "men," Clive knew that it was all right then."[95] Although Bud is left in the room, alone and still angry, drunk, and confused,[96] what has been signalled here by the word "men" is a retreat into the fraternity's milieu of homosocial safety. Again, the language of the passage contains the dichotomy of "girls" and "men."

Packer supplies a contrast with the frat men in the shape of Charlie Edmondson, whom Mitch likes. He is an independent, and not bound by fraternity rules. However, this does not make him anything of a free spirit, unlike Lucifer from the unconventional fraternity. Charlie and Mitch had dated socially, with little more happening than an awkward goodnight kiss.[97] Mitch and Leda are already lovers, and in response to Mitch's complaint about Leda's sleeping with Jake, Leda admonishes her that she "had better get to know men" so that she would not attract a reputation:

> "There are a lot of people who love both and no one gives a damn, and they just say you're oversexed and they don't care. But they start getting interested when you stick to one sex. Like you've been doing, Mitch. I couldn't love you if you were a Lesbian."

92 Packer, *Spring Fire*. 57–58.
93 Packer, *Spring Fire*. 58.
94 Ibid.
95 Ibid.
96 Packer, *Spring Fire*. 59.
97 Packer, *Spring Fire*. 73.

50   *Male agency*

"I'm not," Mitch said, wondering what the word even meant. "I'm not. I – I just haven't met a man yet who makes me feel the way you do."[98]

Perhaps in response to that admonition, Mitch agrees to a night-time picnic with Charlie. They have with them all the trappings of sexual adventure expected of youngsters of the time – blankets and alcohol,[99] and Charlie gauchely hints he has a condom in his wallet[100] – in an attempt to assuage the "desire for conformity and security" mentioned by Dorr.[101] They move from the blankets to the intimacy of the back seat of Mitch's car,[102] but their attempt at sex fizzles out without adequate explanation by either. "I can't," says Charlie, without explanation, and then "I don't want to talk about it. I don't ever want to talk about it."[103] Later, it becomes clear that Charlie has extreme issues of religious guilt;[104] meanwhile Mitch, consulting a psychology tome in the college library, finds the supposed explanation that a "normal" man finds sex with a lesbian "very difficult, if not impossible," and blames herself for their sexual failure.[105]

As Bob and Granger represent two extremes of manhood in *I am a Lesbian*, Charlie and Bud represent two extremes of specifically young manhood in *Spring Fire*. However, their dichotomy is not between good and bad, but between two extremes of inadequacy, and incomprehension regarding women. They do not have the direct agency that Bob and Granger do in *I am a Lesbian*, but rather a more passive, catalysing effect, both orienting Mitch and Leda toward each other and making possible each young woman's self-image, in particular Mitch's internalised homophobia.[106] *Spring Fire* is basically a book without a moral standpoint. Perhaps that is due to the publisher's insistence on not having a happy ending for the two leading lesbian characters,[107] but then there is no significant happiness for anyone.

---

98 Packer, *Spring Fire*. 80.
99 Packer, *Spring Fire*. 89.
100 Packer, *Spring Fire*. 90.
101 Dorr, "The Perils of the Back Seat: Date Rape, Race and Gender in 1950s America." 29.
102 Dorr, "The Perils of the Back Seat: Date Rape, Race and Gender in 1950s America." Dorr states: "Being in the back seat implied greater degrees of intimacy than even the front seat, as men were not hampered by the steering wheel." 47n82.
103 Packer, *Spring Fire*. 92.
104 Packer, *Spring Fire*. 97–98.
105 Packer, *Spring Fire*. 103–104.
106 Packer, *Spring Fire*. 106. I have drawn attention to Mitch's misdirected research in the library, pp.103–104. Having read the book and having wrongly interpreted her interactions with both Leda and Charlie by it, she writes to Leda that, while she does love her, "*Lesbian* is an ugly word and I hate it" and that she wants to "straighten [herself] out." But the book ends with "she had never really loved her" p.160.
107 Packer, *Spring Fire*. vi.

Male agency 51

There is no "Big Handsome Hero"[108] for either Mitch or Leda to marry, and no foregrounded triumph for heterosexuality beyond business as usual in the fraternities and sororities. There is no epiphany for Bud or Charlie, neither progresses in sexual maturity, each simply contributes to the tragic melodrama of the narrative. That is the extent of their indirect agency. If we are to take notice of Judith Butler's assertion that "gender is *performative* in the sense that it constitutes as an effect the very subject it appears to express,"[109] that it declares and establishes itself at the same time, then Bud and Charlie express and constitute failure. Although their masculinity, as in the gender role that is expected of them, is already "underway" as it were, Butler implies that it cannot be "taken on or off at will."[110] There is little room in that theory for the idea that Bud and Charlie are each attempting to fit themselves into playing a role and have indeed put on and taken off roles as Sande Zeig suggests.[111] That is most obvious in Charlie's abandoning conscious role-playing of the almost ritual act of dating and back-seat sex, though in his case he may simply be reverting to the angst-ridden role of a virginal Christian. His and Bud's failures are precipitated, therefore, by the confused amalgam of competing perceptions of masculinity I referred to earlier. Herein lies the major challenge to male masculinity in *Spring Fire*. The prime masculinity – two separate masculinities in Charlie's case – forced by custom upon the bodies of each man, or adopted by them as roles, does not suit who they really are; but we never get to see either realise any alternative potential.

Generational isolation: the absent father

The notion that Packer's *Spring Fire* started a literary trend is not without merit. It was not the first notable cheap paperback to feature an environment that isolated, or at least corralled, young women; that would have to be the semi-autobiographical *Women's Barracks* by Tereska Torrès,[112] which was about a group of women who joined the Free French forces in World War Two. Its titillating cover artwork by Baryé Phillips caught the eye, and its fame was ensured by its being one of the books named in the

---

108 Bradley and Damon, *Checklist 1960: A Complete, Cumulative Checklist of Lesbian, Variant, and Homosexual Fiction, in English, or Available in English Translation, with Supplements of Related Material, for the Use of Collectors, Students, and Librarians*. Unpaginated. There is a low-key heterosexual resolution, inasmuch as Mitch agrees to go to the movies with Lucifer. Packer, *Spring Fire*. 150.
109 Judith Butler, "Imitation and Gender Insubordination," in *Inside/Out: Lesbian Theories, Gay Theories*, ed. Diana Fuss (Routledge, 1991). 24.
110 Butler, "Imitation and Gender Insubordination." 23–24.
111 See page 13 of Sande Zeig, "The Actor as Activator: Deconstructing gender through gesture," *Women & Performance: A Journal of Feminist Theory* vol.2, no. 2 (1985). This will be examined in greater detail in the section on female masculinity.
112 Tereska Torrès, *Women's Barracks: The Frank Autobiography of a French Girl Soldier* (Fawcett Gold Medal, 1950).

52   Male agency

report of the Gathings Committee.[113] *Spring Fire* was another one named by the committee, adjacent in the same list as *Women's Barracks*. The setting of the cheap fiction of that era in female microcosms sprung from these two novels. Although the army does not appear to have featured much,[114] there were plenty set in prisons,[115] nurses' quarters,[116] the daytime emptiness of middle-class houses,[117] even courting borderline ephebophilia in girls' boarding schools,[118] along with a few set in the privacy of the artist's studio.[119] However, none of these microcosms was exploited to the extent that the college campus was. Ann Bannon, of course, had read *Spring Fire* before she wrote *Odd Girl Out*,[120] and there were novels of varying quality from Rene Levi, Bob Lucerne,[121] Don Holliday, E.S. Seeley, Frank Shield, Greg Caldwell, Joan Ellis,[122] John Dexter, R.V. Cassill, Peggy Swenson, Orrie Hitt, Michael Norday, and Jordan Park – a list that almost reads like a *Who's Who* of mid-twentieth-century cheap paperback writers.

The corral of the sorority has the corresponding and, importantly, adjacent corral of the fraternity, of course, but both environments are isolated generationally. The age bracket is limited to the young adult, to people who are out of the immediate presence of their parents for the first time in their lives. It is in and by this absence that the figure of the father paradoxically makes his presence known. The protagonist of Packer's *Spring Fire*, Susan Mitchell, is known by a shortened version of her father's surname – Mitch – thus reinforcing a sense of the paternal appropriation of a daughter. To have a name bestowed by custom can be seen, as Wittig says, as "a private appropriation ([by] a father) and a collective appropriation of the whole group [...] by the class of men."[123] At least she has a given name, unlike her sorority colleague "Jett Duquette [who] was named after the race horse her uncle had made his first million on."[124] Yet the impression is given that Mitch hardly

---

113 Ezekiel C. Gathings and others, *Report of the Select Committee on Current Pornographic Materials* (U.S. Government, 1952). 16.
114 The only other novel that springs to mind is Pauline Cooper's *The Olive Branch* from 1967.
115 Joan Henry's *Women in Prison*, Nedra Tyre's *Reformatory Girls*, and Kermit Welles's *Reformatory Women*, to give three examples. The semiotics of the titles is very simple.
116 J.D. Ford's *Lesbians in White*, Lee Morrell's *Nurses Quarters*, and Kimberley Kemp's *Intimate Nurse* – same observation about titles.
117 George Simon's *The Third Lust*, Max Collier's *The Discontented*, and Kirby MacLane's *For Women Only*.
118 Jay Vincent's *Girl's School*, Marcia Marcoux's *Velvet Seduction*, and Kimberley Kemp's *Private Party*.
119 Ben West's *Girl Artist*, and Jack Evans's *Studio of Lust*.
120 Ann Bannon, *Odd Girl Out* (Cleis, 2001). vi.
121 Lucerne's campus-set novel is also titled *Odd Girl Out*.
122 Ellis used the setting at least three times.
123 Wittig, *The Straight Mind and other essays*. xv.
124 Packer, *Spring Fire*. 47.

Male agency 53

knows her father; he may be lucky and skilful rather than intelligent, but he is also

> a man who was strange to other men and to most women and to Mitch. She could imagine that she and her father had never known each other, and yet they had spent many long hours together when she was on vacation from school, in the summer, and when he visited on his rare trips that brought him to her vicinity.[125]

Paradoxically, the thought of waking up at home and fancying that she hears her father saying, "What a sleepy-head you are, black-eyed Susan!" seems to be an anchoring reality while her new life at college is "cold and hard, as though this room and this house and this whole new life were a dream."[126] However, all the sorority need to know about Edward Mitchell is that he's a millionaire, and that makes her a "potential Tri Ep."[127] To them, the important factor is not something of Mitch's own character: "Well, believe me, if she were anyone but Edward Mitchell's daughter, she'd get a nice, fat round blackball from yours truly. She's hickey! I mean absolutely hickey!"[128] The possibility of cash endowments from a successful businessman, a Rotarian, a member of his local Country Club, Business Club, and P.T.A.,[129] to the sorority, and his social respectability appear to be the only necessary criteria. The daughter of a successful architect is a good candidate for a place in a sorority,[130] a young woman who comes from a town named after her great-great-grandfather is ideal.[131] To put it cynically, and almost in answer to Leda's vernacular question, "Do we have to pledge the girl just because her father is worth a mint?"[132] the equally vernacular answer "They'll like you fine at the sorority if your father's got dough" will do nicely.[133]

What seems to be important, as far as the remote father-figure is concerned, is the end product of the college system. Valerie Taylor's cynical name for it is "the Female Factory," a term spoken by a working-class observer of the well-heeled young women and their college, the taxi driver in *Whisper Their Love*,[134] where the curriculum "had been planned, or had

---

125 Packer, *Spring Fire*. 60.
126 Packer, *Spring Fire*. 37–38. "Black-eyed Susan," the common name for a member of the sunflower family, occurs more than once in *Spring Fire*, but always when Mitch is imagining what her father might say; see page 61 for example.
127 Packer, *Spring Fire*. 13.
128 Packer, *Spring Fire*. 11. Here "hickey" is a slur for someone provincial or rural.
129 Packer, *Spring Fire*. 4.
130 Joan Ellis, *Girls Dormitory* (Midwood, 1963). 29.
131 R.V. Cassill, *Dormitory Women* (Signet, 1959). 12.
132 Packer, *Spring Fire*. 4.
133 Cassill, *Dormitory Women*. 13.
134 Taylor, *Whisper Their Love*. 28.

54 Male agency

grown, to develop attractive wives in the junior executive, ten-thousand-dollar bracket."[135] Mitch's father is expecting her to grow up, to become "a real lady" when she comes home;[136] this phrase comes back to her at and after the ball, where Bud Roberts, a fraternity man, has been slipping spirits into her punch, with her knowledge, and she was "the lady her father wanted her to be."[137] This comes shortly before he rapes her on the cellar floor.[138] Though this trauma leads, in part, to Mitch and Leda holding each other for the first time as lovers,[139] Mitch is emotionally alone, with no grounding in parental intimacy; she imagines being able to toss the fact of "having sexual intercourse" in the cellar casually into an exchange with her father:

> Even after she had thought of such a scene and played with it in her mind and rejected it as impossible, she felt the danger of the thought. She felt that now she was grown, as her father had always said she would be and as she had thought she would never grow. She was grown and there was no more time to say "When I grow up," and now she could say, "When I grew up," and tell what it was like, because it was over. It was over and when it is over you do not talk. You do not say what it was like. Not when it's like this.[140]

When she imagines another conversation with him, she begging to come home, what comes into her mind is his saying "a big girl like you isn't homesick," the word "girl" negating her having grown up, or his relying on "the signs that hung round the walls of his office: "A quitter never wins and a winner never quits." "Keep on keeping on." "If someone hands you a lemon, squeeze it and start a lemonade stand"."[141] Eventually, of course, she does not quit, though this is less likely to be anything to do with the daughter-father relationship as conceived by Packer, and more a factor of Fawcett Gold Medal's editorial dictation of the narrative structure.

The development of the most prominent father-figure in the texts discussed in this book – Ann Bannon's Merrill Landon – has its basis in Bannon's reading of the hard-headed father in *Spring Fire*. The dismissive *idée fixe* we have of Landon as "cold," "violent," and "cruel,"[142] and the abiding image

---

135 Taylor, *Whisper Their Love*. 38.
136 Packer, *Spring Fire*. 16. This reminds us that "*on ne naît pas femme, on le devient.*" Simone de Beauvoir, *Le Deuxième Sexe*, vol. 2 (Éditions Gallimard, 1976). 13.
137 Packer, *Spring Fire*. 52.
138 Packer, *Spring Fire*. 54.
139 Packer, *Spring Fire*. 59.
140 Packer, *Spring Fire*. 61.
141 Packer, *Spring Fire*. 94.
142 Here I quote the only adjectives used in a brief mention in an article by Jeff Weinstein. They are not unjustifiable, but they are typical of the superficial view of Merrill Landon. Jeff Weinstein, "In Praise of Pulp," *Voice Literary Supplement*(October 1983). 8.

Male agency   55

of their sexual confrontation in a hotel bedroom,[143] belie the complex character that eventually emerges in a detailed reading. On the occasion of our first remote meeting with him, Landon's letters to his daughter Laura make her happy,[144] but his wanting her to be popular is a factor of his manipulative attitude to her, shown most clearly in his attempts to get her to contact Charlie Ayers, the son of one of a former college friend with whom he has been in contact ever since his college days.[145] His attitude to her friendship with Beth is similar:

> That's the kind of friendship you should cultivate, Laura, with people who can really do you some good. This girl sounds like a real go-getter – president of the Student Union and etc. That's quite an honour for the girl, isn't it? She can probably do a lot for you – get you into the right activities and so forth. I'd treat her well, if I were you.[146]

Laura's reaction to that is to sigh "with exasperation over her father's ideas of friendship; if it weren't useful somehow it just wasn't friendship, only a waste of time."[147] Landon's attitude to his daughter even proves useful, however, when Beth diverts the persistent wheedling of their roommate Emily to reveal their "secret,"[148] by providing the credible story of his vetoing Laura's transfer out of journalism school – Laura takes a "perverse pleasure" in his inadvertently rescuing her lesbian affair, thinking "It was as good a thing as he ever did for her."[149]

The shock of the paternal presence: Merrill Landon's agency

In *I am a Woman*[150] Ann Bannon moves away from the female homosocial microcosm of the sorority house of *Odd Girl Out* and puts her protagonist into what was for her a new world – New York City, and in particular Greenwich Village. But instead of introducing the new environment, despite

---

143 Ann Bannon, *I am a Woman* (Cleis, 2002). 208. Please bear with my interim description of the incident as a "sexual confrontation." I do not seek to de-emphasise it, but rather to reserve judgment at this stage in the book.
144 Bannon, *Odd Girl Out*. 17.
145 Bannon, *Odd Girl Out*. 34, 124.
146 Bannon, *Odd Girl Out*. 17.
147 Bannon, *Odd Girl Out*. 17. Young men remote from their fathers are not exempted from this pressure. Charlie receives a letter from his father instructing him to give Laura Landon "a good time." 53.
148 Bannon, *Odd Girl Out*. 89. The "secret" is, of course, Beth's and Laura's love affair.
149 Bannon, *Odd Girl Out*. 90.
150 The title of the novel was imposed by the publisher. The title and paratext in full, as seen on the cover, it ran "I am a woman in love with a woman – must society reject me?" It implies a first-person narrative, whereas in fact the novel is entirely in the third-person or free indirect speech.

56 *Male agency*

the back cover blurb of the original Gold Medal edition which, under the actual heading "New World," speaks about "home" being "a dimly lit and badly ventilated bar on a back street in Greenwich Village," she spends the first three or four pages of the novel writing about Merrill Landon. In the earlier novel he had been an absent influence, as most fathers were for their daughters in novels like these, whose time at college was their first sojourn away from home. Bannon casts Landon as one of the most important secondary characters in the novel in the opening short, sharp sentences of the book:

> Tell your father to go to hell. Try it. It's a rotten hard thing to do, even if he deserves it. Merrill Landon did. He was an out-and-out bastard, but like most of the breed, he didn't know it. He said he was a good father: sensible, firm, and just. He said everything he did was for Laura's own good. He took her opposition for a sign that he was right, and the more she opposed him, the righter he swore he was.[151]

The fact that he never showed her any physical affection,[152] even though he was the only man she had ever tried to love,[153] sets the reader up for the shock of the physical contact and sexual confusion later in the novel. Merrill, though he has "never kissed her [...] never touched her,"[154] nor ever shown affection to anyone,[155] has in fact reacted in entirely another physical way: "He had struck her more than once, and his anger with her sometimes reached such heights that she trembled in terror, expecting him to brutalise her. But it never went that far."[156] Here I must note that the word "struck" is a difficult point to a modern readership; back then the readership may well have been less sensitive to the idea of male parental authority expressed in physical chastisement even of a daughter in young adulthood. What is stated here may be (no more than) what in Britain used to be known as 'a clip round the ear', given on a handful of occasions.[157] Today even one such incidence would be enough to damn a man as an irredeemable brute and render him liable to criminal prosecution. This is not, however, a point I wish to labour, I merely wish to sound a note of caution about making cultural assumptions.

---

151 Ann Bannon, *Journey to a Woman* (Cleis, 2003). 1.
152 Ibid.
153 Bannon, *Journey to a Woman*. 2.
154 Bannon, *Journey to a Woman*. 1.
155 Bannon, *Journey to a Woman*. 105.
156 Bannon, *Journey to a Woman*. 3–4.
157 Beebo, however, has the impression that he has been "beating the hell out of her since she was five years old." Bannon, *I am a Woman*. 211. Landon himself says later, "Because I discipline you now and then? Isn't that a father's prerogative?" 202. To Laura it went beyond discipline: "Spanking! It was more than that and you know it!" 205.

Male agency   57

To Laura, who is from that earlier culture, it is the "straight-laced bitter version of fatherly affection that hurt her more than his fits of temper."[158]

Bannon does not present this dysfunctional relationship between Laura and her father as a simple matter of the dynamics of generational or gender power, but rather roots it in a trauma in the past of Laura's family. In a passage where punctuation marks and paragraph separation are a little clumsy, Bannon describes how Laura's father, whenever Laura dares to resist him, persistently brings up the accident in which his wife and son were drowned but she was saved. It is incidents like this piece of back-story that prompt some critics to speak of "melodrama" as opposed to realism, or at least of melodrama manifesting as unintentional realism in Bannon's novels, which dichotomy Christopher Nealon points out.[159] I attribute this minor clumsiness to Bannon's exuberance, the same exuberance that makes her come up with plosive alliteration in phrases like "plastic popguns out in Pasadena,"[160] or strings of unpunctuated adjectives – "big wild angry sobs"[161] – or anacoluthon such as "Her hands went up to Tris's bare arms, over the bandeau and down that silky midriff, and then they went round Tris's waist and pulled her close and kissed her."[162] Militating, on the other hand, for the author's melodramatic tendency is the fact that in *Odd Girl Out* Laura's parents were described as divorced, whereas in her second novel she contrives this tragic back-story. Her subsequent reaction was that it served her right for not rereading her first novel before writing her second.[163]

Merrill Landon's smiles of approval occur but are rare; more frequent are his retorts of "Act your age."[164] He is in no doubt of the dynamics of the parent–offspring relationship. To Laura, however, his rages are "tantrums."[165] He considers himself the adult and Laura the child, but here Bannon uses a word associated with toddler behaviour, and later he smashes a glass ash tray in a fit of anger as an infant might smash a toy.[166] Ironically, it is a similar object with which Laura hits him over the head in their confrontation in his hotel room.[167] Laura's relationship with her father follows her throughout

---

158 Bannon, *I am a Woman*. 1.
159 Christopher Nealon, *Foundlings: Lesbian and Gay Historical Emotion before Stonewall* (Duke University Press, 2001). 146, 156.
160 Bannon, *Journey to a Woman*. 7.
161 Ann Bannon, *Women in the Shadows* (Cleis, 2002). 149.
162 Bannon, *Women in the Shadows*. 50.
163 Personal email, 1st June 2019. Diane Hamer noticed anomalies such as this, giving her opinion that this indicated "the extent to which Bannon shifted, between novels, in her ideas about the significance of certain historical factors in the production of individual lesbian identities." Diane Hamer, ""I am a woman": Ann Bannon and the writing of lesbian identity," in *Lesbian and Gay Writing*, ed. Mark Lilly (Macmillan, 1990). 73n15.
164 Bannon, *I am a Woman*. 2.
165 Ibid.
166 Bannon, *I am a Woman*. 3.
167 Bannon, *I am a Woman*. 208.

58   Male agency

the book, although there are times when he is recalled to her mind, with a start, by something someone else says,[168] or by the realisation that she has absorbed his principle for "doing things the whole way" or not at all,[169] or by conversations where she feel obliged to justify herself.[170] Sometimes she has to get a little drunk to numb the harshness of her thoughts about him,[171] but even so "the spectre of a hated father" can even appear in the middle of an erotic episode.[172] At other times, his influence is more subtle, such as when Laura angrily tells Beebo "Don't talk to me as if I were an irresponsible child!"[173] This could be due more to her resentment at always having been told to act her age than to anything specific that Beebo has said to her. Merrill Landon's opinion of her, as she understands it, influences her self-image:

> She grew up convinced she was as plain as her father seemed to think, and when she looked into the mirror she didn't see her own reflection. She saw what she thought she looked like; a mask, a cliché left over from adolescence. It embarrassed her when people told her she was pretty.[174]

This almost recalls the self-image of the second Mrs. de Winter in Daphne du Maurier's *Rebecca*, except that in this case it is not an unspoken name that has been handed down to the protagonist by her father, but her negative opinion of herself.[175] Bannon's free indirect style lends itself to musings of this type, and they occur throughout her novels.

Throughout *I am a Woman*, Merrill Landon dominates Laura's thoughts and actions as much as if not more than her sexual attraction to Beebo Brinker. His code of "Either you did a thing the whole way or you didn't do it at all" has rubbed off on her,[176] yet ironically she can't hold down a job in New York. With as much regularity as the words "hate" and "hatred" appear in the text, to describe how Laura feels about her father, the word "love" appears. She tries to wish her hate away, whispering to herself, "Why

---

168 Bannon, *I am a Woman*. 17.
169 Bannon, *I am a Woman*. 12.
170 Bannon, *I am a Woman*. 22.
171 Bannon, *I am a Woman*. 49.
172 Bannon, *I am a Woman*. 140.
173 Bannon, *I am a Woman*. 96.
174 Bannon, *I am a Woman*. 100.
175 Bannon had read du Maurier as enthusiastically as any other young woman, though she preferred *Frenchman's Creek* to *Rebecca*. Personal email, 28th December 2020. Laura is in denial about her prettiness, exactly as the second Mrs de Winter is despite Max's describing her as "very pretty." Daphne du Maurier, *Rebecca* (Virago, 2003). 110. The difference of course is that Laura's negativity is because of, not despite, the opinion of the book's dominant man.
176 Bannon, *I am a Woman*. 12.

did we have to hate each other? We're all we have ... Father ..."[177] She has spent nights "torching for a love gone wrong,"[178] He is the only man in her life, the only man she had ever seriously tried to love.[179] Her "stifled love" for him is juxtaposed with her hatred and fear.[180] Even when shame and rejection made her want to kill him, she longed to be "allowed to love him."[181] When eventually she sees him outside the McAlton Hotel, there is an inevitability to the fact that it is his compelling face she is "condemned to love."[182] She likes to imagine him before the trauma as being "generous and gentle and kind," and perhaps he was, but she has no clear memory of that.[183] What she does remember clearly, from the same summer as the accident, is both happy and poignant:

> I can remember sitting on his shoulders when we went to a Fourth of July parade. It was that same summer, before our vacation. I remember he hoisted me up and bought me a balloon and held me while the parade went by so I could see. Afterwards he walked around and talked to his friends, and he didn't make me get down. I felt like a queen on a throne. It's been my one good memory of him, to this day. But Mother was with us. Maybe he did it for her sake.[184]

With the last two short sentences of that passage, Laura takes away any credit for a true gesture of affection. Right at the end of *I am a Woman*, there is a kind of catharsis for her; hatred has run its course, as to her mind her relationship with her father has, but even so her love for him remains:

> No, no, I don't hate him [...] I can't anymore. I never will again. I understand now, so much. Nothing ever made sense before, but now I understand. He was weaker than I was [...] He was more afraid of me than I was of him [...] I don't know quite how I feel about him now. I won't know for a long time, I guess. But I still love him. I always loved him, even when I hated him the most. I only hope we never meet again. I can stand it if I never have to see him again.[185]

---

177 Bannon, *I am a Woman*. 117.
178 Bannon, *I am a Woman*. 1. However, it is not entirely clear from the context whether this refers to the ruins of the father-daughter love, or to those of her relationship with Beth.
179 Bannon, *I am a Woman*. 2.
180 Bannon, *I am a Woman*. 133.
181 Bannon, *I am a Woman*. 155.
182 Bannon, *I am a Woman*. 167.
183 Bannon, *I am a Woman*. 119.
184 Ibid.
185 Bannon, *I am a Woman*. 224.

60   *Male agency*

This passage, as poignant as her childhood memory, signals a degree of closure, but not that Bannon has done with the character of Merrill Landon, as his presence is felt again later in the corpus. However, before following him into *Journey to a Woman*, I want to deal specifically with the peripeteia of *I am a Woman* – the incident in the hotel bedroom.

The presence of Merrill Landon in New York is due to a business convention, held at the McAlton Hotel. Bannon describes Laura sitting in the subway, her fists clenched in her lap, her face like a mask, covering the torment that the news has brought her, her thoughts emphasised in italics – "*Merrill Landon. My father. My father is coming to New York. He never misses these damn things, he goes every year. Oh, God help me.*"[186] Her father's name runs through her mind "like a robot tune from a TV commercial,"[187] and she feels compelled to go to the hotel to see him. The conventional interpretation of the outcome of her first visit is to damn Landon's callousness. The message that he denies her existence is relayed to her by a hotel employee: "He says he has no daughter, Miss," the clerk drawled. He grinned. "Tough luck. Want to try someone else?"[188] The inference is that she is a sex worker, and she flees in tears. Later, taking his denial literally, she says,

> I always knew he was a hard man [...] but I never dreamed he'd go as far as this. I always thought, in spite of everything, in spite of all the bitterness and misery we've had together, that he must love me a little. After all, I'm all he has left ... of my mother, my brother ... his family.[189]

However, the conventional interpretation of the incident is simplistic. At this point we have no idea what Landon actually said to the desk clerk. It may well have been a bald denial intended to hurt, but without knowledge of the inference the clerk would draw, it may have been carelessly-expressed, or indeed it might have been the result of a seeming game of "Telephone" on the part of the clerk. Landon has no idea his daughter is living in New York,[190] and might have said so to the clerk – Laura, in her confusion, has forgotten that fact. The damage, or rather that further piece of damage to an already damaged relationship, has been done, but nevertheless Laura's mind is "wholly occupied"[191] with her father, she is "so absorbed in her father, that nobody else seemed real."[192] Catching sight of him later, it does not occur to her to give him the benefit of the doubt, but her compulsion to permit herself

186 Bannon, *I am a Woman*. 114.
187 Bannon, *I am a Woman*. 115.
188 Bannon, *I am a Woman*. 117.
189 Bannon, *I am a Woman*. 119.
190 Bannon, *I am a Woman*. 114.
191 Bannon, *I am a Woman*. 133.
192 Bannon, *I am a Woman*. 170.

Male agency 61

"the luxury of looking hard at him, his big maleness, his strong face that could never be called handsome and yet compelled interest"[193] is overwhelming. She has actually entered the hotel lobby again to see him, and having turned away, she deliberately turns back to look at him, at which point he cries out her name "in his big rough voice,"[194] and she flees again. Later, however, the import of his cry does not occur to her:

> She knew she didn't want to talk to him, to show him any forgiveness at all, to satisfy his curiosity about her – if he had any. She only wanted a glimpse of him; she wanted to reassure herself that he was still in New York, even though she knew he was. And she knew he might not see her if she hung around his hotel. And she was ashamed that he should see her and know how important he was, even after his cruel denial of her.[195]

She does not realise that his calling out to her not only reverses that denial but is a very demonstrative acknowledgement. He continues to absorb her and occupy her mind, "haunting" her – "the fact of her father's physical presence in New York obliterated other considerations. He was waiting for her around every corner, in every doorway" – and in her imagination he has enough power to command the police to watch for her and arrest her.[196] His calling out has gone beyond acknowledgement and has become a powerful appropriation, in which even her psyche belongs to him.[197]

Inevitably, this leads to a second confrontation – "Abruptly she found herself standing outside the McAlton in the last hour of daylight," with a complete lack of surprise and apparently without having made a conscious decision to go there.[198] Leaning against the wall of the hotel, she looks like "a tired young career girl" waiting for her date and is taken as such by the hotel doorman.[199] Although this is less unflattering than the previous misidentification by an employee of the McAlton as a sex worker, and is welcomed by her as a potential excuse to pass some time in chat, it is an identification that assumes a relationship with a man. Bannon describes her as "almost automatically" entering the hotel and going straight to the elevator, convincing herself, as she rides up to the fourteenth floor, that her father is "a human

---

193 Bannon, *I am a Woman*. 167.
194 Bannon, *I am a Woman*. 168.
195 Bannon, *I am a Woman*. 170.
196 Bannon, *I am a Woman*. 184.
197 See Colette Guillaumin, "Practique du pouvoir et idee de Nature: (1) L'appropriation des femmes," *Nouvelles Questions Feministes*, no. 2 (1978). 6, 11.
198 Bannon, *I am a Woman*. 196.
199 Bannon, *I am a Woman*. 197.

62 *Male agency*

being, not the devil."[200] In his hotel room, for the most part their conversation is a bout of unequal verbal fencing:

> Sooner or later all her arguments were doomed. She never won with him. The sheer physical fact of him, massive and dominant, exhausted her after a while. "I – I never wanted to hate you, Father. You were all I had. I wanted to love you. But you wouldn't let me."[201]

It is within this one-sided *scherma* that she confronts him about the message relayed by the desk clerk. She asks him why he said he had no daughter, to which he replies, "To teach you a lesson," and then reminds her, "You wanted it that way, Laura," referring to her leaving without trace, and later writing a note to tell him to go to hell.[202] To him, the denial had been nothing more than part of the thrust-and-riposte of their relationship, a movement that, in his eyes, scored a hit, and here he believes that he has scored another. The first crack in his defences comes when she tells him he made life intolerable for her, to which he answers that he didn't mean to – "It was an extraordinary admission completely unexpected, and she looked at him speechless for a moment" – and the crack opens up to allow them to speak of his dead wife:

> "Did you treat my mother this way?" she whispered. "Her life must have been hell."
>
> He looked at her for a minute as though he would strangle her. She stood her ground, pale and frightened, until he relented suddenly and turned his profile to her, looking out of the window. "Your mother," he said painfully, "was my wife. I adored her [...] I never struck her."[203]

This is the moment when Landon's suppressed emotions are revealed. *Pace* Weinstein, he is not "cold,"[204] he is far from emotionless, but rather governed by a love and a devastating loss. When he tries to persuade her to come back to Chicago with him, it is at that point that she reveals that she is "a homosexual:"[205]

---

200 Bannon, *I am a Woman*. 198.
201 Bannon, *I am a Woman*. 202.
202 Bannon, *I am a Woman*. 203, 204.
203 Bannon, *I am a Woman*. 204.
204 Weinstein, "In Praise of Pulp." 8.
205 Bannon, *I am a Woman*. 206. This is a very direct and deliberate choice, not "queer," not "lesbian," but a descriptor with the maximum number of syllables to reinforce its directness.

It was her bid for freedom; she had to show this courage, this awful truth to him, or she would never walk away from him. She would spend all her life in a panic of fear lest he find her out. "I'm in love with my roommate. I've made love –"

"All right, all right, all right!" she shouted. His voice was rough and his face contorted. He turned away from her and put his hands over his face. She watched him, every muscle tight and aching.

At last he let his hands drop and said quietly, "Did I do that to you, Laura?"

Without hesitating, without even certain knowledge, but only the huge need to hurt him, she said, "Yes."[206]

It is uncertain which one of them has "every muscle tight and aching," but Landon's putting his hands over his face will not be the last time we see this particular gesture of despair. His asking whether his treatment of her brought about her homosexuality and her affirmative reply, although the latter is intended to hurt, pays lip service to a deterministic, almost pop-Freudian view. When he looks at her again, his face is "pained and full of gentleness,"[207] and what passes between them over the next couple of pages is an extraordinary tenderness, but one that teeters on the brink of something far more dangerous to both of them.

They hold each other, she weeps on his shoulder,[208] he says that he never hated her, never wanted her to go, wants her to come back to Chicago with him no matter that she is different from other girls[209]– "You don't have to love a man" – and she clings to him, "astonished, fearful, grateful, anxious, a whirlwind of confused feelings churning inside her."[210] The danger lies in his conflating Laura and his dead wife: "You never looked like me at all. Every time I look at you I see her face. Her fragile, delicate face. Her eyes, her hair."[211] After years of suppression, Landon says that it is he, not Laura, who deserved punishment and that had been punished, that he has been unbearably lonely without his wife.[212] The conflation is realised when he seizes her hair and kisses her hard on the mouth, but this moment is over almost as soon as it has begun, as he releases her, turns away, puts his face in his hands

---

206 Bannon, *I am a Woman*. 206.
207 Bannon, *I am a Woman*. 206.
208 I am interested to note at this point, that despite Landon's supposed dominating physicality Laura is tall enough to cry on his shoulder.
209 Despite the above fact, he uses the term "girls," which has already been noted as a way of asserting male seniority.
210 Bannon, *I am a Woman*. 207.
211 Ibid.
212 Bannon, *I am a Woman*. 207–208.

64 *Male agency*

– a repetition of the gesture of despair – and sobs his wife's name.[213] Landon is in many ways the masculinity crisis personified. His forceful insistence on everything being done right, his own apparent principle of business success which he has tried repeatedly to foist upon Laura, casts him as a would-be Howard Roark, a ruggedly aggressive personification of the kind of masculinity that emerged at the turn of the nineteenth-to-twentieth century.[214] This persona is, however, a brittle one. As a younger man his social milieu was that of the "companionate nuclear family," which by the mid-twentieth-century was challenging the earlier model.[215] Landon is unsuited to an *ego-contra-mundum* existence; if Laura's recollections are anything to go by, he was relaxed and happy when a member of a cereal packet family of husband, wife, and two children.[216] His unwanted flip from a newer to an older pattern of masculinity is a profound psychological change. His confrontation with Laura has revealed the brittleness of his persona and brought him beyond breaking point. He may even realise that as a journalist – as someone whose *métier* is to merely narrate what other people do – he produces, creates, and sells nothing tangible, but emulates the style of men who do.[217] If we consider Merrill Landon to be the most conventionally, aggressively, obviously masculine man in Bannon's corpus, then in breaking him Bannon delivers a profound challenge to masculinity.

Laura's next action is not taken to defend herself from an incestuous assault – that moment has passed. However, emulating Mitch, the protagonist of *Spring Fire*,[218] she picks up the nearest moveable object to use as a weapon:

> Laura was shaking almost convulsively. At the sound of her mother's name she grabbed the thick and heavy glass ashtray from the dresser, picking it up with both hands. She rushed at him, unable to think or reason, and brought the ashtray down on the crown of his head with all the revolted force in her body. He slumped to the floor without a sound.[219]

---

213 Bannon, *I am a Woman.* 208.
214 Gilbert, *Men in the Middle: Searching for Masculinity in the 1950s.* 26.
215 Gilbert, *Men in the Middle: Searching for Masculinity in the 1950s.* 16.
216 This issue of family conformity is dealt with in Chapter IV. For an exposition of the "cereal packet" family, see Edmund Leach, "The cereal packet norm," *The Guardian*, January 29 1968.
217 Gilbert, *Men in the Middle: Searching for Masculinity in the 1950s.* 202. Here Gilbert is quoting Auguste Comte Spectorsky, from an unpublished proposal for The *Exurbanites*. Auguste Comte Spectorsky, "The New York Commuter", 1954, Spectorsky MSS Box 12, Research Materials: The Exurbanites, U of Wyoming.
218 Vin Packer was Bannon's mentor, to some extent. Packer, *Spring Fire.* 32.
219 Bannon, *I am a Woman.* 208.

Male agency 65

It is not possible for Merrill Landon to be brought any lower. This is the peripeteia of the novel. Laura never sees her father again and is eventually able to achieve catharsis.[220]

Redemption for the absentee father?

Laura may never see Merrill Landon again, but she hears from him. In his message relayed to her there is no resentment. He makes only passing mention to the blow to his head, which could have killed him.[221] It is a changed and chastened man who can only think of saying sorry, and hoping that *he* did not hurt *her*,[222] a man who now can acknowledge the weakness in himself that has now been revealed to his daughter.[223]

There is scant reference to Merrill Landon in Bannon's next book, *Women in the Shadows*. Bannon does seem to revert to the idea of Landon as Laura's "huge heavy domineering father, with his aggressive maleness stamped all over his body,"[224] but the tension in *Women in the Shadows* is between Laura and Beebo, and there is no real need for the father–daughter issue. Initially, when Landon is mentioned in *Journey to a Woman*, there appears to be a recap of the schism between him and his daughter. Landon "blamed her and was very hard on her," her being his daughter and not his wife was her "crime," and she was "was a constant threat to his virtue, a painful reminder of his dead wife."[225] Bannon repeats Laura's pop-Freudian accusation that it was Landon's attitude to her that put her off men and made her a lesbian – that her sexuality is consequential, not essential – but then says that when they had found out the "very worst of each other," the knowledge, "though it hurt, washed away the bitterness."[226] Then comes this passage:

220 Bannon, *I am a Woman*. 224.
221 Bannon, *I am a Woman*. He is concussed and is receiving the attention of a doctor. Laura had been terrified that she had killed him, but is relieved that he is alive. Bannon, *I am a Woman*. 222.
222 Bannon, *I am a Woman*. 223.
223 Bannon, *I am a Woman*. 224.
224 Bannon, *Women in the Shadows*. 111.
225 Bannon, *Journey to a Woman*. 99.
226 Bannon, *Journey to a Woman*. 99. This consequentiality is stressed again not long after the more redemptive passage cited below. Bannon says, on page 101, "His perverted love for her had twisted her whole personality. He had controlled his terrible desire for years, but it has cost Laura a normal childhood." Again, Bannon opts for a quasi-Freudian apologia for Laura's homosexuality, and for the first time in the corpus directly says that Landon had had a sexual longing for her for years. This my-father-made-me-a-lesbian view does not quite ring true. What does appear here is the equation of normality with mental health, and with homosexuality as a condition, as, in fact, code 302.0 of the WHO classification of diseases did up to 1977, although care should be taken with the word "disease" in this context – see Jenny J van Drimmelen-Krabbe et al., "Letter: Homosexuality in the International Classification of Diseases: A Clarification," *JAMA* 272, no. twenty-one (1994).

66   *Male agency*

> Over the chasm of years and miles, Merrill Landon had come to love his daughter in a new way. He had never tried to pursue her, after that one shattering night in a New York hotel room when they had revealed themselves to each other, but he had spent the long years since then wondering about her, wondering how she might be living and with whom. His thoughts were mostly tender, sometimes resentful, always lonely. But he was proud and a little afraid of himself with her, and he would not seek her out again.[227]

Bannon's expression here is a little hyperbolic. Characters in her novels do travel distances – Landon himself lives in Chicago yet the confrontation between him and Laura in *I am a Woman* takes place in New York, so distance is hardly chasmic in itself. As for the "chasm of years" and "long years," it is surely somewhat less than a decade between their confrontation and the infancy of her daughter. However, the main point of this paragraph is the simple fact that Landon has come to love his daughter in a new way. If we are to take his pride as being in her, rather than in himself and in his resolution not to see her any more, then he sees her not as a reflection of or a conflation with his dead wife, but for the first time as a person in her own right. In effect he relinquishes much of his ownership, his appropriation, of her, and in doing so he also relinquishes the masculine role that society expects of him.

It is the agency of Beth, seeking Laura, that brings him into the plot of *Journey to a Woman*. She contacts him, goes to see him, and is struck by his physicality: "In his heavy features she saw very little of Laura, who resembled most her mother. And yet there was something there, faint but visible, that kept the shivers coming in Beth."[228] This reaction makes it worth mentioning that Landon's conflation of Laura with his dead wife is not the only occasion on which Bannon uses conflation as a device. Although the melding of Laura and Ellie in Landon's mind is the most obvious, the most melodramatic, Laura sees Beth in Marcie,[229] notwithstanding that they are unrelated. The little likeness to Laura that Beth sees in Merrill Landon makes her shiver, and Beth's effusive reaction to Betsy Mann's resemblance to Laura makes the child back away, "frightened at her strange behaviour."[230] The following exchange between Beth and Landon is interesting:

227 Bannon, *Journey to a Woman*. 99.
228 Bannon, *Journey to a Woman*. 100.
229 Bannon, *I am a Woman*. 25.
230 Bannon, *Journey to a Woman*. 168–169. Further down page 169, Beth recovers herself and refrains from hugging Betsy again.

Male agency   67

"Mr. Landon," she said, looking at him with all the subterfuges stripped from her. "Why are you kind to me? Why don't you despise me for what I did to your daughter?"

"For what *you* did to her?" He gave a scornful little laugh that turned against himself. "If I were guiltless myself I could despise anyone I pleased. But I'm not guiltless [...] If it hadn't been you it would have been somebody else, Beth. You know that, of course. Laura is a Lesbian. Sooner or later she would have understood that, whether with your help or without it."[231]

Bannon appears to move towards an essentialist view of Laura's sexuality, when she gives Landon this view of inevitability. "That's her nature," he says, of Laura's moving on from her former partnership with Beth.[232] As Landon and Beth continue to talk, Bannon starts to surprise us. Landon understands Beth's language, which makes it easy for her to talk to him,[233] his knowing by the quivering of her lip that she was understating things for him shows him to be perspicacious,[234] his advice to her to make plans and his offer of a loan shows him to be both practical and generous.[235] Throughout their interaction, he is wholly honest about his feelings and his failings:

"Are we a pair of cowards, Mr. Landon?" she said. "Or are we braver than everybody else?"

"Cowards, of course," he said. "We aren't really brave at all. But we do have a certain strength. You set out to find yourself, and that takes strength. I found myself long ago and had the strength to live with what I found – not a pleasant task. He grinned at her and suddenly she liked him. She liked him very much and in that instant she saw Laura in his face, his smile, again.[236]

They part as "a pair of conspirators [...] friends,"[237] and it is as much Bannon who has begun to like him as it is Beth. Later he is described as reserved and cautious, but thankful that Beth has found his daughter,[238] of whom he had

---

231 Bannon, *Journey to a Woman*. 103.
232 Bannon, *Journey to a Woman*. 104.
233 Ibid.
234 Bannon, *Journey to a Woman*. 105.
235 Bannon, *Journey to a Woman*. 105, 106.
236 Bannon, *Journey to a Woman*. 107. The lack of quotation mark after "task" is a typographical error in the Cleis edition.
237 Bannon, *Journey to a Woman*. 107–108.
238 Bannon, *Journey to a Woman*. 200.

68 Male agency

spoken "so lovingly."[239] To Laura, of course, he is still "[m]y bastard of a father who still loves me in spite of everything," and whom she wonders why she still loves.[240] A kind of redemption has come for Merrill Landon by the end of *Journey to a Woman*, and when Bannon mentions another father in her overall prequel it is Beebo's – "My father [...] is a damn good man. He loves me and he tries to understand me. He's the only one who does."[241] – she has completely finished with father-daughter conflicts. The challenge of the "huge heavy domineering father, with his aggressive maleness stamped all over his body"[242] and the mantle of masculinity the father-figure has worn across most of the corpus has been dissipated.

The failure of masculinity?

The male characters dealt with in this chapter have battled with the expectations of 1950s masculinity, and by and large their battles have been lost. They are not the only significant male characters in the novels under study, and I have omitted some from detailed examination in this section. The Hollywood husband Leo Bogardus and the pizza business owner Pete Pasquini, both from Ann Bannon's final novel *Beebo Brinker*, are two such. Christopher Nealon says of Bogardus that he does not resort to the language of what is natural or godly to denounce homosexuality, via Beebo, but rather defends the structure, not the origin.[243] However, in Chapter IV I will use him as an example of someone who does not maintain a structure so much as shore up a façade. Pete Pasquini's major trait is the fetishisation of lesbians, and though it is tempting to say that this represents his own unresolved gender issues,[244] it is much more likely that Bannon held him up as a distorting mirror to the casual male consumers of lesbian-themed paperbacks.[245] Another omitted character is Randy Salem's Johnnie, from *Chris*. He is ingenuous, almost childlike, and indeed is Chris's childhood friend. At well over six feet tall, gangly, with a shock of red hair, and an appearance that is "homely"[246] if not "ugly,"[247] he is said to have ended up with Chris's cast-off lovers in the past. In the narrative, he actively takes away from her one of the lovers

---

239 Bannon, *Journey to a Woman*. 167.
240 Bannon, *Journey to a Woman*. 245.
241 Ann Bannon, *Beebo Brinker* (Cleis, 2001). 12.
242 Bannon, *Women in the Shadows*. 111.
243 Nealon, *Foundlings: Lesbian and Gay Historical Emotion before Stonewall*. 163.
244 His wife says to him, "You married me to prove you was a man, and once we left the church, you figure you proved it." Bannon, *Beebo Brinker*. 116.
245 Bannon provides a scene where he attempts to "prove" his friendship by trying to make love to Beebo against the door of his truck. When she almost faints, he sits her down and puts her head between her legs, protesting his friendship; but the damage is done and his clumsy assault gets him nowhere. Bannon, *Beebo Brinker*. 161–162.
246 Randy Salem, *Chris* (Naiad, 1989). 122.
247 Salem, *Chris*. 124.

Male agency 69

she is torn between, and in doing so is a one-man challenge to the idea of the "Big Handsome Hero"[248] and to the loafered suavity of "Grey Gregg and Big Tom D and Rabbit Man."[249] He takes away Carol by gentleness, with none of the brute force assumed to be the male role, no engraved invitation to a violation, and none of the relaxed confidence of the Ivy League frat man. His success is the exception that tests the general rule of failure.

Another omission, so far, is Ann Bannon's ubiquitous Jack Mann. Christopher Nealon says that Mann's role is to mix dry wit and an outsider's perspective into her narratives,[250] but Bannon herself says that he hides behind wisecracks,[251] and indeed he can be infuriatingly indirect. She claims he is not "pushy," on the page following an exchange in which he insists on picking up Laura at eight o'clock and on not taking no for an answer.[252] Despite being held out as Bannon's Mr Nice Guy, critics and commentatorsoften ignore his propensity for violence.[253] However, I wish to deal with Jack Mann also in Chapter IV, as a specific dynamic, and in a comparable context to that of Leo Bogardus, and therefore I will not deal here with the more generally rehearsed aspects of his character.

This chapter began by referring to "the complex social structures that wed masculinity to maleness and to power and domination,"[254] without offering a definition of "masculinity" or, for that matter, offering a description of the complex social structures in place. The song lyrics at the head of this section imply that masculinity is as simple as the notion of being "brave and free." The entry for "masculinity" in the Oxford English Dictionary contains the words, "the assemblage of qualities regarded as characteristic of men."[255] However, a dictionary entry is not a definition of what a word ought to mean, but a record of how it is used. Moreover that entry does not list any of the qualities, and talks of their being those "regarded" as characteristic of men. The implication is that the list may change, as may the scope or con-

---

248 Bradley and Damon, *Checklist 1960: A Complete, Cumulative Checklist of Lesbian, Variant, and Homosexual Fiction, in English, or Available in English Translation, with Supplements of Related Material, for the Use of Collectors, Students, and Librarians.*

249 Packer, *Spring Fire.* 36.

250 Nealon, *Foundlings: Lesbian and Gay Historical Emotion before Stonewall.* 164.

251 Bannon, *I am a Woman.* 47.

252 Bannon, *I am a Woman.* 47, 46. In fact Jack's attitude to Laura is overbearing throughout this novel, if not throughout the corpus. I have noted that in *I am a Woman* everybody bullies Laura.

253 When he hears that Merrill Landon has "hurt" Laura, his assumption was that Landon had done her physical harm, and his reaction was to say, "I wish I could break his head for him." Bannon, *I am a Woman.* 223. He actually does extreme violence to someone – kneeing him in the genitals and beating his face to a pulp – in a chapter excised from *Women in the Shadows* but published as an extract in a magazine. Ann Bannon, "The Nice Kid," *ONE Magazine* vol.9, no. 1 (1961). 26.

254 Halberstam, *Female Masculinity.* 2.

255 "masculinity,"in *Oxford English Dictionary* (3rd: Oxford U P, 2021).

70 *Male agency*

stitution of whomever it is who "regard[s]" those qualities. If Ann Bannon can be taken to speak for all the authors in this study, and their female contemporaries, then heterosexual men, the majority, are summed up thus:

> As for straight men, alas, I was never very kind to them; they represented the wardens of society, the stern, self-righteous "moralists," the reprovers, the naysayers, the judgment-passers, the anhedonic social cops one had to circumvent to make it to the ball.[256]

But that is not the picture that emerges from the texts. Even Lora Sela's one-dimensional male characters don't quite fit that description, inadequate and lacking in social context as they are. Vin Packer's Bud Roberts may be a rapist, but his troubled conscience makes him more relatable than Ayn Rand's Howard Roark who, though from mainstream literature, is as much of a fantasy figure as any character in the male-authored "virile adventures."[257] Bannon's Merrill Landon, with his impressive male bulk, suppresses trauma and emotion, attempting a kind of masculine stoicism that eventually breaks him. All these characters were created at a time of masculinity crisis and male panic, and they are emblematic of that crisis and that panic. Masculinity was being re-imagined, supposedly to align with nature but in reality trying to define nature; and thus the very concept of masculinity was flimsy – is flimsy in the novels – or is like an ouroboros, circular and incapable of resolution. If masculinity is such a bad fit for the bodies assumed to wear and wield it, for the characters with so much agency in the novels, a proposition emerges that it is not necessarily a quality that resides solely in those bodies. This is the proposition that comes under study in the next chapter.

256 In the Afterword to Bannon, *Women in the Shadows.* 200.
257 Keller, "Pulp Politics: Strategies of Vision in Pro-Lesbian Pulp Novels 1955–1965." 2.

Male agency 71

Bibliography

Baker, David. "Rock Rebels and Delinquents: The Emergence of the Rock Rebel in 1950s "Youth Problem" Films." *Continuum* 19, no. 1 (2005): 39–54.

Bannon, Ann. *Beebo Brinker*. Cleis, 2001.

———. *I am a Woman*. Cleis, 2002.

———. *Journey to a Woman*. Cleis, 2003.

———. "The Nice Kid." *ONE Magazine* 9, no. 1 (1961): 23–28.

———. *Odd Girl Out*. Cleis, 2001.

———. *Women in the Shadows*. Cleis, 2002.

Berliner, Michael S., ed. *Letters of Ayn Rand*. Dutton, 1995.

Bradley, Marion Zimmer, and Gene Damon. *Checklist 1960: A Complete, Cumulative Checklist of Lesbian, Variant, and Homosexual Fiction, in English, or Available in English Translation, with Supplements of Related Material, for the Use of Collectors, Students, and Librarians*. Self-published by Marion Zimmer Bradley, 1960.

Branden, Barbara. "Ayn Rand: The Reluctant Feminist." In *Feminist Interpretations of Ayn Rand*, edited by Mimi Reisel Gladstein and Chris Matthew Sciabarra, 25–45. Pennsylvania State University Press, 1999.

Brandt, Kate. *Happy Endings: Lesbian Writers Talk About Their Lives and Work*. Naiad, 1993.

Brown, Susan Love. "Ayn Rand and Rape." *The Journal of Ayn Rand Studies* 15, no. 1 (2015): 3–22.

Butler, Judith. "Imitation and Gender Insubordination." In *Inside/Out: Lesbian Theories, Gay Theories*, edited by Diana Fuss, 13–31. Routledge, 1991.

Cassill, R.V. *Dormitory Women*. Signet, 1959.

de Beauvoir, Simone. *Le Deuxième Sexe*. Vol. 2: Éditions Gallimard, 1976.

Dorr, Lisa Lindquist. "The Perils of the Back Seat: Date Rape, Race and Gender in 1950s America." *Gender & History* 20, no. 1 (2008): 22–47.

du Maurier, Daphne. *Rebecca*. Virago, 2003.

Ellis, Joan. *Girls Dormitory*. Midwood, 1963.

Foucault, Michel. *Abnormal: Lectures at the College De France, 1974–1975*. Translated by Graham Burchell. Edited by Valerio Marchetti and Antonella Salomoni. Verso, 2016.

———. *The Order of Things*. Translated by not named. Verso, 1994.

———. "What Is an Author?" In *The Foucault Reader: An Introduction to Foucault's Thought*, edited by Paul Rabinow, 101–20. Penguin, 1991.

Gathings, Ezekiel C., and others. *Report of the Select Committee on Current Pornographic Materials*. U.S. Government, 1952.

Gilbert, James. *Men in the Middle: Searching for Masculinity in the 1950s*. University of Chicago Press, 2005.

Guillaumin, Colette. "Practique Du Pouvoir Et Idee De Nature: (1) L'appropriation Des Femmes." *Nouvelles Questions Feministes*, no. 2 (1978): 5–30.

Halberstam, Jack. *Female Masculinity*. Duke University Press, 1998.

Hamer, Diane. "'I am a Woman': Ann Bannon and the Writing of Lesbian Identity." In *Lesbian and Gay Writing*, edited by Mark Lilly. Macmillan, 1990, 47–75.

Hermes, Joke. "Sexuality in Lesbian Romance Fiction." *Feminist Review*, no. 42 (1992): 49–66.

Keller, Yvonne. "Pulp Politics: Strategies of Vision in Pro-Lesbian Pulp Novels 1955–1965." In *The Queer Sixties*, edited by Patricia Juliana Smith, 1–25. Routledge, 1999.

Leach, Edmund. "The Cereal Packet Norm." *The Guardian*, 29 January 1968, 8.

Moskin, J. Robert. "Why Do Women Dominate Him?" In *The Decline of the American Male*. Random House, 1958, 3–24.

72   *Male agency*

Nealon, Christopher. *Foundlings: Lesbian and Gay Historical Emotion Before Stonewall*. Duke University Press, 2001.

Oxford English Dictionary. 3rd ed. Oxford University Press, 2021.

Packer, Vin. *Spring Fire*. Cleis, 2004.

Rodgers, Richard, and Oscar Hammerstein. "I Enjoy Being a Girl." 1958.

Salem, Randy. *Chris*. Naiad, 1989.

Sela, Lora. *I am a Lesbian*. Saber, 1959.

Spectorsky, Auguste Comte. *The Exurbanites*. Lippincott, 1954.

———. "The New York Commuter." Research Materials: The Exurbanites.

Steinmetz, Melissa A. "National Insecurity in the Nuclear Age: Cold War Manhood and the Gendered Discourse of U.S. Survival, 1945–1960." Doctor of Philosophy, Kent State, 2014.

Taylor, Valerie. *Whisper Their Love*. Little Sister's Classics. Arsenal Pulp Press, 2006.

Torrès, Tereska. *Women's Barracks: The Frank Autobiography of a French Girl Soldier*. Fawcett Gold Medal, 1950.

unattributed. "*I am a Lesbian*." Review. *The Ladder* (January 1959): 17.

van Drimmelen-Krabbe, Jenny J., T. Bedirhan Ustun, David H. Thompson, Adre L'Hours, John Orley, and Norman Sartorius. "Letter: Homosexuality in the International Classification of Diseases: A Clarification." *JAMA* 272, no. 21 (1994): 1660.

Vidor, King. "The Fountainhead." Warner Bros, 1949.

Weinstein, Jeff. "In Praise of Pulp." *Voice Literary Supplement* (October 1983): 8–9.

Whitbread, Jane. "A Report on Current Attitudes to Chastity." *Mademoiselle*, no. 49 (1959): 37–40.

Wittig, Monique. *The Straight Mind and Other Essays*. Beacon, 1992.

Zeig, Sande. "The Actor as Activator: Deconstructing Gender Through Gesture." *Women & Performance: A Journal of Feminist Theory* 2, no. 2 (1985): 12–17.

II Female masculinity

Bannon, beebo, and butchness

I can drive, but can I be a boy?[1]

The background to Beebo

The previous chapter concluded with the inadequacy of the dictionary entry for "masculinity," and with an acknowledgement that, notwithstanding the abundance of male agency in the narratives, masculinity sat awkwardly on the bodies of the male characters, like an ill-fitting suit. Masculinity, as several critics point out, is not an easy characteristic to comprehend. For example, Halberstam says that "although we seem to have a difficult time defining masculinity, as a society we have little trouble in recognising it."[2] Gayle Rubin puts forward the view that society's attitude to gender constantly reinforces itself:

> I should make it clear that I do not consider any behaviour, trait, or mannerism to be inherently "male" or "female," and that my operating assumption is that cultures assign behaviors to one or another gender category, and then attribute gendered significance to various behaviors. Individuals can then express gender conformity, gender deviance, gender rebellion, and many other messages by manipulating gender meanings and taxonomies.[3]

Eve Kosofsky Sedgwick maintains that "when something is about masculinity, it is not always 'about men',"[4] going on to say that she considers that "it is important to drive a wedge in, early and often and if possible conclusively,

---

1 Ann Bannon, *Beebo Brinker* (Cleis, 2001). 24.
2 Jack Halberstam, *Female Masculinity* (Duke University Press, 1998). 1.
3 Gayle Rubin, "Of Catamites and Kings: Reflections on Butch, Gender, and Boundaries," in *Transgender Studies Reader*, ed. Susan Stryker & Stephen Whittle (Routledge, 2006). 480n6
4 Eve Kosofsky Sedgwick, "Gosh, Boy George, You Must Be Awfully Secure in Your Masculinity," in *Constructing Masculinity*, ed. Brian Wallis Maurice Berger, Simon Watson (Routledge, 1995). 12.

DOI: 10.4324/9781003422679-3

74   *Female masculinity*

between the two topics, masculinity and men, whose relation to one another it is so difficult not to presume."[5] I concur with Sedgwick, certainly as regards the project in hand in this book, which sets out to find, *inter alia*, whether the novels of a particular era do challenge the situating of masculinity within particular bodies. However, I also fully understand the difficulty, for two reasons. First, the presumption that Sedgwick speaks of, the recognition that Halberstam concedes, and the constant reinforcing Rubin points out, are due to the sheer weight of numbers of men that appear to demonstrate or perform what we recognise; by a feedback loop of definition, masculinity has therefore come to be a code for that which is culturally expected of men. This has a dampening effect on our seeing it any other way, no matter how cogent or forceful the arguments, and even no matter how unsuccessful any particular men seem to be at expressing it. Second, there is the more subtle factor of the very etymology of the word. Even when we refer to "female masculinity" we are forced to use a word that descends from an archaic Latin word, *mas/masculus*, meaning a male.[6] For that very reason we are obliged to qualify it, as Halberstam does in her book title, with the epithet "female," when we wish to describe women who appear to demonstrate or perform it. To sever the link entirely, and indeed to extend the range of behaviours, attitudes, and appearances, there would need to be a word that did not have that origin.[7] Even if we satisfied that need, the controversy about masculinity would not go away; "gender critical" feminists such as Sheila Jeffreys maintain that all forms of masculinity are problematic, and seek to eradicate it as a manifestation in bodies both male and female.[8]

This chapter will focus on the female masculinity of Beebo Brinker, the significant butch figure in the corpus of novels by Ann Bannon, and also on some of Bannon's other notable female characters who deviate from the butch persona while nevertheless having aspects to their character which may be recognised to varying degrees as masculine, or what might nowadays be

---

5 Sedgwick, "Gosh, Boy George, You Must Be Awfully Secure in Your Masculinity." 12.

6 The very fact that the diminutive suffix "-*ulus*" is there suggests the longevity of the categorisation of a person by sex at birth.

7 There is a similar problem in any case with the epithet "female," which has its roots in a word meaning "to suckle." Thus, no matter how this is put, it is encumbered with the biological binary.

8 "All forms of masculinity are problematic" is a phrase often attributed to Jeffreys, but nowhere can I find it correctly referenced. However, she does counter the plural form "masculinities" by saying, "The use of the plural, however, suggests that not all varieties of masculinity are problematic, and that some might be saved. Since I define masculinity as the behaviour of male dominance, I am interested in eliminating it rather than saving any variety at all [...]" This is probably the shortest definition of masculinity on offer anywhere, and, being at the same time both narrow and sweeping, is no more convincing than any other. Sheila Jeffreys, *Unpacking queer politics: a lesbian feminist perspective* (Polity Press in association with Blackwell, 2003). 7.

Female masculinity 75

termed transmasculine.[9] The novels under consideration use a vocabulary from before the theories of Halberstam, Noble, Rubin, et al. were devised and made public in their writings, and before epicene pronouns became prominent in modern gender politics. Therefore, this and subsequent chapters will stick mainly to the usage of the episteme within which they were written and read, as far as possible, including in the use of pronouns. Ann Bannon refers to her principal butch character as "she," and I consider that it is crucial to make use of this in order to show the tension between the characteristic and the body that carries it. I will not, however, use the generic masculine or any such construction when there is a clear common or vernacular alternative available – for example using "they." There will be some exceptions to this general practice, usually in direct quotation, and notably when citing Leslie Feinberg in a critical context, whose principal character in *Stone Butch Blues* is a "he-she"[10] and sometimes "a he – a man without a past";[11] also clearly preferred pronouns of other persons quoted.

As background to considering Bannon's characters, this chapter will look at the emerging language and culture of butch and femme, and the problems of self-definition that went with them. It will introduce the concept of "ki-ki" and show how the characters challenge each other's ideas of what is masculine and what is feminine. With close attention to the texts, it will consider body type and clothes, and Jack Mann's declaration about Beebo's boyish body that there was "nothing wrong with it," suggesting in conclusion that there is indeed a strong undercurrent in these novels that moves gender away from particular bodies.

Placing Beebo Brinker in the twentieth century

Beebo Brinker, feted by many as one of the salient butch characters in twentieth-century literature – the word most frequently used is "iconic"[12] – is

9 This is a comparative neologism that does not yet appear in mainstream dictionaries. The Nonbinary Wiki web site says: "Transmasculine, sometimes abbreviated to transmasc, is an umbrella term that refers to those who were assigned female at birth, and whose gender is masculine and/or who express themselves in a masculine way. Transmasculine people feel a connection with masculinity, *but do not always identify as male*. Transmasculine people can include, but are not limited to: trans men, demiboys, multigender people, genderfluid people, and nonbinary people, as long as they identify with masculinity. Transfeminine is the feminine equivalent of transmasculine." (my emphasis). "Nonbinary Wiki: Transmasculine," 2020, tinyurl.com/trmawiki.

10 Leslie Feinberg, *Stone Butch Blues* (Firebrand, 1993). 2 et seq. This term occurs in the narrative time of the novel as a pejorative used by Jess's male workmates, but appears earlier in the novel's discourse as a self-descriptor, in a letter written by the protagonist.

11 Feinberg, *Stone Butch Blues*. 222.

12 Katherine V. Forrest, ed., *Lesbian Pulp Fiction: The Sexually Intrepid World of Lesbian Paperback Novels 1950-1965* (Cleis, 2005). xviii. This is only one example; others include Melina Alice Moore, who calls Beebo "the most iconic lesbian character of the 1950s.

76 Female masculinity

situated in time roughly half way between two other representative butches, Stephen Gordon in Radclyffe Hall's *The Well of Loneliness* (1928), and Jess Goldberg in Leslie Feinberg's *Stone Butch Blues (1993)*. More modern enthusiasts of Ann Bannon's writings focus so much on the character of Beebo, that the corpus has been retrospectively described as the "Beebo Brinker Chronicles," a set of "five lesbian pulp novels."[13] Indeed, the introduction to the 2001 Cleis edition of *Odd Girl Out* is blazoned "Introduction: The Beebo Brinker Chronicles,"[14] notwithstanding the fact that the character herself doesn't appear in that book. Bannon in fact wrote six novels, in four of which Beebo Brinker appears; in one she enters the plot fairly near the end, and in only one is she the protagonist. Laura Landon, on the other hand, appears in five of the novels, and a case can be made for her being the protagonist in three of them. Laura is a peripheral character in only one novel in Bannon's corpus, *The Marriage* – the novel most critics omit from that corpus, due to its central theme being something other than lesbianism, and the only one not to have been republished after its introduction by Gold Medal in 1960. Whilst I do not wish to diminish Beebo's status as a character representative of her type, nor the way in which she has captured the imagination of Bannon's partisan readers, nor indeed her appearance as a principal in the corpus, Laura's equal or more prominent appearance is the reason why I consistently refer to all six novels as the "Landon-Brinkeriad." Not to do so would be tantamount to dismissing Laura's importance in Bannon's project,[15] and her importance to the novels' exploration of sexuality and gender.

Several distinctions may be drawn between Stephen, Beebo, and Jess, and also some parallels noted. One important consideration is that Stephen and Jess were drawn from the authors' direct experiences of masculinity in a female body. Beebo, by contrast, is a fantasy character created from Bannon's imagination. In an interview, Bannon called Beebo her "dream girl" and said that while she was on her "furtive trips" to New York, she

[...] was already daydreaming about someone like Beebo [...] I've described her as a sort of blend of Tarzan star Johnny Weissmuller and classic beauty Ingrid Bergman. Meld those two into one fabulous

---

Melina Alice Moore, "'A Boy Inside It': Beebo Brinker and the Transmasculine Narratives of Ann Bannon's Lesbian Pulp," *GLQ: A Journal of Lesbian and Gay Studies* 25, no. 4 (2019). 573. Anna Livia says Beebo is "often exalted as the perfect butch." Anna Livia, "'I Ought to Throw a Buick at You': Fictional Representations of Butch/Femme Speech," in *Gender Articulated: Language and the Socially Constructed Self*, ed. Kira Hall and Mary Bucholtz (Routledge). 260.

13 Nicola Luksic, "Authors look back at the heyday of lesbian pulp: Trashy and tragic," *daily-extra.com* (2005), tinyurl.com/LuksicPulp. No page numbers.

14 Ann Bannon, *Odd Girl Out* (Cleis, 2001). v.

15 Best expressed as the principle that "homosexuals, male and female, are as vastly diversified in temperament, interests, social and financial status, and intelligence as heterosexuals." Ann Bannon, "Secrets of the Gay Novel," *One: The Homosexual Viewpoint* 9, no. 7 (1961). 8.

female, put a sword and buckler on her and you've got my gutsy young butch, Beebo Brinker. An archetype, maybe – but I never get tired of looking for her.[16]

Beebo was born of the author's own "sheer need," and Bannon asked "Was there anybody like her anywhere? Big, bold, handsome, the quintessential 1950s buccaneer butch, she was a heller and I adored her."[17] The answer to Bannon's question – was there anybody like her? – is therefore, when compared to Stephen Gordon and Jess Goldberg, and in strict reality, no. Michelle Ann Abate, in her book *Tomboy*, states that Beebo, with her confident swagger, short hair, and men's clothes epitomises lesbian butchness in the post-WW2 era;[18] she goes on to say that for femmes, Beebo was whom they fantasised about dating, and butches fantasised about embodying her tough, transgressive character.[19] As compelling a fantasy figure as she is, therefore, she can hardly be described as quintessential – she is wholly fictional, a representation of what one particular author thinks a butch lesbian is or should be and, as is discussed later, far from ideal as a role model or a fantasy lover. When Beebo was first imagined, Bannon did not concern herself with the whys and wherefores of butchness; Beebo was launched into the world of the cheap paperback fully grown, a personal fantasy becoming a matter of textual fact.

Another difference between Stephen, Beebo, and Jess, and indeed between their authors, is that of class. Radclyffe Hall is from, and Stephen Gordon represents, English aristocracy. Leslie Feinberg is from, and Jess Goldberg represents, the Jewish-American working-class. Ann Bannon was a "Big Ten college girl" who aspired to a career in journalism[20] and had a conventional marriage, and Beebo Brinker was the daughter of a veterinarian in rural Wisconsin, in a relationship with the former college girl Laura in *I am a Woman* and *Women in the Shadows*; although Beebo was expelled from school, and accepted menial work as an elevator operator along with working-class status, she once had an inclination to be a doctor, and both her author and she can be said fairly to be, and broadly to represent, the American middle class.[21] To a marked extent, therefore, Beebo Brinker

---

16 Merryn Johns, "Pulp Pioneer: Ann Bannon reflects on writing lesbian fiction in the 1950s," *Curve: The Lesbian Magazine* 21, no. 2 (2011). 72.

17 Ann Bannon, *I am a Woman* (Cleis, 2002). v. To reinforce this sense of Beebo as a fantasy lover, it is worth noting that Bannon herself says "I think I had a kind of love affair with Beebo." Kate Brandt, *Happy Endings: Lesbian Writers Talk About Their Lives and Work* (Naiad, 1993). 78.

18 Michelle Ann Abate, *Tomboys: A Literary and Cultural History* (Temple University Press, 2008). 177.

19 Abate, *Tomboys: A Literary and Cultural History*. 177

20 Personal email, 30th September 2018.

21 Bannon, *Beebo Brinker*. 14, 15. Gayle Rubin disagrees, calling Beebo "exemplary of white, working-class butchness." Rubin, "Of Catamites and Kings: Reflections on Butch, Gender,

78   Female masculinity

can be considered safe, insulated from the harshness of factory work, poverty, beatings, arrests, and violation that typified the life of the young Jess Goldberg. If the quintessence of the post-WW2 butch is anywhere in fiction, it is in the latter's harsh, putatively semi-autobiographical[22] reality, compared to which the fantasy of Beebo's stunning looks, her relationship with the film star Venus[23] and with the well-off journalist's daughter Laura, and her life swaggering through the New York bars seems almost chic, her imagined masculinity made up of whole cloth.

The Atlantic, and the post-War situation in the United States, where unaccompanied working-class women were beginning to frequent bars,[24] divide Hall and her creation from the milieu that was already firmly in place when Bannon wrote her novels. A decade before Bannon's debut, one of that milieu's own denizens could be heard both defining and questioning the subculture they had set up; writing to Lisa Ben's[25] mimeographed and hand-circulated journal *Vice Versa* in 1947, a reader whom the editor identifies as "Laurajean Ermayne" and who, one assumes therefore, is known to her, says:

> Has it ever occurred to you, my sisters, that the names by which we call ourselves lack dignity? I refer to "butch" and "fluff" and such. They are such slanglish words, yet we have no better [...] Take the butches. I've thought of a word, see what you think of it: <u>Lescourts</u>. First of all, it may be regarded as a combination of "lesbian" and "escort". It is the butch who is the escort, so—Then, too, you can look at it from the standpoint of courting, which is also in the butch's line [...] I've

and Boundaries." 480n18. However, Beebo's employment and status is by choice, not by constraint of social circumstances. Her sojourn in Hollywood even allows her exceptionally to experience the periphery of celebrity, an American equivalent of aristocracy.

22 Jean Bobby Noble reports that when he asked Feinberg "Did it really happen like that?" Feinberg's reply was "I always answer that question with another question: 'What's at stake for you in that question?'" Jean Bobby Noble, *Masculinity without Men? Female Masculinity in Twentieth-Century Fictions* (UBC Press, 2004). 97. However, ze also said in an interview that ze "couldn't have written a fictional work without having lived the non-fictional realities." See Gretchen Lee, "Pink and Blue: Interview with Leslie Feinberg," *Curve: The Lesbian Magazine* 8, no. 5 (1998). 31.

23 Bannon, *Beebo Brinker*. 131 et seq.

24 Madeline Davis and Elizabeth Lapovsky Kennedy, "Oral History and the Study of Sexuality in the Lesbian Community: Buffalo, New York,1940-1960," *Feminist Studies* 12, no. 1 (1986). 7. Davis and Kennedy, whose article deals with one city in particular, point out that the very fact that the denizens of the bars were working-class meant that documentary records are non-existent, and the writers had to seek oral evidence. It is much easier for a researcher to find documentary sources relating to legal restrictions and moral objections to women frequenting bars, than evidence of the bar culture itself. Davis and Kennedy also say, on page 8, that there were more bars in Buffalo in the 1940s and 1950s than there were when they wrote their article.

25 The *nom-de-plume* of Edythe Eyde.

Female masculinity 79

another suggestion: <u>Clyffe</u>. How about being called a clyffe, if you're the tom-boy type? It's a masculine name, for one thing; the main thing is, it comes from Rad<u>clyffe</u>, honouring our Matron Saint.[26]

The correspondent notes the "masculine" accretion to the butch, lescourt, clyffe, or tom-boy persona, and refers back to their aristocratic, British antecedent. The gulf between Radclyffe Hall's real and Stephen Gordon's fictitious worlds and the California of Lisa Ben and Laurajean Ermayne – a gulf which includes not simply nationality and class, but also an ocean, a continent, and a major culturally destructive war – seems very great, but in fact we are considering a gap of just under twenty years since the publication of *The Well of Loneliness*, less if one takes into account the publication problems the novel had in the United States. By 1951 it was available in the United States as a cheap paperback, published by Perma Books. Vin Packer had read it by the time she signed to Fawcett Gold Medal in 1952.[27] Valerie Taylor recalled in 1998 that she had "always thought *The Well of Loneliness* was rather a bad book."[28] Ann Bannon, by the late 1950s, had only read two books on the theme of lesbianism, one being Packer's and the other being Hall's,[29] although in her interview with Warren Etheredge she mentioned also having read *Women's Barracks* by Tereska Torrès, and called *The Well of Loneliness* "the grimmest, dreariest book ever written about two women in love."[30] Another paperback writer, a contemporary of Bannon's and Taylor's, Paula Christian, considered that *The Well of Loneliness* "wallowed in self-pity."[31] Although other books with lesbianism as a theme had been published at roughly the same time as *The Well of Loneliness* notably, in America, Djuna Barnes's *Ladies Almanack* with a character in it based on

---

26 Laurajean Ermayne, "Letter," *Vice Versa* 1, no. 6 (1947), queermusicheritage.com/viceversa6 .html. 9. Punctuation and emphasis original. A writer of this name went on to contribute articles to *The Ladder*, but there is an indication that the name was assumed, as it is reputed to be a pen name of Forrest J. Akerman; see Judith Mayne, *Framed: Lesbians, Feminists, and Media Culture* (U of Minnesota P, 2000). xix. Matt Yockey, "Dr. Ackula or: How I learned to stop worrying and love fandom," *The Journal of Fandom Studies* 1, no. 1 (2012). 102. Readers of *The Ladder* once complained about a film review in which Ermayne had used the words "Lez" and "butch," and had expressed voyeuristic enjoyment of sex scenes. Elizabeth A. Smith, "Butches, Femmes, and Feminists: The Politics of Lesbian Sexuality," *NWSA Journal* 1, no. 3 (1989). 408.

27 Vin Packer, *Spring Fire* (Cleis, 2004). vii.

28 Valerie Taylor, *Whisper Their Love*, Little Sister's Classics, (Arsenal Pulp Press, 2006). 239. Taylor gave her opinion curtly thus: "[...] all this nonsense about being predisposed before birth because your father wanted a son. I don't regard a lesbian as an imitation of a man, either. Women are women, thank God."

29 Bannon, *Odd Girl Out*. vi.

30 Ann Bannon, "The High Bar with Warren Etheredge: Interview with Ann Bannon," interview by Warren Etheredge, 2012, tinyurl.com/BannonEdge.

31 In Eric Garber, "Those Wonderful Lesbian Pulps: A Roundtable Discussion," *The San Francisco Bay Area Gay & Lesbian Historical Society Newsletter* 4, no. 4 (1989). 4.

80 *Female masculinity*

Radclyffe Hall, *The Well of Loneliness* was the only such book that achieved any great fame until *Women's Barracks* by Tereska Torres in 1950 and Packer's under-the-critical-radar success with *Spring Fire* in 1952.[32] It is not surprising to see *The Well of Loneliness* being drawn on by someone in an effort to restructure the vocabulary of the emerging butch-femme scene.[33] Lisa Ben, replying to her correspondent in *Vice Versa*, says "How the terms "butch" and "fluff" originated will probably never be explained."[34] She had heard the terms "Orders" and "Masons" before, but was similarly unsure of their origins.[35] Paula Blank notes an obscure usage of "lesbian rule" or "lesbian square" to refer to a "mason's rule of lead," but that as an origin would be beyond tenuous.[36] Packer and Bannon, relative outsiders at the time each wrote her first novel, could not expect either to replace Hall or, in Bannon's case, to speak for butch-femme bar culture. It was up to Feinberg, later, to give a voice to those women deeply embedded in the scene, to speak throughout *Stone Butch Blues* of the "he-she,"[37] to document what it was like to undergo hormone treatment simply to "pass," and to feel no longer like a he-she but like "a man without a past."[38] Even then, looking back from the 1990s, the vocabulary was still a problem, as Feinberg's characters say, "I wish we had our own words to describe ourselves," and contradictorily "I don't need another label."[39] It is important to bear in mind that throughout the era of the cheap paperback there was no satisfactory vocabulary to use, to describe with any adequacy the complexities of body, sexuality, and gender. That was the ground on which Bannon had to lay her foundation.

Butches, bodily abnormality, and costume

Both Stephen Gordon and Beebo Brinker appear to be trapped by the statistical abnormality of the shape of their bodies, so much so that their creators felt it worthwhile to make a point of liberally mentioning that abnormality.

---

32 By and large, books published only in paperback were not reviewed in newspapers and journals.
33 This was not only the case within the milieu and sub-culture. See Robert Silverberg's attempted coinage of "lover" and "beloved," as noted before. L. T. Woodward, *Twilight Women* (Lancer, 1963). 39.
34 Ermayne, "Letter." 9.
35 Ermayne, "Letter." 10.
36 Paula Blank, "The Proverbial 'Lesbian': Queering Etymology in Contemporary Critical Practice," *Modern Philology* 109, no. 1 (2011), tinyurl.com/PaulaBlank. 128.
37 Feinberg, *Stone Butch Blues*. 2 et seq.
38 Feinberg, *Stone Butch Blues*. 222. Jess does not identify as a binary man; his (at this point) transition is social, not medically defined, and therefore the gender he is exploring is trans-masculine and nonbinary. I consider this an important point to remember when looking at butch characters in earlier literature, such as the Landon-Brinkeriad.
39 Feinberg, *Stone Butch Blues*. 254.

Stephen at birth was a "narrow-hipped, wide-shouldered little tadpole,"[40] and as a youngster was ungainly and boyish, with "funny gawky legs," someone who enjoyed dressing up as the young Lord Nelson.[41] The young Beebo, in Ann Bannon's final novel, the prequel *Beebo Brinker*, is given, by the grace of the author, the redemptive quality of being "a handsome girl" and "big-tall"[42] – certainly taller than the first metropolitan butch she nearly bumps into[43] – of "regular features"[44] and "good-looking."[45] I use the word 'redemptive' deliberately, as her behaviour in the earlier-written novels in which she is at various stages of adulthood is possessive, cruel, and self-destructive. Bannon herself said of what she had written into Beebo, "When she was at her destructive worst, I was using her as a dumping ground for my own frustrations."[46] This prequel is very much Beebo's *apologia*. Having, in Bannon's imagination, the physique of a Weissmuller,[47] the adult Beebo's presence is noticeable:

> Beebo cut a rather startling figure, even in her own milieu in the Village. Uptown, where everybody looked or tried to look perfectly conventional and ordinary, she was painfully obvious […] There wasn't much Beebo could do about her looks, and rather than hide them she had finally surrendered to nature and even exaggerated them. It was a question which would have made her stand out more – trying to hide her looks or playing them up. At least playing them up didn't expose her to the condescending pity that hiding them would have.[48]

Both Stephen and Beebo therefore "play up" their physicalities, adding gesture to them. In her preface to *The Straight Mind and other essays*, Monique Wittig cites Sande Zeig to argue that "the effects of oppression on the body – giving it its form, its gestures, its movement, its motricity, and even its muscles – have their origin in the abstract domain of concepts, through the words that formulate them."[49] In the essay "The Mark of Gender" Wittig says that language "has a plastic action on the real," and that according to Zeig social

---

40 Radclyffe Hall, *The Well of Loneliness* (Penguin Classics, 2015). 5.
41 Hall, *The Well of Loneliness*. 12.
42 Bannon, *Beebo Brinker*. 3.
43 Bannon, *Beebo Brinker*. 4.
44 Bannon, *Beebo Brinker*. 5.
45 Bannon, *Beebo Brinker*. 17.
46 Bannon, *Odd Girl Out*. xi.
47 It is not remarkable to think of Bannon constructing a fantasy lover with Weissmuller's 1.9m physique, when one realises that her first childhood crush, according to her interview with Warren Etheredge (see bibliography), was the Statue of Liberty.
48 Ann Bannon, *Journey to a Woman* (Cleis, 2003). 214.
49 Monique Wittig, *The Straight Mind and other essays* (Beacon, 1992). xv.

82 *Female masculinity*

gestures are the result of that phenomenon.[50] In characterising the body as "the actor's tool," Zeig says

> Gestures are [...] as material as clothing which one may "put on" and "take off." Gestures are a concrete means of producing meaning, both the gestures that have been assigned to us and those that have not been assigned to us.[51]

Though the thrust of Zeig's article is the use of gesture to combat the oppression of "gender" and "sex," she and Wittig have highlighted the way in which language and motricity – the faculty of movement by the parts of the body – are in a constant feedback loop, causing us to move how we are expected to move, and to describe those movements according to the hegemonic code. Thus, in everyday life, when one may not be immediately conscious of performing a role, it is in fact not so easy to put on or take off such gestures. Such expectations extend to what is considered normal in physical appearance. We might innocently refer to one person as "the little chap," if his size was a salient feature, or equally to another person as "the tall girl." An abnormality may give rise to an affectionate even comradely nickname, such as my father's "Woman's Arms" amongst the members of his WWII Yugoslav Partisan unit due to his slender, pale, and largely hairless forearms, or to a more derisive one such as when Andrei Zhdanov dubbed Georgi Malenkov "Malanya," or Melanie, because he had "broad, female hips, a pear shape and a high voice."[52] To feminise a name simply as a vehicle of derision, using the conventional binary opposite as an insult, is of course odious.

The same abnormality may give rise to intense self-loathing, as it seems to do in the fictional case of Stephen Gordon when, having read Krafft-Ebing's *Psychopathia Sexualis*, she regards herself as "hideously maimed and ugly,"[53] whilst her lover Mary Llewellyn is considered "a perfectly normal young woman"[54] in every respect. Elsewhere in fiction the normality even of hips broadened by childbirth – "mare-like" and "a metre across" – can be declared "beautiful," albeit in the opinion of a single character.[55] The fact that the contrasting or apparently misendowed abnormalities are remarkable leads to the speculation that it is not simply that gestures, the language

---

50 Wittig, *The Straight Mind and other essays*. 78.

51 Sande Zeig, "The Actor as Activator: Deconstructing gender through gesture," *Women & Performance: A Journal of Feminist Theory* 2, no. 2 (1985). 13.

52 Simon Sebag Montefiore, *Stalin: The Court of the Red Tsar* (Weidenfeld & Nicolson, 2003).

53 Hall, *The Well of Loneliness*. 223

54 Hall, *The Well of Loneliness*. 381.

55 George Orwell, *Nineteen eighty-four* (Penguin, 1962). 174. Of course, the context matters a great deal in this instance, but the point is that the beauty of the woman is perceived in an exaggeration of what is normal, not of what is abnormal.

Female masculinity 83

that imposes them, the gender roles they support, and the taxonomy that so definitely and severely separates them, that have descended to us by custom from some unknown point in history, but rather two physically distinct breeds, if not in fact then in the ideal, in the supposed norm, and therefore in the normative.[56] This physical distinction serves us badly in many ways, but signally it makes the bearers of such abnormalities as mentioned above carry their difference as something transgressive.

Therefore, when it comes to the tall, boyish Beebo Brinker, it is not simply her assumption of apparently masculine clothes and behaviours that issue a challenge to conventional male masculinity, it is also, importantly, her physical characteristics. The clothes in themselves say less than one might imagine, notwithstanding the street "toughs" who supposedly pick on lesbians, saying that if someone is wearing pants like a man she had better fight like a man.[57] In an often-cited episode in *I am a Woman*,[58] Laura castigates Beebo for being a "little girl trying to be a little boy" because she has taken a job as an elevator attendant, telling her she hasn't "got what it takes," and declaring "You can wear pants till you're blue in the face and it won't change what's underneath."[59] In the episode where Laura says this, Beebo is not wearing pants, but a dress – albeit to please her father, who "likes dames" – so Laura is seeing her in a different light in a situation in which she has "taken off" and "put on," to quote from Zeig above, not gesture but costume.[60] Jack Mann had previously advised Laura, flippantly, to cut her hair, get some desert boots, a car coat, and some men's shirts, saying "that's the uniform [...] Can't join the club without it,"[61] and that she herself was a "boy" in the

---

56 Michel Foucault reminds us that "[The norm] is an element on the basis of which a certain exercise of power is founded and legitimized [bringing] with it a principle of both qualification and correction [and is] is always linked to a positive technique of intervention and transformation, to a sort of normative project" (*Abnormal*, 50).

57 Ann Bannon, *Women in the Shadows* (Cleis, 2002). 54. It is worth remembering that when Beebo refers to these "toughs" she is in fact lying and covering up her false claim of having been raped. The fact remains that their existence is plausible, and one only needs to go to Feinberg's *Stone Butch Blues*, which has parallels with hir own life, to read more graphic and credible accounts of rapes and beatings.

58 To give three examples of regular citation: Christopher Nealon both in an article and in a subsequent chapter of his book. Christopher Nealon, *Foundlings: Lesbian and Gay Historical Emotion before Stonewall* (Duke University Press, 2001). 166; Julian Carter in an article in *GLQ*. Julian Carter, "Gay Marriage and Pulp Fiction: Homonormativity, Disidentification, and Affect in Ann Bannon's Lesbian Novels," *GLQ: A Journal of Lesbian and Gay Studies* 15, no. 4 (2009). 592; S. Lou Stratton in a PhD thesis. S. Lou Stratton, "More Than Throw-Away Fiction: Investigating Lesbian Pulp Fiction through the Lens of a Lesbian Textual Community" (PhD Thesis, University of Birmingham, 2008). 255-256.

59 Bannon, *I am a Woman*. 180-181. It could also be said that Laura is castigating Beebo for appropriating working-class demeanour and appearance, and/or for transgressing the middle-class values she feels they ought to share.

60 Bannon, *I am a Woman*. 178-179.

61 Bannon, *I am a Woman*. 67.

84   *Female masculinity*

"aggressive and violent" way she treated her flatmate Marcie.[62] All of this hardly encourages Laura to comprehend the butch manifestation and the rules of the milieu in which it operates,[63] which is still new to her, with any degree of seriousness. As Laura is a young middle-class woman, her usual milieu would not be in the working-class world.[64] She is also getting her own back for Beebo's appalling behaviour. On Laura's first visit to the club in Greenwich Village frequented by Beebo, the latter flips a ten-cent coin and drops it on the table in front of her.[65] Abate claims this is a "suave strategy to charm Laura."[66] The coin is, of course, to make a telephone call, but Bannon, having been guided on her visits to New York by Marijane Meaker – who herself was not unfamiliar with the club scene, as it was where she had first socialised with Patricia Highsmith[67] – could not have been unaware that many femmes in relationships with butches provided food for the table with income gained from sex work, and that therefore giving a woman money in that environment invokes the connotation of saying "You're a whore." To drop it "insolently"[68] on the table implies, "You're nothing but a whore," and the fact that it is merely a ten cents coin implies, "You're nothing but a cheap whore."[69] When Laura returns the coin on a subsequent visit, smacking it down on the table and showing that she is anything but charmed and Beebo anything but suave, the latter compounds the insult by saying "I always get what I pay for."[70] If by that she means Laura's sexual attention

---

62 Bannon, *I am a Woman*. 66.

63 Lillian Faderman, *Odd Girls and Twilight Lovers: A History of Lesbian Life in Twentieth-Century America* (Columbia UP, 1991). 169. Faderman notes that strict role divisions between butch and femme "are testimony to the essentially conservative nature of a minority group as it attempts to create legitimacy for itself."

64 Faderman, *Odd Girls and Twilight Lovers: A History of Lesbian Life in Twentieth-Century America*. 178. Faderman reminds us that the classes remained as discrete as they were in the "parent culture," i.e. the general society where heterosexuality was culturally dominant. Also 175. Faderman points out that middle-class lesbians had "neither sympathy nor understanding" for butch-femme, and that it was considered "tacky." Laura is not yet particularly familiar with the minority culture.

65 Bannon, *I am a Woman*. 71.

66 Abate, *Tomboys: A Literary and Cultural History*. 176.

67 Marijane Meaker, *Highsmith: A Romance of the 1950s* (Cleis, 2003). 1.

68 Bannon, *I am a Woman*. 71.

69 I recognise that the term "whore" that I have used above is unpleasant and controversial. I listen to, and take note of, all views on the "prostitution" versus "sex work" debate; for example, Kat Banyard's view that "[a] society that acts in law and language as if men who pay to sexually access women are simply consumers, legitimately availing workers of their services, is a society in deep denial about sexual abuse – and the inequality underpinning it." Kat Banyard, "The dangers of rebranding prostitution as 'sex work'," *The Guardian online*, 7th June 2016, tinyurl.com/KatBanyard. Interpreting Beebo's actions as I speculate above would be in line with that culture of abuse, inequality, and commodification. For a wider and more supportive exposition of sex work, see the "Philosophy Tube" vlog on YouTube. *Philosophy Tube: Sex Work*, (Abigail Thorn, 2019).

70 Bannon, *I am a Woman*. 82.

Female masculinity   85

then it would appear that she does; in a subsequent episode in which Laura is the initiator and both gives and takes the lead in what Bannon calls "a lovely mad duet," usurping Beebo's butch dominance.[71] By then, of course, payment has been returned, and the sex that follows is severed completely from the strategy. However Laura, according to Beebo, has been calling out Beth's name during the episode,[72] and Beebo then describes Laura's behaviour with the flippant and uncomplimentary phrase "like a sow in rutting season."[73] The following morning, their next sexual encounter – under the circumstances it is hard to call it lovemaking – happens despite Laura's saying "No," and despite her blows, her sharp nails, and her fistfuls of hair.[74] Albeit Laura succumbs, releasing pent-up feelings, she has been overcome physically, and what she succumbs to is as much a violation as anything at the hands of a man might be. Sexual aggression had, in the 1950s, become an important aspect of white masculinity and sexual adventure, and many behaviours common at the time would nowadays be considered date rape.[75] So it is not surprising to find forceful insistence on sex as some sort of cultural given in any novel of the 1950s and 1960s, even one with a pro-lesbian outlook. A useful direct comparison with Beebo's physical insistence would be the episode between Charlie and Beth in *Journey to a Woman*[76] in which Charlie forces but Beth succumbs, having pointedly referred to it as *"rape."*[77] Beebo seems to have been retaliating for Laura's previous usurpation of her status of initiator. Lillian Faderman categorises Beebo as a "stone butch," but these exchanges between her and Laura show that any such stone-ness, if it exists at all in Beebo, is precarious.[78]

The standard critical interpretation of Laura's pointed comment about Beebo wearing pants comes from Christopher Nealon in *Foundlings*:

---

71 Bannon, *I am a Woman*. 94.
72 Bannon, *I am a Woman*. 96.
73 Bannon, *I am a Woman*. 98.
74 Ibid.
75 This is not to suggest that male sexual aggression was unique to the 1950s. See the previous chapter of this book on male characters, in particular references to Lisa Lindquist Dorr, "The Perils of the Back Seat: Date Rape, Race and Gender in 1950s America," *Gender & History* 20, no. 1 (2008). 28, 29.
76 Bannon, *Journey to a Woman*. 12-13.
77 Bannon, *Journey to a Woman*. 12. Author's emphasis.
78 Faderman, *Odd Girls and Twilight Lovers: A History of Lesbian Life in Twentieth-Century America*. 266. Faderman comments: "The stone butch, for example, who was so popular in novels of the 1950s and '60s such as Ann Bannon's Beebo Brinker series, was passé as a figure in the 1980s lesbian novel." There is actually no indication in the novels that "stone butch" fits Beebo as a description; there is no hint of her "packing" nor using a strap-on, and every indication that she was capable of and enjoyed sexual responsiveness. Ironically, within two years of Faderman making her statement, Leslie Feinberg's *Stone Butch Blues*, the novel that foregrounded working-class butch-femme culture for the first time, was published.

86   *Female masculinity*

"Internalised homophobia" hardly does justice to this vituperation, which violently literalizes and decontextualizes Beebo from exactly the features of her sexuality – her work, her clothes – that make her butchness three-dimensional and alive. By insisting on this terribly narrow story of gender inversion, by taking the elevators out of Beebo's sexuality, Laura returns them both to a brutal ground floor in which desire is always the desire for something real, instead of something living, and every demand is a demand for total validation, for total destruction – in which there is no distinction between hatred and self-hatred.[79]

"Internalized homophobia" and "vituperation" however only fit Laura's outburst if one isolates it from the rest of the novel and misinterprets it as a manifestation of self-hatred. To accept a challenge to Beebo from a woman herself clearly oriented towards women as any kind of "homophobia," one has to accept Beebo as a standard for lesbianism, an individual representative within Bannon's corpus of some kind of homonormative state. Bannon has sufficient skill as a novelist not to fall into that trap. All her lesbian characters, even the most apparently self-assured, are shown as journeying towards self-discovery, not in some kind of normative stasis; Bannon herself used the term "*Bildungsroman*" to describe the Landon-Brinkeriad.[80] Tatiana Prorokova, in her chapter in *Literatures of Madness*, reverses the accusation of "internalized homophobia" and turns it toward Beebo:

> Beebo is clearly a victim of homophobic society; yet she is also portrayed as a victim of herself and her internalized homophobia. Her inability to believe in happiness with a faithful lover drives her crazy and makes her harm herself and those around her.[81]

In causing Beebo to commit such acts of desperation as killing a pet dog, if not two, and faking a rape and the loss of her virginity,[82] Bannon's dumping of her own frustrations on her is extreme, and she is certainly not setting her up as the yardstick of lesbianism, despite wishing to see her as the "quintessential" butch.[83] After the death of the second dog, one that Jack had given to Beebo to replace the first, Jack and Laura have the following exchange:

---

79 Nealon, *Foundlings: Lesbian and Gay Historical Emotion before Stonewall.* 166.

80 Bannon, interview.

81 Tatiana Prorokova, "Alcoholic, Mad, Disabled: Constructing Lesbian Identity in Ann Bannon's 'The Beebo Brinker Chronicles'," in *Literatures of Madness: Disability Studies and Mental Health*, ed. Elizabeth J. Donaldson (Palgrave Macmillan, 2018). 139.

82 Bannon, *Women in the Shadows.* 52-57.

83 Bannon, *I am a Woman.* v. Bannon later regretted these episodes, saying in a 1991 interview: "Beebo really, in a way, had my nervous breakdown for me [...] I think I was just overwhelmed with grief and anger that I was not able to express. Nobody ever knew that." Brandt, *Happy Endings: Lesbian Writers Talk About Their Lives and Work.* 80.

He heaped his scorn on Beebo. "Damn!" he said. "Damn silly hysterical female. I thought Beebo had more sense than most women."

"Just because she's not *like* most women?" Laura cried. "Jack, you make me furious! The more mannish a woman is, the more sense you think she's got! [...] She's not a damn silly female. You damn silly *man*!"[84]

Jack's remark is misogynistic and implies that "sense" is measured in male terms. Laura's defence of Beebo is superficially a declaration that mannishness does not give a woman more sense, or equal sense, but its underlying argument is that human frailty trumps any consideration of sex or gender; this is, in its own right, a challenge to Jack's notions of masculinity. However, it is hard now to see anything iconic about Beebo or to see someone to exalt as "the perfect butch,"[85] or as "the most sympathetic and articulate character" in the corpus,[86] or as a person whom femmes would fantasise about dating;[87] but as Cherry Smyth says, "[m]any of us indulge in an archaeology of desire, divining role models and icons from the past,"[88] without stopping to consider whether those icons are appropriate. Beebo, who claims she always gets what she pays for, signally gets no such thing, if that is not simply sex but a stable and contented relationship; she only achieves a resigned happiness when she ceases to strive for it, the striving having put lines on her "tired handsome" and "fine, worn" face.[89]

Regarding "what's underneath" Beebo's pants, Ann Bannon herself says that Beebo did not want to change that; answering those who claim Beebo as trans, Bannon says that this is "simply not the case," and that Beebo "loved the swagger and the flouting of conventional expectation, but she didn't have the conviction or the motivation to be trans."[90] As was previously noted, Beebo could give and take in lesbian erotism, though her eventual reaction to Laura's usurpation was a violent one. Bannon's assessment, noted above, is

---

84 Bannon, *Women in the Shadows*. 161.
85 Livia, "'I Ought to Throw a Buick at You': Fictional Representations of Butch/Femme Speech." 260.
86 Suzanna Danuta Walters, "As Her Hand Crept Slowly up Her Thigh: Ann Bannon and the Politics of Pulp," *Social Text*, no. 23 (1989). 93.
87 Abate, *Tomboys: A Literary and Cultural History*. 177.
88 Cherry Smyth, "How Do We Look? Imaging Butch/Femme," in *butch/femme: inside lesbian gender*, ed. Sally R. Munt (Cassell, 1998). 88.
89 Bannon, *Journey to a Woman*. 250, 251.
90 Personal email, 4th October 2017. I am presuming here that both those who claimed Beebo as trans and Bannon herself are referring to binary transgender, i.e. as formerly termed "transsexual," and not to any wider definition, such as is suggested by Halberstam: "It is not a matter of whose gender is variable and whose is fixed; rather the term "trans*" puts pressure on all modes of gendered embodiment and refuses to choose between the identitarian and the contingent forms of trans identity." Jack Halberstam, *Trans** (U of California P, 2018). xiii.

88   *Female masculinity*

that Beebo is a butch woman, and not a (potential) trans man; if we accept this, Laura's diatribe is Bannon's and her protagonist's way of calling on Beebo to own her female body, which can be responsive, and which her give-and-take suggests she did not actually despise, even though it clashed violently with her sense of her role. Neither does Laura "[decontextualize] Beebo from exactly the features of her sexuality – her work, her clothes – that make her butchness three-dimensional and alive."[91] "Three-dimensional" is an unfortunately poor term to use of a job that consists of one-dimensional travel; it is a menial task, one of travel without ever achieving a destination, and rather making Beebo's butchness "alive" her work ties it to utter pointlessness. Nealon says, "by taking the elevators out of Beebo's sexuality, Laura returns them both to a brutal ground floor in which desire is always the desire for something real [...]"[92] ignoring the fact that in Beebo's employment there can never be anything other than a return to the brutal ground floor at the end of each working day. That is what is real for Beebo, it is her quotidian existence, and whether Laura mentions it can have no effect. It is Beebo, then, who is insisting on this narrow, one-dimensional gender inversion; Laura, at the end of her tether and having had plenty to drink may be doing the ranting,[93] but Bannon is using her to give Beebo a wake-up call. It is one to which Beebo probably fails to listen throughout the rest of the Landon-Brinkeriad, if her subsequent behaviour in *Women in the Shadows* is anything to judge by. It is only at the winding up of the narrative time of the Landon-Brinkeriad, at the final page of *Journey to a Woman*, that Beebo at last chooses to leave the elevator and walks out of the lobby, hand-in-hand with another woman.[94]

In highlighting Laura's diatribe, critics tend to fail to mention that Laura hurls the same jibe about what is underneath someone's pants at a male elevator operator.[95] It would be too easy to say that in the second incident Laura is distraught after her encounter with her father and somehow mistakes the elevator operator for Beebo, notwithstanding the different location, and whilst forgetting that she was inebriated when confronting Beebo; thus the two challenges, one affected by distraction and the other by drink, are clearly comparable. Laura challenges both sexes on the issue of whether

---

91 Nealon, *Foundlings: Lesbian and Gay Historical Emotion before Stonewall.* 166.
92 Nealon, *Foundlings: Lesbian and Gay Historical Emotion before Stonewall.* 166.
93 Bannon, *I am a Woman.* 178.
94 Bannon, *Journey to a Woman.* 252.
95 Bannon, *I am a Woman.* 208, 213. Melissa Sky's 2006 thesis is an exception, although she contends that Laura is "clearly confusing the boy with her lover, Beebo." Melissa Sky, "Twilight Tales: Ann Bannon's Lesbian Pulp Series 'The Beebo Brinker Chronicles'" (PhD Thesis, McMaster University, 2006). 145. This is an interesting interpretation that parallels her father's conflation of her with her dead mother. However, the fact that her father has just forced a kiss on her makes the argument for Laura's cursing the inadequacy of male masculinity generally, as signalled by pants, stronger than Sky's interpretation.

Female masculinity 89

clothes determine gender, and thus challenges the male-masculine-normality vector. Pants are only a sign;[96] they can only stand for masculinity, they are not masculinity in themselves, and Bannon insists in free indirect mode that "It was futile. Beebo *was* a woman, no matter how many pairs of pants hung in her closet, no matter how she swaggered or swore."[97] Here Bannon's focalisation is through the thoughts of Laura, weeping silently in frustration with her face in her hands.

Beebo's own stated view of butchness is a totalised and totalising one, demonstrated in her early attitude to Beth. In *Journey to a Woman*, the character Nina had appreciated the older Beth's "long, strong limbs," and had seen something in Beth that was "fashionably boyish."[98] That was sufficient for Nina to say, "You know what you'd be if you let yourself go? [...] You'd be a butch. You'd cut your hair off real short and live in the Village."[99] Beth is certainly strong enough to lift the suicidal, one-time lover Vega down from a window casement.[100] In *Odd Girl Out* Beth's description was one of boyishness or at least unconventionality. She had close-cropped hair,[101] was tall,[102] informal, fitted no mould, and was not shy of swearing,[103] habitually went without underwear,[104] walked with long, smooth strides,[105] drank coke from the bottle,[106] and had a strong laugh.[107] She had played a kind of protector's role to Laura, assuming actions conventionally expected of a male escort:

> Beth had then led Laura down to the basement. She was enjoying this new role of guide and guardian, enjoying even more Laura's unquestioning acceptance of it. They found themselves playing a pleasant little game without ever having to refer to the rules: when they reached the door to the back stairs together, Laura stopped, as if automatically, and let Beth hold the door for her. Laura, who tried almost instinctively to be more polite than anybody else, readily gave up all the small faintly

---

96 Daniel Chandler, *Semiotics*, The Basics, (Routledge, 2002). 241. I am using Chandler's definition of "sign," as "a meaningful unit which is interpreted as 'standing for' something other than itself. Signs are found in the physical form of words, images, sounds, acts or objects (this physical form is sometimes known as the sign vehicle). Signs have no *intrinsic* meaning and become signs only when sign-users invest them with meaning with reference to a recognized code." In the two incidents, pants could be said to have a metonymic function.

97 Bannon, *Women in the Shadows*. 57.

98 Bannon, *Journey to a Woman*. 117.

99 Bannon, *Journey to a Woman*. 135. This is in keeping with Jack Mann's attitude to butch style, Bannon, *I am a Woman*. 67.

100 Bannon, *Journey to a Woman*. 72. Not that the emaciated Vega actually weighs much.

101 Bannon, *Odd Girl Out*. 1.

102 Bannon, *Odd Girl Out*. 3.

103 Bannon, *Odd Girl Out*. 7.

104 Bannon, *Odd Girl Out*. 8.

105 Bannon, *Odd Girl Out*. 16.

106 Bannon, *Odd Girl Out*. 10.

107 Bannon, *Odd Girl Out*. 36.

90   *Female masculinity*

masculine courtesies to Beth, as if it were the most natural thing in the world, as if Beth expected it of her.[108]

When they went to the cinema, Beth's helping Laura out of her coat whilst seeing to her own became a kind of ritual for them,[109] Beth the tomboy shaping subtly into the kind of character Bannon would eventually amplify into Beebo. This performance of a role was one that indeed marked out a butch-femme relationship, and in time came to be ridiculed by feminists a decade or so after the Landon-Brinkeriad was written, as Leslie Feinberg portrayed in *Stone Butch Blues*: "One of the women at the dance made fun of the butch I was with because she helped me off with my coat. I was so upset we left right away."[110] But when Beth tells Beebo of Nina's assessment, Beebo retorts, "Good God, you're no butch!"[111] Perhaps afraid of being usurped, as she knew she could be, and thus have her butchness destabilised, she negates Beth's right to anything in her inclinations that tends towards the protector's role, and with that any part in female masculinity. Yet there is no hint, beyond Beth's discovering that she preferred to do domestic chores for Beebo than for her husband Charlie,[112] that she is about to relinquish her own character and settle down as Beebo's femme. Indeed, both Beth and Beebo seem typical of Bannon's connecting her female characters' behavioural traits with their physical characteristics. Beebo, however, by her five-word outburst to Beth, appears to want to put forward herself, her inclinations, and her behaviour, as the only definition of butchness.

Whilst it might take another three decades for Feinberg's salient butch Jess to acknowledge that "there's lots of ways for butches to be,"[113] Laura has already challenged Beebo by her refusal to be a stereotypical femme. "I don't want you to dress me as a damn princess" she says.[114] Alley Hector maintains that Beebo and Laura "seem to represent fairly rigid models of butch and femme."[115] But rather than femme, Laura and Beth both represent individual

---

108 Bannon, *Odd Girl Out*. 9.
109 Bannon, *Odd Girl Out*. 45.
110 Feinberg, *Stone Butch Blues*. 214.
111 Bannon, *Journey to a Woman*. 157.
112 Bannon, *Journey to a Woman*. 158-159.
113 Feinberg, *Stone Butch Blues*. 282.
114 Bannon, *Women in the Shadows*. 29. Julian Carter notes this resistance to playing femme to Beebo's butch, also noting that Laura's femininity is conventional: "In Bannon's fictional world, most lesbians conform to dominant cultural expectations of what middle-class white women in the United States ought to do and be. Their femininity is ordinary, not elaborated according to the subcultural codes that mark working-class femmes." Carter, "Gay Marriage and Pulp Fiction: Homonormativity, Disidentification, and Affect in Ann Bannon's Lesbian Novels." 587.
115 Alley Hector, "The Odd Girls' Journey Out of the Shadows: Lesbi-Pulp Novels," in *Sticking it to the Man: Revolution and Counterculture in Pulp and Popular Fiction, 1950 to 1980*, ed. Andrew Nette and Iain McIntyre (PM Press, 2020). 34. This book is not a major work

Female masculinity   91

aspects of the ambiguous and ill-defined "ki-ki" category. This is another term that defies etymology. Possibly it is from the Magyar word for "each," being a repetition of the word for "who" in that language – finding its way into vernacular American English via a handful of unknown immigrants – signifying someone who can switch between butch and femme; equally it could be a shortening and corruption of "AC/DC," meaning bisexual. The popular web site distionary.com traces the origin to the 1930s when apparently, it could be applied to a gay man who could be either passive or dominating, going on to document the migration of its meaning.[116] Marie Cartier defines it simply as "a term used in pre-Stonewall butch-femme bar culture to refer to someone who did not identify specifically as butch or femme."[117] Julia Penelope, in an article in *Off Our Backs* in 1993, gives, along with other quick definitions of "butch," the following definition of ki-ki:

> [...] Lesbians switched back and forth [...] depending on who they were lovers with at the time. If they were attracted to a [...] femme, they were butch; if they were sleeping with a butch, they were femme [...] We referred to such Lesbians as *ki-ki*, *bluffs* (a blend of *butch* + *fluff*), or *switch-hitters* (also used them [sic], as now, to refer to bisexuals).[118]

Valerie Taylor used the same definition in her 1964 novel *Journey to Fulfillment*, having one of her characters say, "I'm kiki. I can be either, depending who I'm with."[119] A New England woman recalled that the term was also applied to two butches or two femmes who were lovers, often under clandestine circumstances due to the hostility of those in their community who demanded that one only select a partner who was "heterogendered."[120] *Vice Versa*'s December 1947 issue carried an anonymously-authored short story entitled "Kiki," about a young woman who "did not know that Fate

---

of criticism, and I disagree with many of this writer's conclusions, but it is interesting. Hector's chapter appears at smith.academia.edu/AlleyHector as a longer essay and, unlike the book, with proper citations, leading to interesting sources, but with no indication that it has been published anywhere before. The essay was apparently written when she was an undergraduate.

116 unattributed, "Kiki," in *dictionary.com* (2018). https://www.dictionary.com/e/slang/kiki/.
117 Marie Cartier, "Baby, You Are My Religion: The Emergence of "Theology" in Pre-Stonewall Butch-Femme / Gay Women's Bar Culture and Community" (PhD Claremont Graduate University, 2010). 159 n528. In a later footnote on page 167, Cartier also refers to a long-since deleted 2009 contribution to the urbandictionary.com that gave the pronunciation of the letter "i" as "y" (in "why"). As the spelling "ky-ky" exists only in a minority of cases, I tend to doubt this pronunciation, given its lateness.
118 Julia Penelope, "Whose Past Are We Reclaiming?," *Off Our Backs* 23, no. 8 (1993), tinyurl.com/jupenpast. 12.
119 Valerie Taylor, *Journey to Fulfillment* (Volute, 1982). 45.
120 Faderman, *Odd Girls and Twilight Lovers: A History of Lesbian Life in Twentieth-Century America*. 168.

92   *Female masculinity*

had named her for what she was: Kiki – the kind of Radclyffe girl with a dual nature; now masculine, now feminine,"[121] which is rather a misinterpretation of Radclyffe Hall and her creation Stephen Gordon. According to S. Lou Stratton's 2018 thesis, Ann Aldrich (another pseudonym for Ann Bannon's mentor Marijane Meaker) was a "self-identified ki-ki lesbian in her twenties," noting that ki-ki meant a lesbian who did not fall into either the butch or the femme category.[122] To Audre Lorde the rules of the "dyke-chic scene" were "every bit as cutthroat as the tyrannies of [the] Seventh Avenue" fashion world;[123] resolutely individualistic and determined not to conform to either stereotype, she recollected in *Zami*, "For the regulars at the Colony and the Swing we were Ky-Ky girls because we didn't play roles,"[124] and:

> We were both part of the 'freaky' bunch of lesbians who weren't into role-playing, and who the butches and femmes, Black and white, disparaged with the term Ky-Ky, or AC/DC. Ky-Ky was the same name that was used for gay-girls who slept with johns for money. Prostitutes.[125]

Commenting on Lorde's statement, Kerry MacNeil notes that she does not explore her assumptions about the term further, nor her feelings about being linked with sex workers; Lorde may use the link to distance herself from the normative tendency of butch-femme culture, or indeed she may resent it.[126] The presence of ki-ki women, who could feel free to "put on" and "put off" at will appearances and behaviours that the bar culture considered either butch or femme, or who recognised these elements in their psyche to varying degrees as non-totalising traits, or who could make a style of their own, often was a destabilising influence in the eyes of the denizens who conformed to the culture's internal rules. Gayle Rubin notes that as in what was considered normal heterosexual relationships so also in normative butch-femme relationships, both sets of expected behaviours "were located within a system in which gender role, sexual orientation, and erotic behaviour were presumed

---

121 unattributed, "Kiki," *Vice Versa* 1, no. 7 (1947), queermusicheritage.com/viceversa7.html. 2.

122 Stratton, "More Than Throw-Away Fiction: Investigating Lesbian Pulp Fiction through the Lens of a Lesbian Textual Community." 125, 125n9. Kennedy and Davis also categorise ki-ki as "neither-nor," but then confusingly go on to say that ki-ki "did not refer to an abandonment of role-defined sex," in effect they parlay "neither-nor" into "either-or;" either way, they agree that ki-ki "disrupted the butch-fem social order." Elizabeth Lapovsky Kennedy and Madeline D. Davis, *Boots of Leather, Slippers of Gold: The History of a Lesbian Community* (Penguin, 1993). 212-213.

123 Audre Lorde, *Zami: a new spelling of my name* (Pandora, 2003). 211.

124 Lorde, *Zami: a new spelling of my name*. 181.

125 Lorde, *Zami: a new spelling of my name*. 154.

126 Kerry MacNeil, "Bathroom Lines, Ky-Ky Girls, and Struggles: Butch/Femme Aesthetics, Identity Politics and Positionalities in Audre Lorde's Zami: A New Spelling of My Name and Joan Nestle's A Restricted Country," *Journal of Lesbian Studies* 1, no. 3-4 (1997). 83.

Female masculinity   93

to exist only in certain fixed relationships to one another. Variations existed and were recognized but were considered aberrant."[127] According to Lillian Faderman, butches and femmes laughed at middle-class ki-ki women for their "wishy-washy self-presentation.[128]

Laura Landon, as a middle-class ki-ki woman who is capable of taking the initiative in lovemaking and refuses to be costumed to please her partner, draws pleasure from turning her gaze on the clientele of "a favourite hangout in Greenwich Village."[129] Here is Bannon's description, again focalising on Laura:

> All she wanted to do was sit there quietly and look at them … those lovely girls, dozens of them, with ripe lips and rounded hips in tight pants or smooth skirts. And the big ones, the butches, who acted like men and expected to be treated as such. They were the ones who excited Laura the most, when it came right down to it.[130]

She overturns scopophilia by removing the male entirely from the act of gazing, and by usurping his place as the gazer upon women. Under her gaze firstly are women of socially acceptable and expected beauty. Bannon is clear that Laura does admire this type of woman. She admires Sunny, the principal female character in *The Marriage* and "the kind of girl you marry,"[131] and admits that she held her close and kissed her hair "like a sister,"[132] though Bannon may have insinuated this into the narrative there in order to keep her lesbian readers, and her readers who simply like to read about lesbians, on board.[133] But also, and in particular, Laura admires women of transgressive beauty in the Greenwich Village hangout, the butches. In the latter is a double overturning, inasmuch as she not only usurps the male privilege of gazing, but also she is a woman gazing at female masculinity and not, as normality and normativity might sanction, at conventionally male masculinity. Such a display of frank interest could, under other circumstances, be considered a *faux pas*, however. Beth, accompanied by novelist Nina on her first visit to a bar in Greenwich Village, is openly curious about everything and everyone. To her persistent questions, Nina replies, "Quiet […] they'll

---

127 Rubin, "Of Catamites and Kings: Reflections on Butch, Gender, and Boundaries." 475.
128 Faderman, *Odd Girls and Twilight Lovers: A History of Lesbian Life in Twentieth-Century America*. 179.
129 Bannon, *Women in the Shadows*. 127.
130 Bannon, *Women in the Shadows*. 127.
131 Ann Bannon, *The Marriage* (Fawcett Gold Medal, 1960). 20.
132 Bannon, *The Marriage*. 8.
133 Possibly also at the urging of an editor from Fawcett Gold Medal, more likely Dick Carroll than Leona Hedler. It is important to remember that these books exist within what Meredith Miller reminds us is "a capitalist consumer culture which exploits lesbians for profit. ("Secret Agents," 38)

94 *Female masculinity*

think we're cops [...]"[134] – women who did not adhere to the cultural rules in this milieu were instantly under suspicion, as even this milieu was, in its own microcosmic fashion, an example of Foucault's "normative project."[135] When Nina silences her, Beth is actually not gazing at the women but at the men in the bar, and asking if they are "Johns," i.e. potential clients for sex workers, but nonetheless she is daring to gaze.[136] Monique Wittig in *The Straight Mind*, citing Paola Tabet, makes the point that "there is a continuum between so-called prostitutes and lesbians as a class of women who are not privately appropriated but are still collectively the object of heterosexual oppression,"[137] which accords with Lorde's first-hand observations, quoted earlier. Bannon must have been aware of this, of the encroachment of sex work into the bar scene, and yet allowed Beebo Brinker to make her contemptuous gesture with the coin in *I am a Woman*.[138] Beebo is eventually obliged, by experience, to give up not her butchness but the authority over a partner that the stereotype implies, the authority she has tried to maintain by contemptuous gestures and by cruel fakery more than by the force of her character.[139]

Writing of the end of male appropriation of masculinity, Jean Bobby Noble says that "[...] anatomy, identity, and authority no longer function as synonyms for each other [...]"[140] Bannon shows that this is as true for the butch who stops striving as it is for men who must now accept the wider ambit of masculinity; Beebo does not dominate Beth, and Beth, for all we know, may go on to moderate Beebo. It is significant that at the end of the narrative they leave "hand-in-hand,"[141] which is a signal of mutuality and equality, an experience in which both can be toucher and touched.[142] At that moment,

---

134 Bannon, *Journey to a Woman*. 118.
135 Michel Foucault, *Abnormal: lectures at the College de France, 1974-1975*, trans. Graham Burchell, ed. Valerio Marchetti and Antonella Salomoni (Verso, 2016). 50.
136 Bannon, *Journey to a Woman*. 117.
137 Wittig, *The Straight Mind and other essays*. xv.
138 Bannon, *I am a Woman*. 71.
139 I offer one caveat to equating Beth in *Odd Girl Out*, with Beth recuperated for *Journey to a Woman*, in that Bannon incorporated something of her own experience into both Laura in the former and Beth in the latter. In the introduction to the Cleis edition of *Journey* she says "For any writer, all of our various characters are "us" when we create them. I have always responded that Beth [in *Odd Girl Out*] was based, physically and socially at least, on a former sorority roommate [...] That said, however, perhaps it is fair to allow that there is a lot of me in Beth [in *Journey*] and a lot of her problems are the ones I was wrestling with in my twenties [...] We differed most in two ways: she spoke to her husband about her fears and misgivings while I swallowed mine [...]" vii.
140 Noble, *Masculinity without Men? Female Masculinity in Twentieth-Century Fictions*. x.
141 Bannon, *Journey to a Woman*. 252.
142 Anya Daly, "A Phenomenological Grounding of Feminist Ethics," *The Journal of the British Society for Phenomenology* 50, no. 1 (2019). 10. And Maurice Merleau-Ponty, *The Phenomenology of Perception*, trans. Colin Smith (Routledge, 2006). 410. Both cited, although my point here is a simpler one than Merleau-Ponty's "reversibility thesis."

Female masculinity 95

each woman owns who she is, each bringing herself intact into a possible relationship. At this point, the lesson has been learned that masculinity is not there to overwhelm, but to be respected in a situation of give-and-take. This mutuality between two women, both of whom have masculine traits to a greater or lesser degree, is perhaps Bannon's happiest 'happy ending', and as such is her most direct challenge to the "Big Handsome Hero who eventually converts [...] girls to 'normality' with some secret formula of caresses."[143] It is also a challenge to the idea that butchness is nothing more than one half of a system that signals a particular erotic desire in a relationship, what Gayle Rubin calls "an indissoluble unity."[144] Joan Nestle, eloquent and forthright in standing up for the butch-femme lifestyle, said "a butch lesbian wearing men's clothes in the 1950s was not a man wearing man's clothes; she was a woman who created an original style to signal to other women what she was capable of doing – taking erotic responsibility."[145] But even that, with all due respect to Nestle, is a totalising declaration. The idea that butchness ought to be confined to a set of rules in a sub-culture, forcefully challenged by Feinberg in *Stone Butch Blues* – "I always wanted all of us who were different to be the same. I can't believe I rejected a butch friend because she took a butch lover"[146] – is first challenged here by Bannon, three decades previously in Beebo and Beth's final exit together. Bannon's stance is more one of curiosity, testing butchness to see how it stands up, as an idea, under inquiry; and curiosity, as Joan Nestle herself says, "is the respect one life pays to another."[147]

Bannon's readers did not get to know how the relationship between Beth and Beebo developed, though there was a late hint that they would. In the introduction to the 2002 Cleis edition of *Journey to a Woman*, she wrote of Beebo and Beth:

> [...] I can reassure you that Beebo and Beth, at the end of *Journey to a Woman*, made it out happy and intact. How do I know this? Because I know where they are now: sitting on the pages of a manuscript written some years ago and awaiting resurrection and revision [...] I should have written a novel then that pursued them into their life together, Now, I will.[148]

---

143 Marion Zimmer Bradley and Gene Damon, *Checklist 1960: A Complete, Cumulative Checklist of Lesbian, Variant, and Homosexual Fiction, in English, or Available in English Translation, with Supplements of Related Material, for the Use of Collectors, Students, and Librarians* (Self-published by Marion Zimmer Bradley, 1960). No page numbers.

144 Rubin, "Of Catamites and Kings: Reflections on Butch, Gender, and Boundaries." 475.

145 Joan Nestle, "The Fem Question," in *Pleasure and Danger: Exploring Female Sexuality*, ed. Carole S. Vance (Routledge, 1985). 235.

146 Feinberg, *Stone Butch Blues*. 271.

147 Nestle, "The Fem Question." 234.

148 Bannon, *Journey to a Woman*. xii.

96 *Female masculinity*

Writing to me in 2018, however, the existence of any such further novel was far from her mind; she said that she had never written a follow-up to *Journey to a Woman* but had decided to get away from the stresses of gay life in the 1950s and 1960s, and instead write something that was "a kind of romp after the grimmer tales," referring of course to *Beebo Brinker*.[149] She did draft another novel during her career in University administration, but she felt that it lacked the drive of her youthful work, and indeed the perceptions about gender and sexuality had changed and were still changing – "I would rather look ahead than back"[150] – so it was never submitted for publication. The intention she declared in 2003, by that "Now, I will," did not bear fruit either, and I speculate that these references could be to the same manuscript or to a memoir she was preparing.[151] Writing a prequel instead meant that the ending of *Journey to a Woman* is the closest that Bannon comes to a true resolution of the Landon-Brinkeriad. Speaking of lesbian-themed paperbacks in general in her essay about the "Implied Lesbian Reader," Meredith Miller said that some of them had "reassuringly" heterosexual resolutions but increasingly some didn't,[152] and in any case "as Peter Brooks has famously pointed out, it is in the middle of plots that we work out the real ideological struggles of culture."[153] Endings in Bannon, from the standard, editorially-dictated splitting up of the lesbian couple and triumph of the male suitor in *Odd Girl Out*, through the setting up of a faux-heteronormative marriage in *Women in the Shadows*, to the all-female, egalitarian exit of *Journey to a Woman*, are in themselves indicative of an ideological struggle, however. In imagining the young Beebo Brinker, Bannon sets aside the resolution, and reintroduces and reinforces the tension between body, gender, and sexuality.

The body of Beebo, Beth, and others: "There's nothing wrong with it"[154]

There is one moment, well on in the overall narrative, that could be cited as introducing the idea of the adult Beebo's transsexualism.[155] It comes in

---

149 Personal email, 3rd December 2018.
150 Same email.
151 Bannon, interview.
152 Meredith Miller, "Secret Agents and Public Victims: The Implied Lesbian Reader," *The Journal of Popular Culture* 35, no. 1 (2001). 46.
153 Miller, "Secret Agents and Public Victims: The Implied Lesbian Reader." 46. Miller offers no reference, and this point is not precisely stated in such words in *Reading for the Plot*. But Peter Brooks confirmed (personal email 26th November 2019) that the middle section of plots is something he returns to throughout the book, particularly in the chapter on *Great Expectations* by Charles Dickens.
154 Bannon, *Beebo Brinker*. 51.
155 I have chosen "transsexualism" over "transsexuality" simply because the definition of the former, according to the OED, carries the sense of "the fact of [...] wishing to live as a member of the opposite sex." In the context of this book, I am confining variants of "transgender" to the OED definition of designating someone "whose sense of personal identity and

Women in the Shadows, when Beebo exclaims, "I'd sell my soul to be an honest-to-God male. I could marry Laura! I could marry her. Give her my name. Give her kids ... oh, wouldn't that be lovely? So lovely ..."[156] This appears to be a plain wish for maleness, even though it is a fleeting one and the adult Beebo never repeats it. Bannon's own opinion, or intention, as previously noted, is that Beebo "didn't have the conviction or the motivation to be trans."[157] However motivation is evident enough in the brief line of dialogue above, and it is not lack of it that puts a barrier in the way, but rather circumstances, because she lives and moves in a social milieu of women who prefer women; Laura loves the physicality of that, loves being made love to by a woman like Beebo. And as Beebo points out after the above, her being magically transformed into a man – a man from birth, at that, not someone whose gender is reassigned – would be of no use simply because Laura loves women. Laura, right at the beginning of the book, has already declared that she would never marry a man,[158] though this is ironic, given that the book ends with her marrying Jack Mann and their planning to have a child by artificial insemination. Some of the language in Beebo's declaration is significant: "Give her my name. Give her kids ..."[159] Beebo does not say "Share a name. Have children with her." Rather she stresses the active, the acting upon, the giving, the naming, relegating Laura to the passive, the acted upon, the receiving, the named. In short, Beebo appears to want to take possession of Laura in the way that Wittig says a man does, buying into the heterosexual idea of "a political regime which rests on the submission and the appropriation of women."[160] This could be no more than simply using the hegemonic code and speaking conventionally. An alternative interpretation is that Beebo's position is somewhat analogous to that of a "service top," which is someone, usually in a gay male relationship, who "tops under the direction of an eager bottom,"[161] inasmuch as the word "give" implies a longing to be generous, to give of oneself in a voluntary relationship of dominance and submission.[162] However, at the point in the narrative where Beebo makes this declaration, Laura is far from eager, and Beebo's angst even echoes the contemporaneous "male panic"[163] that plagued the sex she seems to aspire to.

---

gender does not correspond to that person's sex at birth, or which does not otherwise conform to conventional notions of sex and gender."

156 Bannon, *Women in the Shadows.* 27.
157 Personal email, 4th October 2017.
158 Bannon, *Women in the Shadows.* 2.
159 Bannon, *Women in the Shadows.* 27. My emphasis.
160 Wittig, *The Straight Mind and other essays.* xiii, xv.
161 Carissa Rodriguez, "It's Symptomatic," *Document* (May 13 2015), tinyurl.com/RodriguezSym.
162 I am grateful to my colleague Katerina García-Walsh for this interpretation. Private conversation, 12th September 2021.
163 James Gilbert, *Men in the Middle: Searching for Masculinity in the 1950s* (U of Chicago P, 2005). 3.

98   *Female masculinity*

When Bannon crafted her prequel, she made the young Beebo – Betty Jean Brinker, farm girl from Wisconsin – experiment with masculinity and with "passing" in a flash-back, long before there was any thought in her mind about a relationship with a woman, or a marriage, or children. On the brink of puberty, she borrows her brother's clothes and her father's press pass, gets a "real man's haircut," and bluffs her way into the Chicago livestock exhibition.[164] All goes well – her height and boyish looks convince people that she is a cub reporter – until she apparently falls ill. The doctor who attends discovers that she is having her first period, and her disguise is of no further use.[165] It is of no consequence that she was functioning and accepted within a particular gender, because as soon as her pretence is discovered the functioning and acceptance is nullified. But discovery of pretence is only an excuse for a more basic prejudice against someone of her sex category acting in ways considered appropriate only for the other. Halberstam reminds us that "tomboyism for girls is generally tolerated until it threatens to interfere with the onset of adolescent femininity. At that point, all attachments to preadolescent freedoms and masculine activities must be dropped."[166] The late-teenage Beebo that appears on the corner of Gay Street and Queer Street, clad in a skirt and carrying a wicker suitcase,[167] and who emerges gradually throughout the novel as a young butch, is a retrospective rehabilitation of the later

164 Bannon, *Beebo Brinker*. 52-53.
165 Bannon, *Beebo Brinker*. 54. Halberstam, referencing a 1978 study by Suzanne J. Kessler and Wendy McKenna, says that they note, "far ahead of poststructuralist gender theory, that biology is not the key to gender attribution. Instead of gender attribution, a split-second assessment, being based on genitalia, they note, genitalia are mostly assumed." Halberstam, *Trans**. 58-59. Beebo's genitalia are assumed in this episode before they are medically discovered. They are likewise assumed by whomever employs her as an elevator operator; according to Jack Mann, "They think she's a boy." Bannon, *I am a Woman*. 178. Norena Shopland calls this tendency to assume, "selective attention." Norena Shopland, *A History of Women in Men's Clothing: From Cross-dressing to Empowerment* (Pen & Sword History, 2021). 23. Kessler and McKenna themselves make the point that gender attributions "are almost always made in the absence of information about genitals" – as they are in the case of Beebo – but their subsequent point that "most people do not change their gender attributions even if they discover that someone does not have the "appropriate" genitals" is the opposite of what happens to Beebo. Suzanne J. Kessler and Wendy McKenna, *Gender: An Ethnomethodological Approach* (U of Chicago P, 1978). 17.
166 Halberstam, *Female Masculinity*. 268.
167 Bannon, *Beebo Brinker*. 3, 10. The street signs are shown on the original cover illustration rather than named on the page. The illustration is sometimes criticised for not portraying a butch character (see Melissa Sky, "Cover Charge: Selling Sex and Survival in Lesbian Pulp Fiction," in *Judging a Book by its Cover: Fans, Publishers, Designers, and the Marketing of Fiction*, ed. Nicole Matthews and Nickianne Moody (Ashgate, 2007). 132). However, Beebo had not yet put on that appearance. Her depiction is quite accurate, although her height is difficult to gauge. Her hair is black and wavy (see page 5) rather than curly, as described on page 3. Her skirt is mentioned in passing on page 10 and her wicker suitcase on page 3. By 1999 Ann Bannon herself had forgotten all this, calling the cover a "megabomb": Ann Bannon, "Foreword," in *Strange Sisters: The Art of Lesbian Pulp Fiction*, ed.

possessive, unkind, self-destructive character. Beyond making this novel the one where Beebo is uncontestably the protagonist, an important factor of this rehabilitation is the amount of physical description Bannon devotes to her. She is "a handsome girl [...] in her late teens, big-tall, with dark curly hair"[168] and "good looking."[169] We read that there was "intelligence in her regular features, but a pleasant country innocence."[170] She has a laugh "that must have carried across country fields,"[171] muscular angles,[172] and big hands.[173] She is a "big, beautiful, strange girl"[174] who had been strong enough to throw prowlers out of her father's farmhouse,[175] and who was "tall [...] tanned and strong"[176] but who only had "marginal femininity."[177] With her "flawless skin"[178] she could still appear ingenuous: "Asleep, she looked younger: still a child, with a child's purity [...]"[179]

But her looks are perceived as dangerous, destabilising the norm. To Leo Bogardus, husband and manager to Hollywood star Venus Bogardus to whom Beebo becomes companion and lover, she is a "freak" and a "mistake of nature," whilst even to Venus those looks are a "problem."[180] Pete Pasquini, her first employer in New York City, says flatly "Girls ain't supposed to be so tall."[181] Pete's reaction is based on society's expectations, which seem to cover more than behaviour and dress. Wittig says "[w]e have been compelled in our bodies and in our minds to correspond, feature by feature, with the *idea* of nature that has been established for us,"[182] and not only in our own minds but in the minds of those who observe us. "I was kicked out of school," says Beebo, "because I looked so much like a boy, they thought I must be acting like one. Chasing girls. Molesting them."[183] Is this – pursuit and molestation – considered to be normal, acceptable behaviour for a boy in a Wisconsin high school in the 1940s?[184] She has "broad shoul-

---

Jaye Zimet (Penguin Books Canada Ltd, 1999). 11. The illustration can be found at tinyurl
.com/BBC0ver.

168 Bannon, *Beebo Brinker*. 3.
169 Bannon, *Beebo Brinker*. 17.
170 Bannon, *Beebo Brinker*. 5.
171 Bannon, *Beebo Brinker*. 9.
172 Bannon, *Beebo Brinker*. 19.
173 Bannon, *Beebo Brinker*. 27.
174 Bannon, *Beebo Brinker*. 68.
175 Bannon, *Beebo Brinker*. 71.
176 Bannon, *Beebo Brinker*. 156.
177 Bannon, *Beebo Brinker*. 62.
178 Bannon, *Beebo Brinker*. 20.
179 Bannon, *Beebo Brinker*. 19-20.
180 Bannon, *Beebo Brinker*. 209.
181 Bannon, *Beebo Brinker*. 26.
182 Wittig, *The Straight Mind and other essays*. 9.
183 Bannon, *Beebo Brinker*. 50.
184 See the earlier chapter that deals with male aggression, *inter alia*, and in particular the references to teenage behaviour in Dorr, "The Perils of the Back Seat: Date Rape, Race and

100 *Female masculinity*

ders and hardly a hint of a bosom"[185] and "felt unassailable in the fortress of her flat-chested, muscular young body."[186] The perceived threat she posed to girls at school is reversed, parlayed into a defensive quality. It takes Jack Mann to resolve the issue: "[...] you're Beebo Brinker, human being. If you *are* gay, that's second. Some girls like you are gay, some aren't. Your body is boyish, but there's nothing *wrong* with it."[187] This is Bannon's taxonomy, expressed via Jack; firstly, homosexuality does not necessarily attach itself to a body type, and secondly the sentiment that there is "nothing *wrong*" with Beebo's body – implying that there is nothing wrong with either her perceived male attributes or her female – is a direct challenge to the notion that health equates to normality and vice versa. Citing Georges Canguilhem's *The Normal and the Pathological*, Karma Lochrie says:

> the nineteenth-century definition of normal already manifests a key con-fusion that would survive into the popular twentieth-century understand-ing of the term. On the one hand, the normal is that which is usual, in the sense of being most prevalent, most quantifiable as common, and most susceptible to averaging. On the other, it is a rule or standard, a type that defines an ideal as well as deviations from that ideal. The one describes a statistical regularity derived from quantitative analysis, the other, an evaluative judgment attached to a model or type. In its nineteenth-cen-tury usage, writes Canguilhem, "normal" was ambiguous, designating both what was regarded as factual and an evaluative judgment at the same time. For example, in medicine, the normal was equivalent to the healthy, the ideal, and the *goal* of medicine. The normal was also defined as habitual, as if to suggest that what was found in a majority of cases was also the ideal to be sought through medical practice.[188]

Notwithstanding Jack is seeking to counter that evaluative judgment, to take Beebo's attention away from the atypicality of her body, it is within that body that gender and sexuality are experienced. Beebo says of her body,

> [...] there's a boy inside it [...] And he has to live without all the mas-culine trimmings other boys take for granted. Jack, long before I knew anything about sex, I knew I wanted to be tall and strong and wear pants and ride horses and have a career ... and never marry a man or learn to cook or raise babies. Never.[189]

    Gender in 1950s America."
185 Bannon, *Beebo Brinker*. 29.
186 Bannon, *Beebo Brinker*. 32.
187 Bannon, *Beebo Brinker*. 51.
188 Karma Lochrie, *Heterosyncrasies: Female Sexuality When Normal Wasn't* (U of Minnesota P, 2005). 3.
189 Bannon, *Beebo Brinker*. 51.

Female masculinity 101

This may be non-sexual but is certainly highly conventionally gendered, the "boy inside" again putting a strain on Bannon's maintaining that Beebo cannot be taken as trans.[190] The reference to horse riding seems to echo the young life of Stephen Gordon, in *The Well of Loneliness*, whom Jean Bobby Noble genders with "he."[191] This is echoed again by the outfit Beebo wears while a protegee of Hollywood Star Venus Bogardus:

> She looked the best in riding gear: a formal tight-waisted jacket and white stock, hard velvet cap, smooth leather boots, jodhpurs. The kind of clothes she used to wear at shows around Juniper Hill. When she won ribbons for jumping other people's horses. She had a lithe elegance that the riding clothes dramatized.[192]

Bannon has Beebo feel "proud of her size, proud of her strength, even proud of her oddly boyish face," going on to say, "She could see interest, even admiration on the faces of many of the girls. She was not used to that kind of reaction in people, and it exhilarated her."[193] Bannon makes this an exceptional feeling, implying perhaps that a young man would have been bred up to expect this kind of reaction in young women. In the mind of one of her early lovers, Paula, Beebo is "too good to be true, too young to know herself, too masculine to be faithful," but equally, "how strong she [is] how sensual and sure; in some ways, wise beyond her years with that hard-won maturity [...]"[194] With Paula who is "soft and submissive,"[195] Beebo could nevertheless respond with a "helpless fury of desire,"[196] and come "crashing to a climax,"[197] or descend to a kind of infantilism when Paula sits on her lap and allows herself to be fed.[198] As a young butch, Beebo wishes to be all things to all women – "I'm as strong and tall as a boy, but I'm not as free as a man. I wanted to be gentle and loving with a woman, but I can't

---

190 Melina Allice Moore was confident enough to challenge Bannon's assertion recently in an article placing Bannon's novels squarely in the trans discourse, speaking of "Beebo's emphatically masculine identification," and asserting that "butch and transmasculine identities overlap and coexist." Moore, "'A Boy Inside It': Beebo Brinker and the Transmasculine Narratives of Ann Bannon's Lesbian Pulp." 569, 576. However, see my earlier footnote on this issue, and in particular the quotation from Halberstam. Halberstam, *Trans**. xiii.

191 Noble, *Masculinity without Men? Female Masculinity in Twentieth-Century Fictions*. 96.

192 Bannon, *Beebo Brinker*. 175. This is the closest that Beebo comes to traversing class barriers, albeit to the faux aristocracy of Hollywood.

193 Bannon, *Beebo Brinker*. 40.

194 Bannon, *Beebo Brinker*. 91. It is worth noting that Paula challenges the idea that fidelity can be a masculine quality.

195 Bannon, *Beebo Brinker*. 88.

196 Bannon, *Beebo Brinker*. 86.

197 Bannon, *Beebo Brinker*. 87. Both this phrase and the one immediately above are somewhat cliched, but they convey the force of the physical reaction. They also reinforce the point that Beebo is not a stone butch and can own her female bodily responses.

198 Bannon, *Beebo Brinker*. 91.

102 *Female masculinity*

be feminine"[199] – but has yet to find her own level in butchness, to "start acting the way she looked."[200] Perhaps in trying to fit in to the bar scene stereotype in the Landon-Brinkeriad sequels she never actually comes close, if the failures up until the potential of the relationship with Beth at the end of *Journey to a Woman* are anything to go by. The bar scene appears intolerant of deviance, and remains so; as has been noted before, it takes Leslie Feinberg to pronounce, thirty years later through hir protagonist Jess Goldberg, that "there's lots of ways for butches to be,"[201] and Gayle Rubin to relate those "ways" to their bodies.[202]

As much as there is nothing wrong with Beebo's boyish body, there is nothing wrong with Beth's "unfeminine" one,[203] nor with the contrastingly diminutive one belonging to the butch the new-in-town Beebo almost collides with on the street,[204] nor with Laura's small-breasted one,[205] nor with any in the corpus with the possible exception of Vega's. Vega is a disturbing presence throughout *Journey to a Woman*, her self-destructive obsession with Beth driving the melodrama of the book's plot. her body is

> a complex of scars that twisted every which way over her chest, like yards of pink ribbons in snarls. She had no breasts, and the operation to remove her lung had left a bad welt that Beth returned to once or twice with a prickle of revulsion. Even Vega's dainty little abdomen had its share. And bones, the poor sharp bones without which the ordinary smooth envelope of tender flesh that most girls take for granted and even rail against when there's too much. Vega's bones were all pitifully plain and frankly outlined.[206]

---

199 Bannon, *Beebo Brinker*. 187. To be "gentle and loving" runs against what is expected of young men. See Dorr, "The Perils of the Back Seat: Date Rape, Race and Gender in 1950s America."

200 Bannon, *Beebo Brinker*. 65.

201 Feinberg, *Stone Butch Blues*. 282.

202 Rubin, "Of Catamites and Kings: Reflections on Butch, Gender, and Boundaries." 470. Rubin says: "Butches vary in how they relate to their female bodies. Some butches are comfortable being pregnant and having kids, while for others the thought of undergoing the female component of mammalian reproduction is utterly repugnant. Some enjoy their breasts while others despise them. Some butches hide their genitals and some refuse penetration. There are butches who abhor tampons, because of their resonance with intercourse; other butches love getting fucked. Some butches are perfectly content in their female bodies, while others may border on or become transsexuals."

203 Bannon, *Beebo Brinker*; Bannon, *Journey to a Woman*. 72.

204 Bannon, *Beebo Brinker*. 4.

205 Bannon, *Women in the Shadows*. 6. Lili, one of Beebo's former lovers, refers to Laura as a "button-breasted bad-tempered little prude."

206 Bannon, *Journey to a Woman*. 71. Vega is based on a real person, though the harsh exaggeration of her character caused Bannon to fall out with that person's family. Personal email, December 8th, 2021.

Female masculinity 103

This tests very severely the overall appropriateness of Jack Mann's dictum. Beth finds that body "repellent and pitiable"[207] and the experience of love-making "a gruesome parody of the happiness she had anticipated."[208] The instant comparison and stark contrast that comes to mind is found in Audre Lorde's *Zami*, in a sexual episode involving Lorde's protagonist and her lover Eudora:

> In the circle of lamplight I looked from her round firm breast with its rosy nipple erect to her scarred chest. The pale keloids of radiation burn lay in the hollow under her shoulder and arm down across her ribs [...] She took my hand and placed it there, squarely, lightly upon her chest. Our hands fell. I bent and kissed her softly upon the scar where our hands had rested.[209]

This was all the more remarkable inasmuch as Lorde wrote that passage shortly after she had been diagnosed and undergone surgery, which makes it a passage not only of great tenderness but of self-tenderness. It is little wonder that Lorde's opinion of the niche of ephemeral lesbian novels of the 1950s, Bannon's included, was that they focused primarily on pain and never "even mentioned the joys."[210]

But if Vega's body is a site for her self-destructiveness,[211] Beebo's for her alcoholism,[212] and Laura's for her feared promiscuity,[213] or for any negative trait, then they are no less appropriate sites for traits and behaviours of other kinds. Nothing about Vega's slenderness, Beebo's height, Laura's small or Lili's full bust automatically signals lesbianism. Nothing about Beth's strength or Beebo's height automatically signals masculinity any more than the hips of "Malanya" or the forearms of "Woman's Arms" signal femininity. The bodies of Laura, Beth, and Beebo are the sites where gender is put to use or performed, each character bringing her own nuance. Each, as we have seen, can be said to access masculinity without assuming an absolute stereotype. Where Beebo tries to enforce stereotypically femme femininity, she fails and is resisted; where she accepts the nuances that Beth brings and takes her hand, she heralds something new, something transmasculine. Laura and Beth leaven

---

207 Bannon, *Journey to a Woman*. 73.
208 Bannon, *Journey to a Woman*. 75.
209 Lorde, *Zami: a new spelling of my name*. 144.
210 Audre Lorde, *Zami: A New Spelling of My Name* (Crossing Press, 1982). 213. Quoted in Nealon, *Foundlings: Lesbian and Gay Historical Emotion before Stonewall*. 196n4.
211 She tries to throw herself from a window at one point, and eventually succeeds in shooting herself dead. Bannon, *Journey to a Woman*. 71, 225.
212 Bannon, *Women in the Shadows*. 13.
213 Bannon, *Women in the Shadows*. 22. Laura's relationship with Beebo, which lasted little more than one year before disintegrating, was the last long-term relationship she has with a woman, using her eventual marriage to Jack as a marriage of convenience.

104   *Female masculinity*

femininity with varying degrees of ki-ki. The undercurrent of a realisation that bodies do not govern gender, one way or another, is there in the major characters of the Landon-Brinkeriad, even though the precise vocabulary to express it is not. With that undercurrent comes a clear pressure on the understanding of gender, in particular masculinity, for the readers of the corpus.

Bibliography

Abate, Michelle Ann. *Tomboys: A Literary and Cultural History*. Temple University Press, 2008.

Bannon, Ann. *Beebo Brinker*. Cleis, 2001.

———. "Foreword." In *Strange Sisters: The Art of Lesbian Pulp Fiction*, edited by Jaye Zimet. Penguin Books Canada Ltd, 1999, 9–15.

———. "The High Bar with Warren Etheredge: Interview with Ann Bannon." By Warren Etheredge. 2012. tinyurl.com/BannonEdge.

———. *I am a Woman*. Cleis, 2002.

———. *Journey to a Woman*. Cleis, 2003.

———. *The Marriage*. Fawcett Gold Medal, 1960.

———. *Odd Girl Out*. Cleis, 2001.

———. "Secrets of the Gay Novel." *One: The Homosexual Viewpoint* 9, no. 7 (1961): 6–12.

———. *Women in the Shadows*. Cleis, 2002.

Banyard, Kat. "The Dangers of Rebranding Prostitution as 'Sex Work'." *The Guardian online*, 7 June 2016. tinyurl.com/KatBanyard.

Blank, Paula. "The Proverbial 'Lesbian': Queering Etymology in Contemporary Critical Practice." *Modern Philology* 109, no. 1 (2011): 108–34. tinyurl.com/PaulaBlank.

Bradley, Marion Zimmer, and Gene Damon. *Checklist 1960: A Complete, Cumulative Checklist of Lesbian, Variant, and Homosexual Fiction, in English, or Available in English Translation, with Supplements of Related Material, for the Use of Collectors, Students, and Librarians*. Self-published by Marion Zimmer Bradley, 1960.

Brandt, Kate. *Happy Endings: Lesbian Writers Talk About Their Lives and Work*. Naiad, 1993.

Carter, Julian. "Gay Marriage and Pulp Fiction: Homonormativity, Disidentification, and Affect in Ann Bannon's Lesbian Novels." *GLQ: A Journal of Lesbian and Gay Studies* 15, no. 4 (2009): 583–609.

Cartier, Marie. "Baby, You Are My Religion: The Emergence of 'Theology' in Pre-Stonewall Butch-Femme / Gay Women's Bar Culture and Community." PhD, Claremont Graduate University, 2010.

Chandler, Daniel. *Semiotics. The Basics*. Routledge, 2002.

Daly, Anya. "A Phenomenological Grounding of Feminist Ethics." *The Journal of the British Society for Phenomenology* 50, no. 1 (2019): 1–18.

Davis, Madeline, and Elizabeth Lapovsky Kennedy. "Oral History and the Study of Sexuality in the Lesbian Community: Buffalo, New York, 1940–1960." *Feminist Studies* 12, no. 1 (1986): 7–26.

Dorr, Lisa Lindquist. "The Perils of the Back Seat: Date Rape, Race and Gender in 1950s America." *Gender & History* 20, no. 1 (2008): 22–47.

Ermayne, Laurajean. "Letter." *Vice Versa* 1, no. 6 (1947): 9. queermusicheritage.com /viceversa6.html.

Faderman, Lillian. *Odd Girls and Twilight Lovers: A History of Lesbian Life in Twentieth-Century America*. Columbia University Press, 1991.

Feinberg, Leslie. *Stone Butch Blues*. Firebrand, 1993.
———. *Stone Butch Blues*. self-published, 2014. tinyurl.com/StoneButchB.
Forrest, Katherine V., ed. *Lesbian Pulp Fiction: The Sexually Intrepid World of Lesbian Paperback Novels 1950–1965*. Cleis, 2005.
Foucault, Michel. *Abnormal: Lectures at the College De France, 1974–1975*. Translated by Graham Burchell. Edited by Valerio Marchetti and Antonella Salomoni. Verso, 2016.
Garber, Eric. "Those Wonderful Lesbian Pulps: A Roundtable Discussion." *The San Francisco Bay Area Gay & Lesbian Historical Society Newsletter* 4, no. 4 (1989): 1, 4–5.
Gilbert, James. *Men in the Middle: Searching for Masculinity in the 1950s*. U of Chicago P, 2005.
Halberstam, Jack. *Female Masculinity*. Duke University Press, 1998.
———. *Trans**. University of California Press, 2018.
Hall, Radclyffe. *The Well of Loneliness*. Penguin Classics, 2015.
Hector, Alley. "The Odd Girls' Journey out of the Shadows: Lesbi-Pulp Novels." In *Sticking It to the Man: Revolution and Counterculture in Pulp and Popular Fiction, 1950 to 1980*, edited by Andrew Nette and Iain McIntyre, 29–35. PM Press, 2020.
Jeffreys, Sheila. *Unpacking Queer Politics: A Lesbian Feminist Perspective*. Polity Press in association with Blackwell, 2003.
Johns, Merryn. "Pulp Pioneer: Ann Bannon Reflects on Writing Lesbian Fiction in the 1950s." *Curve: The Lesbian Magazine* 21, no. 2 (2011): 72–73.
Kennedy, Elizabeth Lapovsky, and Madeline D. Davis. *Boots of Leather, Slippers of Gold: The History of a Lesbian Community*. Penguin, 1993.
Kessler, Suzanne J., and Wendy McKenna. *Gender: An Ethnomethodological Approach*. University of Chicago Press, 1978.
Lee, Gretchen. "Pink and Blue: Interview with Leslie Feinberg." *Curve: The Lesbian Magazine* 8, no. 5 (1998): 39–31.
Livia, Anna. "'I Ought to Throw a Buick at You': Fictional Representations of Butch/Femme Speech." In *Gender Articulated: Language and the Socially Constructed Self*, edited by Kira Hall and Mary Bucholtz, Routledge, 1995. 245–78.
Lochrie, Karma. *Heterosyncrasies: Female Sexuality When Normal Wasn't*. University of Minnesota Press, 2005.
Lorde, Audre. *Zami: A New Spelling of My Name*. Crossing Press, 1982.
———. *Zami: A New Spelling of My Name*. Pandora, 2003.
Luksic, Nicola. "Authors Look Back at the Heyday of Lesbian Pulp: Trashy and Tragic." *dailyextra.com*, 2005. tinyurl.com/LuksicPulp.
MacNeil, Kerry. "Bathroom Lines, Ky-Ky Girls, and Struggles: Butch/Femme Aesthetics, Identity Politics and Positionalities in Audre Lorde's *Zami: A New Spelling of My Name* and Joan Nestle's *A Restricted Country*." *Journal of Lesbian Studies* 1, no. 3–4 (1997): 75–87.
Mayne, Judith. *Framed: Lesbians, Feminists, and Media Culture*. University of Minnesota Press, 2000.
Meaker, Marijane. *Highsmith: A Romance of the 1950s*. Cleis, 2003.
Merleau-Ponty, Maurice. *The Phenomenology of Perception*. Translated by Colin Smith. Routledge, 2006.
Miller, Meredith. "Secret Agents and Public Victims: The Implied Lesbian Reader." *The Journal of Popular Culture* 35, no. 1 (2001): 37–58.
Montefiore, Simon Sebag. *Stalin: The Court of the Red Tsar*. Weidenfeld & Nicolson, 2003.
Moore, Melina Alice. "'A Boy inside It': Beebo Brinker and the Transmasculine Narratives of Ann Bannon's Lesbian Pulp." *GLQ: A Journal of Lesbian and Gay Studies* 25, no. 4 (2019): 569–98.

106 *Female masculinity*

Nealon, Christopher. *Foundlings: Lesbian and Gay Historical Emotion before Stonewall*. Duke University Press, 2001.

Nestle, Joan. "The Fem Question." In *Pleasure and Danger: Exploring Female Sexuality*, edited by Carole S. Vance, 232–41. Routledge, 1985.

Noble, Jean Bobby. *Masculinity without Men? Female Masculinity in Twentieth-Century Fictions*. UBC Press, 2004.

"Nonbinary Wiki: Transmasculine." 2020. tinyurl.com/trmawiki.

Orwell, George. *Nineteen Eighty-Four*. Penguin, 1962.

Packer, Vin. *Spring Fire*. Cleis, 2004.

Penelope, Julia. "Whose Past Are We Reclaiming?". *Off Our Backs* 23, no. 8 (1993): 12–13, 19, 24–25. tinyurl.com/jupenpast.

Prorokova, Tatiana. "Alcoholic, Mad, Disabled: Constructing Lesbian Identity in Ann Bannon's 'the Beebo Brinker Chronicles'." In *Literatures of Madness: Disability Studies and Mental Health*, edited by Elizabeth J. Donaldson, 127–44. Palgrave Macmillan, 2018.

Rodriguez, Carissa. "It's Symptomatic." *Document*, 13 May 2015, online. tinyurl.com/RodriguezSym.

Rubin, Gayle. "Of Catamites and Kings: Reflections on Butch, Gender, and Boundaries." In *Transgender Studies Reader*, edited by Susan Stryker and Stephen Whittle, 471–81. Routledge, 2006.

Sedgwick, Eve Kosofsky. "Gosh, Boy George, You Must Be Awfully Secure in Your Masculinity." In *Constructing Masculinity*, edited by Brian Wallis Maurice Berger and Simon Watson, 11–20. Routledge, 1995.

Shopland, Norena. *A History of Women in Men's Clothing: From Cross-Dressing to Empowerment*. Pen & Sword History, 2021.

Sky, Melissa. "Cover Charge: Selling Sex and Survival in Lesbian Pulp Fiction." In *Judging a Book by Its Cover: Fans, Publishers, Designers, and the Marketing of Fiction*, edited by Nicole Matthews and Nickianne Moody. Routledge, 2007, 129–145.

———. "Twilight Tales: Ann Bannon's Lesbian Pulp Series 'the Beebo Brinker Chronicles'." PhD Thesis, McMaster University, 2006.

Smith, Elizabeth A. "Butches, Femmes, and Feminists: The Politics of Lesbian Sexuality." *NWSA Journal* 1, no. 3 (1989): 398–421.

Smyth, Cherry. "How Do We Look? Imaging Butch/Femme." In *Butch/Femme: Inside Lesbian Gender*, edited by Sally R. Munt, 82–89. Cassell, 1998.

Stratton, S. Lou. "More Than Throw-Away Fiction: Investigating Lesbian Pulp Fiction through the Lens of a Lesbian Textual Community." PhD Thesis, University of Birmingham, 2008.

Taylor, Valerie. *Journey to Fulfillment*. Volute, 1982.

———. *Philosophy Tube: Sex Work*. Thorn, Abigail, 2019.

———. *Whisper Their Love*. Little Sister's Classics. Arsenal Pulp Press, 2006.

———. *dictionary.com*. 2018.

unattributed. "Kiki." *Vice Versa* 1, no. 7 (1947): 2–4. queermusicheritage.com/viceversa7.html.

Walters, Suzanna Danuta. "As Her Hand Crept Slowly up Her Thigh: Ann Bannon and the Politics of Pulp." *Social Text*, no. 23 (1989): 83–101.

Wittig, Monique. *The Straight Mind and Other Essays*. Beacon, 1992.

Woodward, L.T. *Twilight Women*. Lancer, 1963.

Yockey, Matt. "Dr. Ackula or: How I Learned to Stop Worrying and Love Fandom." *The Journal of Fandom Studies* 1, no. 1 (2012): 101–11.

Zeig, Sande. "The Actor as Activator: Deconstructing Gender through Gesture." *Women & Performance: A Journal of Feminist Theory* 2, no. 2 (1985): 12–17.

III Female masculinity beyond Beebo

Tell me, gentle hob'dehoy,
Art thou Girl or art thou Boy?
Art thou Man or art thou Ape;
For thy Gesture and thy Shape.
And thy Features and thy Dress
Such contraries do express

Anon., 18c.[1]

Going beyond Beebo

The overall Introduction to this book introduced the stereotypical conventions of the lesbian-themed paperback, showing how they had been perpetuated as much by both fandom and scholarship as they had by the supposed commercial pressures of the era. Subsequent chapters have shown, by examples, how those stereotypes can be adhered to, in novels such as *Spring Fire* and *Odd Girl Out*, but just as easily bucked and subverted by other novels, as well as challenged by subtle or even occult factors within the supposedly stereotypical ones. The previous chapter specifically challenged the portrayal of butchness in fiction, certainly the "quintessential [...] buccaneer butch,"[2] in Ann Bannon's corpus, and the stereotypical image of out-and-out female masculinity. The picture is complicated further by the fact that even around the era that characters such as Beebo Brinker were being created, outward presentation was not as clear cut as the stereotype would have us believe.[3]

This chapter, pushing beyond the compelling figure of Beebo Brinker, sets out to investigate whether there are challenges to masculinity that do not depend, or do not depend solely, on a masculine presentation, or even on the apparently masculine traits within the contraries of features and dress

---

1 unattributed, "The Petit Maître, 1749," in *Homosexuality in Eighteenth-Century England: A Sourcebook*, ed. Rictor Norton (Rictor Norton (online), 2000).
2 Ann Bannon, *I am a Woman* (Cleis, 2002). v.
3 According to "Reggie," quoted in Elizabeth Lapovsky Kennedy and Madeline D. Davis, *Boots of Leather, Slippers of Gold: The History of a Lesbian Community* (Penguin, 1993). 192.

DOI: 10.4324/9781003422679-4

108 *Female masculinity beyond Beebo*

of the ki-ki manifestation. It points to both subtle and unsubtle tensions and power (im)balances between lesbian couples or couples in temporary lesbian relationships, in novels that both conform to and contradict the stereotype, novels that both laud and excoriate the butch and the masculine woman. In the section **"Bit players, professional women, and predators"** I look at the relationships between the principal female couples in a range of novels,[4] and at the relevance to the discursive field of Simone de Beauvoir's assessment of the relationship between a younger and older woman. The three subsequent sections focus entirely on *Chris* by Randy Salem, again looking at the dynamics of the triangular relationship that dominates the narrative, at the mid-twentieth-century concept of frigidity as understood, both outside and inside the novel, and its use as a weapon against lesbianism. I draw the conclusion that *Chris*, when compared both to pre-war novels such as *The Well of Loneliness* and *We Too Are Drifting* and to the quasi-realism of Ann Bannon's corpus, is radical in its creation of a sapphocentric fantasy world. The final section – **Is dominance a masculine prerogative?** – brings together all this section's dominant women into the male-dominated culture of the nineteen-fifties and sixties.

"Butches" beyond Beebo: Bit players, professional women, and predators

Such diverse novels as Claire Morgan's *The Price of Salt*, Valerie Taylor's *Whisper Their Love*, and E.S. Seeley's *Sorority Sin*, feature lesbian relationships between women none of whom are identifiably butch, but one of whom is clearly dominant. Lora Sela's potboiler *I am a Lesbian* has, as one of its principals Jan, a woman who declares to her lover Melba, "I'm a masculine lesbian [...] You're a feminine lesbian. In our togetherness nature strikes a balance."[5] But characters in that novel are very inadequately developed, and beyond certain behaviours not unlike those Beth had displayed towards Laura in Ann Bannon's *Odd Girl Out*,[6] there is nothing overtly "butch" about Jan. She is in a dominant position, both professionally and in the relationship. Although Gayle Rubin warns against stereotyping butches, and states that the term encompasses individuals with a broad range of investments in masculinity,[7] the relationship between Jan and Melba seems to resemble more that described in the late 1940s by Simone de Beauvoir:

---

4 These include *I am a Lesbian (1959)* by Lora Sela, *Whisper Their Love* (originally 1957) by Valerie Taylor, *Sorority Sin (1965)* by E.S. Seeley, *Girls Dormitory (1963)* by Joan Ellis, and *The Price of Salt (1953)* by Claire Morgan. This is a broad range, varying in type and quality.

5 Lora Sela, *I am a Lesbian* (Saber, 1959). 10.

6 See Chapter II.

7 Gayle Rubin, "Of Catamites and Kings: Reflections on Butch, Gender, and Boundaries," in *Transgender Studies Reader*, ed. Susan Stryker & Stephen Whittle (Routledge, 2006). 472.

Female masculinity beyond Beebo   109

She will turn to a woman, who is less strange and less frightening than the male, but who will have something of male prestige: a woman with a profession, who earns her own living, who makes a certain show in the world, will easily be as fascinating as a man.[8]

Jan's transmasculinity[9] does not particularly manifest itself in clothing and presentation; her hair is in a short style, but she wears "blouses and skirts, or trim, tailored suits;" her stride is graceful, and her voice is a gentle, throaty contralto.[10] The novel does feature a more stereotypical butch as a minor agent. Melba's tormentor, Bob, has bribed a young itinerant, Mac Collins, to turn up at Melba's home pretending to be a present from the absent Jan. Mac is described as looking like a boy, in shirt, jeans, and a motorcycle jacket, sporting a crew-cut hairstyle, and speaking in a kind of clipped, affected hipster slang.[11] Before going on her way, Mac defends Melba from Bob, knocks him unconscious, and delivers him to his own home in his own car.[12]

Mac appears as a transmasculine *deus ex machina*, challenging the supremacy of a sexually inadequate, violent, and ultimately humiliated male, in only a handful of pages. In many other novels butches are relegated to similar "bit parts," and usually not as sympathetic as Mac's. Valerie Taylor's novel *Whisper Their Love*, for example, has a gym instructor who is nicknamed "Butch" by her students, and who has "bony" arms and a tendency both to sarcasm and to invading the protagonist's physical space.[13] Another peripheral butch character appears in the seventeenth chapter of the novel, in which Joyce and Edith, the lesbian 'couple' of the novel, visit a bar which is "[n]ot the kind of place for a respectable girl at one in the morning."[14] The club is full of characters written about with barely-concealed disdain: a pair

---

8 Simone de Beauvoir, *The Second Sex*, trans. Howard Madison Parshley (Picador, 1988). 367. De Beauvoir is speaking specifically of the relationship between a pupil and a teacher, but this may legitimately be extended to other spheres; Jan is in management in the business where Melba is employed. The phrase "as fascinating as a man" is startling, as it almost gives credence to the woman-as-man notion of the butch, and generally makes "male" into a normal or default yardstick.

9 Transmasculinity is explained in a footnote in Chapter II. It includes, but does not equate to, transgender, as transmasculinity can be manifest in people who do not identify themselves as "male." I use the term to describe both Jan and Mac in *I am a Lesbian*, although they are superficially dissimilar.

10 Sela, *I am a Lesbian*. 5. Elizabeth A. Smith notes that such characteristics as "low voice, short hair, tailored clothes [...] appear over and over again" in the fiction published in *The Ladder*, which had a generally anti-butch editorial stance, to signal the more dominant partner in a relationship. Elizabeth A. Smith, "Butches, Femmes, and Feminists: The Politics of Lesbian Sexuality," *NWSA Journal* vol.1, no.3 (1989). 403.

11 Sela, *I am a Lesbian*. 104.

12 Sela, *I am a Lesbian*. 107–108.

13 Valerie Taylor, *Whisper Their Love*, Little Sister's Classics, (Arsenal Pulp Press, 2006). 109,138.

14 Taylor, *Whisper Their Love*. 164.

110   *Female masculinity beyond Beebo*

of little, hollow-chested, pasty-faced gay men, a haggard girl in a cheap fur stole, a seedy bookkeeper-type with his arm round a young man dressed as a woman – all of these characters looking like they needed a bath.[15] At the table next to the bookkeeper and the "transvestite"[16]

> sat two girls about whom there was no doubt. One was thin and flat, with a jutting jaw. The other had heavy lips and a sagging bust. Both had ducktail haircuts like some of the girls at school, but with no softening from waves or little tendril curls. Both wore regular men's overall jeans with fly fronts, heavy pullover sweaters, and one gold ring in the right ear.[17]

The young woman with the heavy lips introduces herself to Joyce and Edith as "Bobbie." She has tried sex with a man once out of heterocuriosity, but that was enough.[18] The following passages show several coincidental, superficial likenesses between Bobbie and Beebo Brinker, firstly:

> "I ain't afraid of work, I was raised on a farm, only it's hard to find a job where they let you dress like you want to.
>
> "Don't you ever wear regular clothes?" Edith asked. She smoothed her skirt with a slender hand. Joyce could imagine her thinking: After all, I'm not *masculine*. I'm *different*.
> "Hell no. What would I do that for?"[19]

Secondly:

> It was while she was living with Karla that she decided to change over to men's clothes. She went to a man's barber shop and got her hair cut. "Real short, you know, he liked to scalp me. Now I like this here D.A. better, it's got more style. I always wanted to be a boy from the time I was little. Boys get all the breaks. Like home, Pa always had the say about everything. Ma never got to open her yap about anything. Work, work, work all the time. It's a man's world."

---

15 Taylor, *Whisper Their Love*. 164–166.
16 Taylor, *Whisper Their Love*. 165. Taylor uses this now rather outmoded term. The reason why the character adopts this particular presentation is left unaddressed, so the term, as a catch-all, will have to do.
17 Taylor, *Whisper Their Love*. 165.
18 Taylor, *Whisper Their Love*. 169.
19 Taylor, *Whisper Their Love*. 167.

Female masculinity beyond Beebo 111

The market fired her for wearing jeans to work under the regular white apron, or maybe it was for trying to make a girl customer who looked lonesome.[20]

Being raised on a farm and wanting the privileges of being a boy are the major similarities.[21] Bobbie is obviously predatory; she invites one of Edith's acquaintances into the toilet, saying "There's a question I want to ask you," and they are gone for some considerable time.[22] When they emerge, the other woman slightly dishevelled, they leave for Bobbie's home, the latter asking the barman to lie for her if her regular girlfriend comes in.[23]

This portrayal more than suggests that the author does not like butches – not that she appears to like anyone much in the milieu of the bar, no matter what their sexuality or presentation. Valerie Taylor was a lesbian herself and is generally credited as being one of the "pro-lesbian" authors. However, her definition of, or preferred standard of lesbianism appears to have been narrow. Her protagonist Joyce voices the opinion that the people she has met in Edith's company display not gender identities and sexualities but pathologies:

The men-women and women-men at Anitra Schultz's party had opened her eyes, and the habitués of Club Marie were only shabbier, dingier examples of the same thing. There were bars and clubs and magazines that catered to these people and enabled them to find each other. Famous scientists had written books about them.[24]

In a 1998 interview, Taylor said of bar culture, "everything was very imitative of heterosexuals," and in the same interview, of lesbianism in general, "I don't regard a lesbian as an imitation of a man, either. Women are women, thank God."[25] Notwithstanding her reputation, *Whisper Their Love* is hard to define as a "pro-lesbian" novel. It is exceptional inasmuch as it deals with such topics as teenage pregnancy, abortion, and suicide, but Bradley and Damon called it "unsympathetic" and "over-written."[26] The final section of the novel consists of John, a young man, persuading Joyce that her lesbianism

---

20 Taylor, *Whisper Their Love*. 168. The vernacular term "make" is explained in Chapter I. "D.A." is short for "duck's ass," and signifies the 1950s "ducktail" hairstyle.
21 I merely point these out as coincidences, rather than suggesting Bannon read Taylor.
22 Taylor, *Whisper Their Love*. 170.
23 Taylor, *Whisper Their Love*. 170.
24 Taylor, *Whisper Their Love*. 185. As well as "famous" scientists having written about them, there were of course many cheap paperback works of faux sexology.
25 Quoted in the appendix to the Arsenal Pulp Press edition of the novel. Taylor, *Whisper Their Love*. 234.
26 Marion Zimmer Bradley and Gene Damon, *Checklist 1960: A Complete, Cumulative Checklist of Lesbian, Variant, and Homosexual Fiction, in English, or Available in English Translation, with Supplements of Related Material, for the Use of Collectors, Students, and Librarians* (Self-published by Marion Zimmer Bradley, 1960). Unnumbered.

112 *Female masculinity beyond Beebo*

was "a manifestation of her infantile sexuality,"[27] and that she was in reality heterosexual. Barbara Grier describes the ending of the novel thus:

> Was this Taylor's way of "sticking it to the man"? Was she expecting this ending to be read ironically at some point? Is this some sort of code? The ending of *Whisper Their Love* reads so obviously as "fiction"; it is so different in tone and pacing from the earlier parts of the book that one can't help but wonder about the author's real motives, beyond ending her story in a way that would allow it to legally pass through the US mail system.[28]

Grier's analysis and Taylor's own explanation of the ending differ sharply. Taylor is clear that Joyce is not a lesbian but is "a young girl looking for a mother image," that she ends up with a "nice young man," that she had planned the ending from the start, and that she did not regard the novel as a lesbian story because Edith was "something of a villain."[29] Edith is as predatory in her own way as butch Bobbie. During her dialogues with John, Joyce says in passing "She's got her next girl picked out already."[30]

Given these unsympathetic portrayals of a butch and a dominant older lesbian, and the narrow view of gender, in a novel by a lesbian writer, it is perhaps unsurprising to find a similar disdain in a male writer's descriptions of the same. E.S. Seeley's *Sorority Sin*, a "virile adventure"[31] with a melodramatic and fiery ending, contains a bar scene with a brief description of a "dyke:"

> Linda gazed across the room. A group of three young men moved towards the bar, still talking in loud tones, and uncovered a table where a girl with extremely short blond hair, wearing a man's shirt, sat smoking a long cigar with the aplomb of a banker. Linda nudged Kay and pointed to the girl.
>
> "Oh, my God. A dyke," Kay said.
> "A what?"
> "Isn't that disgusting? Cigar and all," and Kay's body stiffened angrily.
> "Oh, that's Paul," Igor said.
> "God. A man's name and everything," Kay went on.

---

27 Barbara Grier, writing in the Introduction to Taylor, *Whisper Their Love*. 18.
28 Grier's Introduction again. Taylor, *Whisper Their Love*. 19.
29 In the appended interview, Taylor refers to Edith as "*the* lesbian" (my emphasis) in the novel. Taylor, *Whisper Their Love*. 237, 238.
30 Taylor, *Whisper Their Love*. 220.
31 Yvonne Keller, "Ab/normal Looking: Voyeurism and surveillance in lesbian pulp novels and US Cold War Culture," *Feminist Media Studies* five, no. two (2005). 178.

Female masculinity beyond Beebo   113

"I think her real name is Pauline. But she wants everybody to call her Paul."

"Well I can think of other things to call her. And I think she'd find them more descriptive than complimentary."[32]

The disgust here is being voiced by a character who, although feminine in presentation, is the dominant partner in the lesbian relationship featured in the novel. Saying that "her real name is Pauline" would be considered 'deadnaming' if done nowadays, as if her chosen name of "Paul" is any less "real."[33] Paul attempts to force sex on Kay's partner Linda in the toilet, but Kay intervenes and, without letting her land a single punch, trips her and steps on her hand with a stiletto heel.[34] Seeley depicts Paul's masculinity as ineffective, a mere façade of toughness that can be easily torn away, and finished off by an object of fetishised femininity, the high-heeled shoe. Both Seeley and Taylor associate butchness with the toilet, in an apparent attempt to depict it as something unsavoury. Alice Echols quotes feminist Sally Gearhart as saying, "lesbians have spent untold hours explaining to Middle America that lesbians do not have to worry about venereal disease, do not have sex in public bathrooms ... and do not want to go to the barricades fighting for the lowering of the age of consent."[35] In fact the public bathroom was the scene of routine humiliation for lesbians in the post-war butch-femme culture, according to Joan Nestle.

> But the most searing reminder of our colonized world was the bathroom line. Now I know it stands for all the pain and glory of my time, and I carry that line and the women who endured it deep within me. Because

---

32 E.S. Seeley, *Sorority Sin* (UPD Book Export Inc, 1965). 116–117. Seeley was a minor Hollywood scriptwriter, having provided the screenplay for B movies *Blood on His Lips* (1958) and *Shangri-La* (1961).

33 Deadnaming may be applied to anyone in the transgender and nonbinary communities, and by extension, in retrospect to anyone who has or had a butch or transmasculine presentation. Julia Sinclair-Palm describes it as "calling a trans person by their birth name after they have adopted a new name. The act of deadnaming has the effect of "outing," or making public, a trans person's identity. Deadnaming is sometimes accidental, as when a friend or family member is still adjusting to a trans person's new name and unintentionally calls them by their birth name. However, there are also many times when trans people are addressed by their birth name as a way to aggressively dismiss and reject their gender identity and new name." Julia Sinclair-Palm, "'It's Non-Existent': Haunting in Trans Youth Narratives about Naming," *Bank Street Occasional Paper Series* 2017, no.37 (2017), tinyurl.com/Sinclair-Palm. 5. I am adhering to the pronouns of the episteme, for reasons previously stated, and continuing to use she/her for Paul.

34 Seeley, *Sorority Sin.* 120–121.

35 Echols actually cites a 1979 article by Richard Goldstein in *Village Voice* for this quotation, but I have been unable to access that article. Alice Echols, "The Taming of the Id: Feminist Sexual Politics, 1968–83," in *PLEASURE and DANGER: exploring female sexuality*, ed. Carole S. Vance (Routledge & Kegan Paul, 1984). 61.

114 *Female masculinity beyond Beebo*

we were labelled deviants, our bathroom habits had to be watched. Only one woman at a time was allowed into the toilet because we could not be trusted. Thus the toilet line was born, a twisting horizon of lesbian women waiting for permission to urinate, to shit.[36]

Both Seeley and Taylor pillory their fictional butches as predatory and, in one case, ineffectively aggressive. In their disdain for butches, two writers – one male, one female and lesbian – have recreated the distrust that initiated the "bathroom line," and the world of the "sexual criminal who stood on a bathroom line awaiting her allotted amount of toilet paper."[37]They tap into a damaging social reality of the time.

As Gayle Rubin reminds us, however, butch goes well beyond the stereotypical. I passed over the masculinity of Jan in *I am a Lesbian* mainly because her part in that novel is almost devoid of agency.[38] The quotation from Simone de Beauvoir I used in introducing Jan speaks of "male prestige" and "profession."[39] In the context of these paperbacks, it is worth looking further into de Beauvoir's descriptions of such a woman:[40]

Since she must play a masculine part, it is preferable for the loved woman to be unmarried: marriage does not always discourage the young admirer, but it bothers her; she dislikes having the object of her adoration appear as subjected to the power of a husband or lover [...] but passage to definite eroticism is much easier than when the loved one is masculine [...][41]

The virile woman [...] has the father's authority and transcendence, she is the source and standard of values, she surpasses the world as given, she is divine; but she also remains a woman.[42]

36 Joan Nestle, *A Restricted Country: Essays & Short Stories* (Sheba Feminist Publishers, 1987). 38.
37 Joan Nestle, "The Will to Remember," *Journal of Homosexuality* vol.34, no. 3–4 (1998). 228.
38 The agency in *I am a Lesbian* is largely male, as has been covered in Chapter I.
39 de Beauvoir, *The Second Sex*. 367.
40 I do not reintroduce de Beauvoir here simply because her view is handily close to a description of relationships in the novels. De Beauvoir's writings were part of the discursive field of feminism during the era. Writers such as Valerie Taylor and Ann Bannon had good educational backgrounds, and Bannon recalls having read both *Le Deuxième Sexe* and Betty Friedan's *The Feminine Mystique*. It is not as easy to pin down the more elusive, more ephemeral writers such as Sela/Hales, but there is no reason to assume that they were any less well-read.
41 de Beauvoir, *The Second Sex*. 368.
42 de Beauvoir, *The Second Sex*. 369.

Female masculinity beyond Beebo 115

De Beauvoir seems not to be able to escape the idea that the woman who must play "*un rôle viril*"[43] is somehow less than a man, because the use of the words "masculine" and "virile" implies that "man" is the standard, the default value. She uses the words "virago" and "*damnées*," which Pashley translates as "viriloid" and "female 'homos'."[44] De Beauvoir, as an observer, looks at these relationships from below, from the mindset of the girl who is attracted, albeit more often than not temporarily, to such women. The novels, on the other hand, tend to portray them as active; they are not simply objects of desire, they deliberately attract their younger admirers and potential lovers. They are of the generation of women who were thought to have "invaded the strongholds of masculinity in work, play, sex, and the home,"[45] and even to have taken over the sexual aggression in search of conquest that was men's "one sure proof of masculinity" in a society in which women's roles are indistinguishable from men's.[46]

Apart from Jan in *I am a Lesbian*, with her status in the company for whom her partner works, and Edith in *Whisper Their Love*, who uses her academic status to attract younger women in the student body, there are other characters of this type that are of note. Prolific paperback author Julie Ellis, writing as Joan Ellis amongst other pseudonyms,[47] published the novel *Girls Dormitory* in 1963. The novel is generally thought of as being a "lesbian pulp," but it does not appear at all amongst Ellis's other books in *The Lesbian in Literature*.[48] It does, however, contain almost a whole chapter devoted to a brief affair between Mona, a student, and Jean, an older

---

43 Simone de Beauvoir, *Le Deuxième Sexe*, vol.2 (Éditions Gallimard, 1976). 110.

44 de Beauvoir, *Le Deuxième Sexe*, 2. 190. de Beauvoir, *The Second Sex*. 424. De Beauvoir and Pashley make different use of *diple periestigmene* quotation marks. There are none containing "virago" but there are containing "viriloid," and although "*damnées*" is also contained, only the "homos" element of the translated term is. This tends to alter in translation the original author's emphases.

45 Helen Mayer Hacker, "The New Burdens of Masculinity," *Marriage and Family Living* vol.19 no.3 (1957). 228.

46 Jane Whitbread, "A Report on Current Attitudes to Chastity," *Mademoiselle*, no.49 (1959). 39. This citation has been followed from Lisa Lindquist Dorr's 2008 article; I have deliberately reversed the precedence of the "indistinguishable roles" from Dorr's in order to shift the emphasis from men to women. Lisa Lindquist Dorr, "The Perils of the Back Seat: Date Rape, Race and Gender in 1950s America," *Gender & History* vol.20, no.1 (2008). 31.

47 "Midwood," Lynne Munroe Books, 2020, tinyurl.com/munbookwood. This is a page from a web site belonging to a vintage book dealer in the United States. The page contains a very interesting interview with Julie Ellis. Ellis wrote occasionally under her own name, as well as Joan Ellis, Allison Lord, Jeffrey Lord, Susan Marvin, Susan Marino, Linda Michaels, Jill Monte, and Susan Richard.

48 Ellis has eight entries under her least covert pen name, ranging from the highest to the lowest ranking from the compilers.Gene Damon and Lee Stuart, *The Lesbian in Literature*, 1st ed. (The Ladder, 1967). 22.

116 *Female masculinity beyond Beebo*

woman.[49] They engage in conversation in a bar, Jean having come over to where Mona is sitting – Jean's excuse for introducing herself is that "Men are stupid about a woman alone" in a bar.[50] She makes no secret of the fact that she is "cruising," nor that the bar staff know her and keep men from pestering her.[51] After lovemaking that convinces Mona that she is "just beginning to live," she is shocked to find on the piece of paper that Jean gives her when they part company, "*Mrs Jean Addams*" along with an instruction to "Call before 6 o'clock."[52] Mona's reaction is one of nausea,[53] going well beyond being discouraged or bothered by the fact that Jean is "subjected to the power of a husband."[54] In *Girls Dormitory* however, this power is implied rather than stated. Jean, cynical and predatory, is a world away from those women in similar domestic situations whose ingenuousness and yearning was expressed in the "cries of the heart" in correspondence to Ann Bannon after *Odd Girl Out* was published.[55]

Jean is also a world away from Carol, a principal in Claire Morgan's earlier, well-crafted novel *The Price of Salt*, inasmuch as the power of a husband, implied in Ellis's novel, is overwhelmingly palpable in Morgan's. *The Price of Salt* is a love story involving a young woman, Therese, who works in a Manhattan department store and a more mature woman, Carol, her wealthy customer; the difference in status is one of wealth and social position rather than professional position. The two strike up a relationship, and in order to escape the tense atmosphere in New York – mainly caused by the men in their lives – they go on a road trip, West toward Utah. Carol's husband engages a private investigator to follow them, to bug their hotel rooms, and to gather any evidence which might help his divorce case against Carol. Eventually Carol succumbs to his pressure, returns to New York, and she and Therese break up. Notwithstanding, Carol is humiliated in the divorce and her husband gains custody of their daughter. The husband's control over his wife illustrates what Collette Guillaumin says about "*l'appropriation de la classe des femmes par la classe des hommes,*"[56] which I translate freely as "the forcible ownership of women as a class by men." Even in disowning a woman, the moneyed, bourgeois husband as good as keeps a controlling hand on her life. Moreover, again as Guillaumin says, "*Les enfants appartiennent au père,*"[57] – "children belong to the father" – and in this case the father has appropriated

---

49 Though to Mona she only appears to be in her twenties. Joan Ellis, *Girls Dormitory* (Midwood, 1963). 129.
50 Ellis, *Girls Dormitory*. 129.
51 Ellis, *Girls Dormitory*. 131, 132.
52 Ellis, *Girls Dormitory*. 135. Jean's married name is italicised in the original.
53 Ellis, *Girls Dormitory*. 135.
54 de Beauvoir, *The Second Sex*. 368.
55 Ann Bannon, *Odd Girl Out* (Cleis, 2001). x.
56 Colette Guillaumin, "Practique du pouvoir et idee de Nature: (1) L'appropriation des femmes," *Nouvelles Questions Feministes*, no.2 (1978). 6.
57 Guillaumin, "Practique du pouvoir et idee de Nature: (1) L'appropriation des femmes." 11.

the daughter by economic and legal force. There is, however, an optimistic ending to the narrative. For a start, as Lauren Jae Gutterman points out, the novel upends the power relationship between the married lesbian and her lover that is typical in the plots of lesbian-themed paperbacks, as Therese, the character junior in years and of supposed lesser social status, takes the upper hand and decisive role in the relationship.[58] Therese and Carol are shown to be on the brink of defying male power, even if they can't beat it:

> Carol raised her hand slowly and brushed her hair back, once on either side, and Therese smiled because the gesture was Carol, and it was Carol she loved and would always love. Oh, in a different way now, because she was a different person, and it was like meeting Carol all over again, but it was still Carol and no one else. It would be Carol, in a thousand cities, a thousand houses, in foreign lands where they would go together, in heaven and in hell. Therese waited. Then as she was about to go to her, Carol saw her, seemed to stare at her incredulously a moment while Therese watched the slow smile growing, before her arm lifted suddenly, her hand waved a quick, eager greeting that Therese had never seen before. Therese walked toward her.[59]

Heather Love says that Carol is willing to risk her social position in order to make a life with Therese,[60] but at the ending of the book that is a possibility, not yet a definite risk, and the dynamic at the finale is Therese's rather than Carol's.[61] Love is adding to the narrative, rather than leaving it where the author does. However, the potential is there for Therese and Carol to defy male appropriative power and damn the consequences. Though they may not overcome its conventions, those conventions can be challenged.

Butches beyond Beebo: Christopher Hamilton and the lesbian mesocosm

Risk for the protagonist is also a major factor in the narrative of Randy Salem's *Chris*.[62] The eponymous Chris has the full name Christopher Hamilton, the

---

58 Lauren Jae Gutterman, "Another Enemy Within: Lesbian Wives, or the Hidden Threat to the Nuclear Family in Post-war America," *Gender & History* vol.24, no.2 (2012). 488.

59 Claire Morgan, *The Price of Salt* (Bantam, 1953). 248–249.

60 Heather Love, "Lesbian Fiction 1900--1950," in *A Companion to the Modern American Novel 1900 1950*, ed. John T Matthews (Wiley-Blackwell, 2009). 410.

61 Clara Bradbury-Rance reminds us of the "unpredictability" of the novel and that, as it is focalised through Therese, the "glance of assertive desire" belongs to her, rather than to Carol. Clara Bradbury-Rance, *Lesbian Cinema After Queer Theory* (Edinburgh UP, 2021). 137, 133, 138.

62 Randy Salem was the pen name of Pat Perdue; details about this author do not appear to be given in any sources of academic standing, and I have seen her surname given variously as Perdue, Perdee, and Pardee. She was supposedly the partner of Sally Singer, who also wrote lesbian paperbacks under the name March Hastings.

118 *Female masculinity beyond Beebo*

masculine given name echoing Radclyffe Hall's Stephen Gordon, there being no mention of an earlier one to deadname her by.[63] The novel was published as a paperback original, by Beacon Books, in 1959, immediately after Fawcett Gold Medal published Ann Bannon's *Odd Girl Out*, and contemporarily with their publication of *I am a Woman*. Where Bannon's first novel is conventional within the sub-genre, Salem's *Chris* is revolutionary in form and content.[64] Its treatment of lesbian love and domestic relationships as givens, as an accepted mesocosm within society at large and not as something 'abnormal', and indeed as the major sexuality in the narrative, together with its use of some basic tropes of mainstream romance, sets it apart.[65] As such, it is not primarily concerned with the lesbian's place in society, and the obstacles society places in her way, and 'normality' is not even mentioned. It could be argued that either this novel avoids the issues facing women in its contemporary world, or that by setting them aside it is the most radical novel of its type. That would not be apparent from the cover, however. At the time, publishing houses like Beacon and Midwood were set up to cash in on the success of Fawcett Gold Medal, and competed by using sensational cover art. The cover for *Chris* seems to bear little relation to the content of the book. It is dominated by a highly sexualised, overtly feminine depiction of a young woman leaning forward, her eyes half-closed, her lips pouting and painted a deep red, a décolletage revealing a deep cleavage, and the illustration supported by the words "Life in the limbo of lesbianism" and "An intimate story of the third sex, told with tenderness and unblushing honesty."[66] None of this

---

63 Salem tended to give her protagonists a name that was either traditionally masculine or which suggested masculinity. Hence Chris, Lee in *The Sex Between*, Karel in *Baby Face*, and Jesse in *The Unfortunate Flesh*.

64 Merja Makinen, in arguing that romance is not a conservative genre per se, says that all genres are "potentially and inherently transformable," but equally she concedes that "genre sedimentation" exists; it is the genre canon that is conservative, she explains, whilst the genre itself is "more than, other than, its canonical construction." Merja Makinen, *Feminist Popular Fiction* (Palgrave, 2001). 1, 2, 19. Bannon, having placed her first novel in the sediment of the sub-genre created by Fawcett with Packer's *Spring Fire*, was attempting to change it. Unknown to her, while she strove for some kind of realism, the fantasy world created by Salem had already disturbed the sediment radically.

65 The major trope I am thinking of is the professional relationship in mainstream heterosexual romances between, say, a hospital doctor and a nurse, or an executive and his secretary or P.A. In the case of *Chris*, the relationship is between the assistant to the director of a museum and that museum's high-status associate and sub-contractor for dangerous fieldwork. In another novel by Salem, *The Sex Between*, the major relationship, established early in the text, is between an executive and her secretary. Randy Salem, *The Sex Between* (Midwood, 1962). 8–9. As a caveat, this type of relationship may be stereotypical rather than typical; Rosemary Achmuty points out that even Mills & Boon did not use this trope until the 1970s. Forward to: Jay Dixon, *The Romance Fiction of Mills & Boon 1909-1990s* (Routledge, 2016). x.

66 Randy Salem, *Chris* (Naiad, 1989). Paratext. The Naiad edition does not use the sensationalist artwork of the 1950s, as Cleis does with its Bannon and Packer reprints. However, the publisher does not resist the tropes of 1950s paratext, and uses words like "shadowy" and

Female masculinity beyond Beebo   119

gives any indication that the novel has as its protagonist someone who challenges the male-dominated society outside the novel by largely unchallenged usurpation within it.[67]

Despite this apparent detachment, lip service is paid, in passing, to the social position of men. Men, to Chris, are a disease the world would be better without: "She sometimes dreamed of finding a cure for them, like polio."[68] However, risks for Chris do not come so much from men or their status or power, even though she says that there has never been "a man who didn't believe he could take a girl away from another woman,"[69] but more from the dangers of her profession, from internal factors in her relationships with women, and from her "destructive self-hatred."[70] Most male characters in the book – Dr Jonathan Brandt, director of the marine museum, Johnnie, Chris's friend since childhood, and the old fisherman Clem – seem to accept Chris's relationships with women, which is indicative of Salem's radically imagined sociality. The intrusion of George Randolph into her life, as a potential heterosexual rival "with all the usual equipment,"[71] is more indicative of the problems between her and her partner Dizz, and of Chris's own insecurity, than of the power of men and of heteronormativity.

> Something pounded in her head, an ugly something. What, it said, will happen to me if he can do for her what I can't? What if she goes to bed with him and finds out what it means to be fulfilled? [...] She dared not tell [Dizz] that she was afraid, and that it was not George who made her so, but her own sense of inadequacy.[72]

George occupies a position that is not quite the equivalent *in parvo* of Martin Hallam's in Hall's *The Well of Loneliness*.[73] He is a man with prestige – a

---

"forbidden" in the rear cover blurb: "This classic early novel will draw you back into an era when love between women was a shadowy and forbidden adventure." Given that Christopher Hamilton strides confidently through a world largely devoid of heterosexual convention this is rather a strange statement.

67 The opinion of Bradley and Damon is that in *Chris* "there are almost no hints that there is a heterosexual world outside the gay one," and they judge the novel "[g]ood but unreal.". Bradley and Damon, *Checklist 1960: A Complete, Cumulative Checklist of Lesbian, Variant, and Homosexual Fiction, in English, or Available in English Translation, with Supplements of Related Material, for the Use of Collectors, Students, and Librarians.*

68 Salem, *Chris*. 14. This is almost an adumbration of certain attitudes that would develop within second-wave feminism.

69 Salem, *Chris*. 18.

70 Angela Weir and Elizabeth Wilson, "The Greyhound Bus Station in the Evolution of Lesbian Popular Culture," in *New Lesbian Criticism*, ed. Sally Munt (Harvester Wheatsheaf, 1992). 107.

71 Salem, *Chris*. 18.

72 Salem, *Chris*. 26.

73 Martin Hallam, at the end of *The Well of Loneliness*, is Stephen Gordon's rival for the love of Mary Llewellyn. Stephen cedes to Martin, in order to secure happiness for Mary.

120 *Female masculinity beyond Beebo*

lawyer[74] – but is used as a ploy by Dizz to make Chris jealous. Indeed it is his couture that is in direct rivalry to Chris's, who likes the crease in her slacks,[75] rather than his prestige and sexuality. The latter, along with his romantic presumption, disgusts Dizz on their first and only sexual encounter. "He asked me to marry him [...] I told him no [...] Men are like Lesbians, only worse. I let him kiss me and all he wanted to do was get my pants off. I let him do that too. What difference does it make?"[76] Salem makes Dizz distance herself from "Lesbians;" despite her being in a relationship with Chris, Dizz considers the term to include only stone butches such as her masculine-styled partner, not the likes of herself who are oriented towards them.[77]

Conceived at the same time as Beebo Brinker, Chris shares some of Beebo's physicality and style. Weir and Wilson refer to her as "one of the butchest of women."[78] However it is not in a butch presentation that her power lies. Although she does like creases in her slacks, she does not have Beebo's almost compulsive attachment to pants. She finds no discomfort in slipping into a skirt[79] – she may even find it commonplace, as her donning it appears in the text without further comment – and her confidence in this regard, on not having to put effort into passing for a menial job, is no doubt due to her being a well-known conchologist and marine biologist. Along with her success, in Salem's fantasy world, comes the kind of privilege unknown to Beebo, or to real-life butches such as the denizens of *Stone Butch Blues*. Chris is a person of both athleticism and intellect, an expert swimmer, and a writer of articles.[80] She has looks that make it easy to pick up women in bars,[81] a similar milieu to Beebo's. Despite Chris's comfort in a skirt, Salem tends to dress her in slacks, shirt, and jacket, and writes her self-appraisal as follows:

> She stood dressed in front of a full-length mirror and liked what she saw. Lean and firm, built like a young boy, she did not look like a

---

74 Salem, *Chris*. 15.
75 Salem, *Chris*. 3.
76 Salem, *Chris*. 172.
77 Unlike Beebo Brinker, Chris may be labelled "stone" fairly, as her sexual concern is to bring her partner to climax. It is Chris rather than Beebo, then, who bisects the six decades between *The Well of Loneliness* and *Stone Butch Blues*. As previously stated, it was Lillian Faderman who defined Beebo as stone; Lillian Faderman, *Odd Girls and Twilight Lovers: A History of Lesbian Life in Twentieth-Century America* (Columbia UP, 1991). 266. It is also worth noting that this dichotomy that labels only one half of a partnership as "Lesbian" echoes Valerie Taylor's view that *Whisper Their Love* was not a lesbian story for the simple reason that one of the major characters was "something of a villain," and also L.T. Woodward's pseudo-categories of "lovers" and "beloveds." Taylor, *Whisper Their Love*. 238. L. T. Woodward, *Twilight Women* (Lancer, 1963). 39.
78 Weir and Wilson, "The Greyhound Bus Station in the Evolution of Lesbian Popular Culture." 107.
79 Salem, *Chris*. 31.
80 Salem, *Chris*. 5.
81 Salem, *Chris*. 2.

Female masculinity beyond Beebo   121

thirty-year-old woman. She was all things beautiful, graceful, and desirable. A pet to be doted on and spoiled. The thought amused her and she smiled.[82]

The trope of a woman admiring herself in front of a mirror is supposed to be a 'tell' for a male writer, but in this case the writer has merely adopted a male façade, the masculine "Randy"[83] as a forename, along with a surname associated with the history of early English settlement in America.[84] Add to the slacks and shirt the character's "close-cropped hair,"[85] flat heels,[86] and pea jacket,[87] and the description of Chris could almost fit Beebo. Her height is "five-ten."[88]

That physicality is never a source of discomfort to Christopher, as it can be to Stephen Gordon or Beebo Brinker; there is no need for the equivalent of Jack Mann to tell her that there is "nothing wrong" with her body.[89] Neither is there anything wrong with her intellect, or her relationship to her field of expertise. Carol, the third person in the triangle that is the major issue of the plot, says of Chris's professional writing:

"You write about the sea like others write about a first love, with the same tenderness and doting devotion. What anyone else would make a dull, dry treatise, you render into an elegy [...] Not that I don't know better than to judge you by what you write."[90]

Carol's final sentence above perhaps acknowledges the fact that Chris had met her whilst drunk, and they had just had a one-night stand, or simply that Carol is perceptive enough not to make a superficial judgment. In reply, Chris offers the self-assessment "I'm a disagreeable bitch. I'm snide and sarcastic and sometimes cruel. A lecher and a drunkard to boot."[91] The novel

---

82 Salem, *Chris*. 3.
83 Usually thought of as a familiar form of "Randolph," "Randall," or some such, it has connotations of male sexual arousal in British English that it does not often have in American English, though the OED records its use in *The Grapes of Wrath*.
84 Salem in Massachusetts was an important port in the seventeenth century, and a centre for early European immigration.
85 Salem, *Chris*. 24.
86 Salem, *Chris*. 67.
87 Salem, *Chris*. 116.
88 Salem, *Chris*. 15. One has the impression that Beebo Brinker is taller, but Jeffrey Weinstein refers to Beebo as "five feet ten in sneakers and pants." Jeff Weinstein, "In Praise of Pulp," *Voice Literary Supplement*(1983). 8. The Wikipedia entry for Ann Bannon puts Beebo at "nearly 6 feet (1.8m) tall." "Ann Bannon," Wikipedia, updated 31st January 2020, tinyurl .com/BeeboBannon.
89 Ann Bannon, *Beebo Brinker* (Cleis, 2001). 51.
90 Salem, *Chris*. 7.
91 Salem, *Chris*. 7.

122   *Female masculinity beyond Beebo*

has begun *in medias res* with Chris waking up in bed with Carol, and that fact that this is typical of "every Saturday night for four years" introduces the reader to the effect on Chris's character caused by the problems that exist between Chris and Dizz. Notwithstanding Carol's assessment that Chris works hard at creating the impression of her disagreeable nature,[92] when Chris finds her home empty and comes to the conclusion that Dizz has left her, she sinks into misery, snivelling, and calling her absent partner "No good bitch. No good goddamn slut."[93] As with the relationship of Laura and Beebo in *Women in the Shadows*, however, this partnership is difficult to break.

Chris, Dizz, and the weaponising of frigidity

The principal problem with the relationship between Chris and Dizz is their sexual incompatibility. When they make love, Dizz does not experience orgasm; she lies "unfulfilled" in Chris's arms, and "[t]he moment of greatest joy invariably became one of utter defeat."[94] It is clear that they do make love, or attempt to, but the conclusion of these attempts is always the one that is most devastating for a stone butch. There may be a coded message here in the novel for male readers: if a stone butch is stereotypically supposed to care about her partner's sexual pleasure and fulfilment, and a man stereotypically about his own, then a stone butch's masculinity is the antithesis of a man's, not a copy of it. With thirty-two years between them, the assessment of Bradley and Damon and that of Weir and Wilson is the same – that Dizz is frigid. Bradley and Damon say that Chris's life is "complicated" by her "frigid girlfriend."[95] Weir and Wilson say that "Dizz is frigid. She won't let Chris make love to her,"[96] but that is contradicted by the text. It is probable that Dizz would nowadays be regarded as being in the broad spectrum of asexual sub-identities. Asexuality does not preclude orientation, nor the capacity to love deeply, nor to form long-term relationships such as Dizz's romantic and domestic relationship with Chris, which has lasted more than four years. Nor, when understood as a positive and self-defining sexuality, does it preclude attempts at fulfilling sex, though they might fail. To blame one partner's supposed frigidity for the complication of the partnership is as pointless as blaming the other's highly sexual nature – sexual incompatibility is no one's fault.[97]

---

92 Salem, *Chris*. 8.

93 Salem, *Chris*. 13.

94 Salem, *Chris*. 19, 21.

95 Bradley and Damon, *Checklist 1960: A Complete, Cumulative Checklist of Lesbian, Variant, and Homosexual Fiction, in English, or Available in English Translation, with Supplements of Related Material, for the Use of Collectors, Students, and Librarians*. Unpaginated.

96 Weir and Wilson, "The Greyhound Bus Station in the Evolution of Lesbian Popular Culture." 108.

97 If not precisely asexual, Dizz could simply have the condition known as anorgasmia. In which case their incompatibility is still the fault of neither of them.

Female masculinity beyond Beebo   123

In the faux sexology of the era, lesbianism was often attributed to female frigidity,[98] the inference being that a woman turning to a woman for love and sex was either a fault in herself or the lack of a suitable man to provide the warmth necessary to thaw her. It is worthwhile to consider this cultural background of attitudes to asexuality and "frigidity" in the mid-twentieth century, in order to understand how Chris's and Dizz's relationship fits into the challenges of and to the accepted norms of sexuality and gender. It is only relatively recently that asexuality has been recognised as a legitimate identity rather than simply a condition. The Oxford English Dictionary's bald definition, "Without sexual feelings or desires; not sexually attracted to anyone,"[99] is followed by four examples of contradictory usage, starting at 1862, before a fifth, dated 2012, actually indicates that a person can attach the word as a self-description. Michael D. Storms simply labels "individuals who are asexual" as "those who score low on [heteroeroticism and homoeroticism]."[100] Anthony F. Bogaert's 2006 article "Towards a Conceptual Understanding of Asexuality" concludes that asexuality "should not *necessarily* be synonymous with a pathological state,"[101] but also points out the lack of reliability of self-report,[102] and the closeness of asexuality in manifestation to and overlap with hypoactive sexual desire disorder (HSDD)[103] which, at the time of his writing, was mostly considered a sexual dysfunction in women. It is this cultural emphasis on the lack of desire or sexual function specifically in women, that is most relevant to Chris and Dizz, despite the fact that *Chris* treats lesbian romance and domesticity as a societal given, and the mainstream perceived dysfunction assumes relations between men and women to be central. The term "frigidity" should be considered as having been weaponised in the normative battle for female compliance. Adrienne Rich refers to the "psychoanalytic doctrines of frigidity"[104] that class female asexuality as a pathology. Although the twentieth-century contained significant periods where women emerged in their own right – in particular the nineteen-twenties, when "radical voices [...] sought harmony between the sexes by reforming what seemed the most oppressive elements of Victorian

---

98 Albert Reissner devotes a whole chapter to "Lesbians as Frigid Females" in his work of faux sexology. Albert Reissner, *Female Perversions: Sex and the Lesbian* (Wee Hours, 1965). 128–134.

99 OED online, s.v. "Asexual," accessed February 2021, www.oed.com/view/Entry/11430?redirectedFrom=asexual#eid

100 Michael D. Storms, "Theories of Sexual Orientation," *Journal of Personality and Social Psychology* vol.38 no.5 (1980). 790.

101 Athony F. Bogaert, "Toward a Conceptual Understanding of Asexuality," *Review of General Psychology* vol.10, no.3 (2006). 249, my emphasis.

102 Bogaert, "Toward a Conceptual Understanding of Asexuality." 245. "self-report" is Bogaert's usage.

103 Bogaert, "Toward a Conceptual Understanding of Asexuality." 243.

104 Adrienne Rich, "Compulsory Heterosexuality and Lesbian Existence," *Signs* vol5, no.4 (1980). 639.

124 Female masculinity beyond Beebo

marriage"[105] – this seemingly liberalising shift in cultural paradigm brought with it a different kind of oppression. In the companionate marriage idealised from the nineteen-twenties onward, the sexual enthusiasm and pleasure of both male and female partner were supposed to balance. Gutterman notes Edmund Bergler's 1958 conclusion that lesbianism was a subcategory of frigidity, "in other words, while not all frigid women were lesbians, all lesbians were sexually frigid."[106] An example of this attitude in mainstream psychotherapy in the nineteen-sixties can be found in an article in the *American Journal of Psychotherapy*, which labels "frigidity" as a "sexual disorder" brought about by anxiety, and links it to "homosexual trends" in women.[107] Regarding the manifestation of this cultural attitude in popular fiction, Gutterman notes that by the early nineteen-sixties "the lesbian wife had become a stock character in lesbian paperback originals that usually portrayed lesbian wives as fleeing from adult responsibilities while emasculating their husbands."[108] In addition to the paperback fiction of the era, cheap works of pop-sexology made similar links. Reissner's chapter on "Lesbians as Frigid Females" has already been referred to, and other sexologists repeat the pattern. Dr Benjamin Morse, in his book *The Lesbian* headed a chapter "The Frigid Abstainer,"[109] though the two "case studies" he highlights are indeed abstainers from rather than disinclined towards sex – it is simply significant that he chooses the word for inclusion in his title. M.D. Pourdes does the same with "Frigidity and Impotence,"[110] balancing perceived female and male dysfunctions; frigidity, he states, stems from "a sense of guilt and fear," hammering the point home with "fear of incapability in the performance of the sex act can and in many cases does create a climate for frigidity" and "[...] deeply buried feelings of guilt and fear [...]"[111] He links frigidity

---

105 Christina Simmons, "Companionate Marriage and the Lesbian Threat," *Frontiers: A Journal of Women Studies* vol.4, no.3 (1979). 54.
106 Gutterman, "Another Enemy Within: Lesbian Wives, or the Hidden Threat to the Nuclear Family in Post-war America." 480. Gutterman is referring, without giving a page number, to Edmund Bergler, *Counterfeit-Sex: Homosexuality, Impotence, Frigidity* (Grune and Stratton, 1958).
107 Tom Kraft and Ihsan Al-Issa, "Behavior therapy and the treatment of frigidity," *American journal of psychotherapy* vol.21, no.1 (1967). 116, 119. Although this article appeared in an American journal, the writers were based in London, and the case history was (presumably) that of an English woman. Although this book is principally concerned with an American literary phenomenon, that article shows the pervasiveness of ideas about frigidity in a worldwide context.
108 Gutterman, "Another Enemy Within: Lesbian Wives, or the Hidden Threat to the Nuclear Family in Post-war America." 489.
109 Benjamin Morse, *The Lesbian*, A Monarch Human Behavior Book, (Monarch Books Inc, 1961). 132–136.
110 M.D. Pourdes, *The Deviate Patterns* (Challenge Publications, 1966). 66–76.
111 Pourdes, *The Deviate Patterns*. 66. In this case pop-psychology aligns with professional; see the similarity with Kraft and Al-Issa. In the commercialism of the nineteen-fifties and sixties it should not be surprising to find writers with actual medical knowledge writing potboilers.

Female masculinity beyond Beebo 125

to vaginismus, kleptomania, and "subconscious or conscious homosexual feelings."[112] Yet another chapter heading comes in Carlson Wade's *Sexual Behavior of the Lesbian* – "The Frigid Female Homosexual."[113] Wade calls frigidity "an organic flaw,"[114] declares that it is "a problem that needs treatment by the family doctor or psychiatrist,"[115] and cites Wilhelm Stekel's categories of types of frigid female.[116] The following category is of interest: "*3. The passionate-frigid female* Despite her intense yearning and extreme anxiety, she still cannot achieve an orgasm."[117]

Can this category include Dizz? If it does – and it is possible to see that as a defensible description of the character – then Salem has appropriated the perception of hetero-uxorial frigidity and applied it to her lesbian-inclusive, lesbian-dominant mesocosm. That application in itself challenges heteronormativity and, even if we accept the use by Bradley and Damon, and Weir and Wilson, of the pejorative "frigid," removes "frigidity" from being in any way a "cause" of homosexuality. Before she met Dizz

> Chris had been a carefree, footloose devil. With a graceful ease that could charm the birds off the trees, Chris's life had been a series of one night stands. A whirlwind courtship, promises to be true forever, one lovely night, and off to the next one.[118]

Weir and Wilson, in remarking that *Chris* is not set in the milieu of the 1950s lesbian sub-culture, although its protagonist does regularly visit Greenwich Village bars, state that the novel implies that those visits are "sordid."[119] Yet in the above passage there is no trace of sordidness. What has tainted the visits by the time the novel begins is not the milieu itself, nor indeed is it Chris's promiscuity, but rather it is Chris's self-loathing, that and the complicity of Dizz in Chris's life outside their domesticity – "It had been Dizz's idea that [Chris] go out that first Saturday night." The condition of their relationship owes as much to one as it does to the other.

Radical *Chris* in the continuum of twentieth-century lesbian novels

What I see as the radical nature of the novel, in its departure from strict realism in creating this lesbian mesocosm, which as well as being included

---

112 Pourdes, *The Deviate Patterns*. 68, 71.
113 Carlson Wade, *Sexual Behavior of the Lesbian* (Imperial, 1964). 145–153.
114 Wade, *Sexual Behavior of the Lesbian*. 147.
115 Wade, *Sexual Behavior of the Lesbian*. 152.
116 Stekel was a pupil of Sigmund Freud.
117 Wade, *Sexual Behavior of the Lesbian*. 146.
118 Salem, *Chris*. 166.
119 Weir and Wilson, "The Greyhound Bus Station in the Evolution of Lesbian Popular Culture." 108.

126 *Female masculinity beyond Beebo*

in the societal norm incorporates all the fault lines of heterosexuality, Weir and Wilson see as retrograde. They see it as harking back to Radclyffe Hall's *The Well of Loneliness* and Gale Wilhelm's *We Too Are Drifting*, and that the nature of her work "makes Chris an isolated, although 'special' figure – something of a star – who relates mainly to men."[120] There are some admittable parallels. For example, in both *We Too Are Drifting* and *Chris* the protagonist becomes involved in a love triangle with an established and a new partner, and in both *The Well of Loneliness* and *Chris* the protagonist loses a lover to a male rival, a friend of her youth. As regards relating to men, apart from Johnnie no man in the novel plays any significant part. As previously mentioned, none of them actually threaten her sexuality or her presentation, and she holds her own in their world:

> Chris was remembering proudly how she'd done that lying bastard Blackfield out of an authentic pirate's map. He'd tried to chisel her out of a small fortune. But he had a weakness for rum and poker.[121]

There is little difference between her having "done" the Cratylic Blackfield and his having tried to "chisel" her, in the world of cards and drink with which they are both familiar. The radicalism of the novel lies in Salem's creation of this world where lesbian couples are a given, and a female adventurer is the equal of, or surpasses, any given man.

There is a more disturbing episode in the novel that juxtaposes Chris to a male-dominated environment, and perhaps this, rather than any similarity to Hall or Wilhelm, is where *Chris* is at its least radical. When paying a professional visit to Max Peterson, a former leading marine biologist whose life had been in a downward spiral since the death of his wife, Chris is approached by Jennie. She is described as fat, blonde, drunk, dressed only in a brassiere, but having gorgeous green eyes.[122] She makes overt sexual advances to Chris, which Chris rejects:

> But she knew she had to be calm about it, not take the damn slut and bat her around like she deserved. She had to be polite about it.
>
> Chris put three fingers on each of Jennie's shoulders and pushed her gently away. "No, thanks," she said.
>
> "Big dumb bastard," Jennie said. "Big dumb bastard."
>
> Max slammed the door behind Chris. He approached Jennie. His arm went up and back. The huge hand caught Jennie on the side of the head.

---

120 Weir and Wilson, "The Greyhound Bus Station in the Evolution of Lesbian Popular Culture." 108.
121 Salem, *Chris*. 35.
122 Salem, *Chris*. 72.

Female masculinity beyond Beebo 127

She screamed and dropped the bottle. It smashed and gin soaked into the bare wooden floor.

Jennie glared at Max with hatred. "Big dumb bastard," she said.[123]

Having "a straight man for an audience" and rejecting the woman's advances, Chris sends a message to male readers that, perhaps, this book was not written expressly for their voyeuristic attention. Chris's thoughts however, in free indirect speech, do not read well for a modern readership; they are slut-shaming of a nasty kind, and assume that a woman needs violence to teach her a lesson. If Chris has absorbed this as part and parcel of 'masculinity', then it has to be questioned. Jennie addresses both Chris and Max as "Big dumb bastard," her inarticulacy de-gendering the term and equating the two. Inasmuch as Chris stands by when Max hits Jennie, she is complicit by letting it happen, more so by standing back and letting a man do it. As though to underline Chris's position in relation to the "stench of Jennie" and to "this filthy apartment and this degraded man," Jennie twice calls her "big boy,"[124] but what price this acknowledgement of masculinity in these circumstances? On leaving the apartment Chris hears the door slam, and then a slap and a scream; she shakes her head sadly.[125] Nevertheless she can still be considered complicit; for all her sadness, the closed door does not absolve her. An alternative way of looking at this incident is that Jennie, in making sexual advances, is attempting to usurp a masculine prerogative, which both Chris and Max resent. In the earlier chapter of this book, where I concentrated on male characters, I noted Jane Whitbread's comments – made at about the time *Chris* was published – to the effect that sexual aggression in pursuit of a conquest was men's "one sure proof of masculinity."[126] I also noted a much later comment by Susan Love Brown, dating the cultural acceptance of coercive sexual relations to the mores of the films and fiction of the 1930s and 1940s.[127] The irony of the incident in Max's apartment is that in her drunken approach to Chris, Jennie is probably not doing anything more than can be found in Chris's own regular, Saturday-night behaviour. The first few pages of the novel tell of how sobering up and enduring hangovers is part of that behaviour, and of how when she had picked up Carol the latter had had "two heads and not much of a face" when seen through drunkenness.[128]

It Is possible that Weir and Wilson's opinion of *Chris* – that it harks back to pre-war lesbian novels rather than fitting in with the generality of post-war

---

123 Salem, *Chris*. 73.
124 Salem, *Chris*. 79.
125 Salem, *Chris*. 79.
126 Whitbread, "A Report on Current Attitudes to Chastity." 39.
127 Susan Love Brown, "Ayn Rand and Rape," *The Journal of Ayn Rand Studies* vol.15, no.1 (2015). 4.
128 Salem, *Chris*. 2–3.

128 *Female masculinity beyond Beebo*

cheap paperbacks – is due to their having commented at a time when both *Chris*, alone of Salem's novels, and *We Too Are Drifting* were in print at Naiad Press. Over a five-year period in the late nineteen-fifties and early nineteen-sixties, Salem went on to publish nine more 'paperback original' novels, and although *The Lesbian in Literature* notes that their quality had declined by 1964,[129] it would have been more legitimate if Weir and Wilson had been able to take *Chris* as part of her overall corpus. In all her novels, Salem creates a world that sometimes seems "made up only of women,"[130] through which a capable woman of status strides, emerging head and shoulders above the rest of the cast. Karel Richards in *Baby Face* rises from being a junior executive when the novel begins to being the only credible candidate for the position of a manager of a prestigious branch in Newark NJ.[131] Lee in *The Sex Between* becomes a CEO.[132] Chris Hamilton, though she turns her back on her long-term partner and loses her new one, finds a new, powerful independence and decides to set off on an exotic expedition – the last sentence in the novel is a single, stark word, "Alone."[133] There is also the independence shown by Carol, who gives up Chris; the latter "couldn't help feeling a grudging admiration for Carol – it took courage to give up somebody you love, somebody you know is no damn good for you."[134] The presence or absence of men is sometimes an ambiguity. For example, given such factors as the violence in *The Sex Between*, it is possible to imagine Lee being written with only minor alteration as a male character,[135] though of course this depends on a highly debatable male stereotype.[136] In *Chris*, Carol "might just settle" for Johnnie, or at least that is the hope he voices.[137] The fact that *Baby Face* has no salient male characters at all and is full of sex scenes, and that *The Sex Between* has a happy ending and features a protagonist who has the "power" to quash a heterosexual marriage,[138]points, rather than to Salem's corpus being influenced by novels such as *We Too Are Drifting*, to

---

129 Damon and Stuart, *The Lesbian in Literature*. 61. All of these were still listed in the second edition in 1975. Gene Damon, Jan Watson, and Robin Jordan, *The Lesbian in Literature: a bibliography*, 2nd ed. (The Ladder, 1975). 75. Also the third edition in 1981. Barbara Grier, *The Lesbian in Literature*, 3rd ed. (The Naiad Press, 1981). 133.

130 Randy Salem, *Baby Face* (Softcover Library, 1964). 7.

131 Salem, *Baby Face*. 153.

132 Salem, *The Sex Between*. 188.

133 Salem, *Chris*. 211.

134 Salem, *Chris*. 184.

135 I am grateful to Lisa Vecoli, formerly of the Tretter Collection at the University of Minnesota and herself a long-time collector of lesbian paperbacks, for drawing my attention to this.

136 See the references to sexual aggression, in the chapter of this book dealing with male agency, by Lisa Lindquist Dorr and by Susan Love Brown.

137 Salem, *Chris*. 184.

138 Salem, *The Sex Between*. 176.

Female masculinity beyond Beebo   129

their being conceived as sheer escapism, an alternative to Bannon's corpus that never even mention the joys of lesbian love.[139]

Is dominance a masculine prerogative?

The idea or ideal of the companionate marriage, a partnership of sexual and social equals, did not last beyond the societal upheavals that followed the nineteen-twenties – the Depression and a major international war.[140] The concept of such a partnership, in which an intellectually and sexually ful-filled woman stands alongside an intellectually and sexually fulfilled man, is a somewhat bourgeois concept. In fact, Sociologists had coined the term "com-panionate marriage" in the nineteen-twenties "to describe a transformation in the social and economic functions of marriage for middle-class, and pre-dominantly white, American families."[141] In the war years, working-class American women staffed the industrial assembly lines, living lives remote from their husbands, and whether their married lives had ever approached the ideal of "companionate" was irrelevant. After the war, according to Finch and Summerfield, the aim of social reconstruction was to consolidate family life and to build a future in which marriage and the home would be the foundations of a better life.[142] However, Roberta Yusba, whom I men-tioned briefly in the Introduction as helping to create the stereotype of les-bian-themed paperbacks, expressed that consolidation thus:

> The end of the war brought sudden and intense repression. The image of Rosie the Riveter was being replaced in the media by an Ozzie and Harriet-type nuclear family. Women were pressured to return to a tra-ditional home, raise families, appreciate the plentiful consumer goods,

---

139 Audre Lorde, *Zami: A New Spelling of My Name* (Crossing Press, 1982). 213. I shall add a caveat at this point. I asked Ann Bannon, during our email correspondence, whether her fan mail contained appreciation of her works as erotic; she answered "Of course [...]" but did not really elaborate on that. The reason I mention that is that Salem's *Baby Face*, though written in the mid-1960s, less than five years after Bannon was firmly established as a writer, with its plethora of sex scenes, the only coyness of which is that genitals are not specifically mentioned, is open to interpretation as having been written as a catchpenny for voyeuristic men as much as escapism for women.

140 Janet Finch and Penny Summerfield would disagree with my view, arguing that the compan-ionate marriage was emerging from the end of World War II, to become the most distinctive feature of domestic life of the period. However, see my arguments that follow from this point. Janet Finch and Penny Summerfield, "Social reconstruction and the emergence of companionate marriage, 1945--59," in *Marriage, Domestic Life & Social Change: Writings for Jacqueline Burgoyne (1944 88)*, ed. David Clark (Routledge). 6.

141 Rebecca L. Davis, ""Not Marriage at All, but Simple Harlotry": The Companionate Mar-riage Controversy," *Journal of American History* vol.94, no.4 (2008). 1138.

142 Finch and Summerfield, "Social reconstruction and the emergence of companionate mar-riage, 1945–59." 6.

130   *Female masculinity beyond Beebo*

move to the suburbs on low-cost GI loans, and give their jobs back to the men.[143]

Although some propaganda asserted that women could have "careers, or cradle, or both,"[144] and in the portrayal of the domestic set-up there was an echo of the companionate ideal, there could be no escaping the fact that it was the *paterfamilias* and all the trappings of respectability that were re-emerging.[145] There were comparatively liberal aspects to *The Adventures of Ozzie and Harriet* of course, notably their attitude to the rock and roll career of their son Ricky,[146] but in publicity photographs of the family, Ozzie is always pictured in a dominant position. Chapter I has already noted that the post-war years saw a "masculinity crisis" and a "male panic,"[147] and a reassertion in the media of sexual dominance amongst (young) males,[148] and of the prerogative of a man to head families and relationships.

The presence of a dominant person in a lesbian couple, such as has been highlighted in this chapter, is therefore a direct challenge to the culture of the dominant, male-based masculinity of the era, regardless of whether the female dominant enjoys success in the narrative. The novels have presented a varied picture. In Taylor's *Whisper Their Love* and Seeley's *Sorority Sin*, butches are shown as unsavoury, and both butches and dominant older women as predatory and pathological, although otherwise the two novels are unlike in many other aspects. In Sela's *I am a Lesbian*, despite its dubious literary merit, a peripheral butch character is shown in a positive light, and a socially dominant, self-described "masculine" woman ends up in a successful relationship. Ellis's *Girls Dormitory* and Morgan's *The Price of Salt* have contrasting views of married lesbians. In both cases the husbands are virtually faceless – literally so in the case of the cover art of *The Price of Salt*, where a male figure stands off, in. the middle-background, lit from behind with his face in shadow, and figuratively so in *Girls Dormitory*, in which he is implied merely by her title "Mrs." The economic and familial power wielded by the dominant female character in *The Price of Salt* is considerable, yet it does not stop the lesbian relationship nor, as was mentioned earlier, the power dynamic within that relationship flipping. In *Girls Dormitory*

---

143   Roberta Yusba, "Twilight Tales: Lesbian Pulps 1950–1960," *On Our Backs*, no. Summer 1985. 30.

144   According to a documentary film quoted in Aerlyn Weissman and Lynne Fernie, "Forbidden Love: The Unashamed Stories of Lesbian Lives," (National Film Board of Canada, 1993).

145   Ann Bannon attested to this in her own married life, using that very Latin term. Personal email, 22nd September 2020.

146   James Joslyn and John Pendleton, "The Adventures of Ozzie and Harriet," *The Journal of Popular Culture* vol.7, no.1 (1973). 36.

147   James Gilbert, *Men in the Middle: Searching for Masculinity in the 1950s* (U of Chicago P, 2005). 25.

148   See Lisa Lindquist Dorr, also quoted in Chapter I: Dorr, "The Perils of the Back Seat: Date Rape, Race and Gender in 1950s America." 31, 35.

Female masculinity beyond Beebo 131

the relationship simply fails with the revelation of marital status. The unique figure of Christopher Hamilton in *Chris*, although sacrificing two relationships, emerges as a strong and independent figure. The casual reader of the era could expect the kaleidoscopic within the stereotypical.

Bibliography

"Ann Bannon." Wikipedia, Updated 31 January 2020. tinyurl.com/BeeboBannon.

Bannon, Ann. *Beebo Brinker*. Cleis, 2001.

———. *I am a Woman*. Cleis, 2002.

———. *Odd Girl Out*. Cleis, 2001.

Bergler, Edmund. *Counterfeit-Sex: Homosexuality, Impotence, Frigidity*. Grune and Stratton, 1958.

Bogaert, Athony F. "Toward a Conceptual Understanding of Asexuality." *Review of General Psychology* 10, no. 3 (2006): 241–50.

Bradbury-Rance, Clara. *Lesbian Cinema after Queer Theory*. Edinburgh University Press, 2021.

Bradley, Marion Zimmer, and Gene Damon. *Checklist 1960: A Complete, Cumulative Checklist of Lesbian, Variant, and Homosexual Fiction, in English, or Available in English Translation, with Supplements of Related Material, for the Use of Collectors, Students, and Librarians*. Self-published by Marion Zimmer Bradley, 1960.

Brown, Susan Love. "Ayn Rand and Rape." *The Journal of Ayn Rand Studies* 15, no. 1 (2015): 3–22.

Damon, Gene, and Lee Stuart. *The Lesbian in Literature*. 1st ed. The Ladder, 1967.

Damon, Gene, Jan Watson, and Robin Jordan. *The Lesbian in Literature: A Bibliography*. 2nd ed. The Ladder, 1975.

Davis, Rebecca L. "'Not Marriage at All, but Simple Harlotry': The Companionate Marriage Controversy." *Journal of American History* 94, no. 4 (2008): 1137–63.

de Beauvoir, Simone. *Le Deuxième Sexe*. Vol. 2. Éditions Gallimard, 1976.

———. *The Second Sex*. Translated by Howard Madison Parshley. Picador, 1988.

Dixon, Jay. *The Romance Fiction of Mills & Boon 1909–1990s*. Routledge, 2016.

Dorr, Lisa Lindquist. "The Perils of the Back Seat: Date Rape, Race and Gender in 1950s America." *Gender & History* 20, no. 1 (2008): 22–47.

Echols, Alice. "The Taming of the Id: Feminist Sexual Politics, 1968–83." In *Pleasure and Danger: Exploring Female Sexuality*, edited by Carole S. Vance, 50–72. Routledge & Kegan Paul, 1984.

Ellis, Joan. *Girls Dormitory*. Midwood, 1963.

Faderman, Lillian. *Odd Girls and Twilight Lovers: A History of Lesbian Life in Twentieth-Century America*. Columbia University Press, 1991.

Finch, Janet, and Penny Summerfield. "Social Reconstruction and the Emergence of Companionate Marriage, 1945–59." In *Marriage, Domestic Life & Social Change: Writings for Jacqueline Burgoyne (1944–88)*, edited by David Clark, 6–27. Routledge.

Gilbert, James. *Men in the Middle: Searching for Masculinity in the 1950s*. U of Chicago P, 2005.

Grier, Barbara. *The Lesbian in Literature*. 3rd ed. The Naiad Press, 1981.

Guillaumin, Colette. "Practique Du Pouvoir Et Idee De Nature: (1) L'appropriation Des Femmes." *Nouvelles Questions Feministes*, no. 2 (1978).

Gutterman, Lauren Jae. "Another Enemy Within: Lesbian Wives, or the Hidden Threat to the Nuclear Family in Post-War America." *Gender & History* 24, no. 2 (2012): 475–501.

132 *Female masculinity beyond Beebo*

Hacker, Helen Mayer. "The New Burdens of Masculinity." *Marriage and Family Living* 19, no. 3 (1957): 227–33.

Joslyn, James, and John Pendleton. "The Adventures of Ozzie and Harriet." *The Journal of Popular Culture* 7, no. 1 (1973): 23–41.

Keller, Yvonne. "Ab/Normal Looking: Voyeurism and Surveillance in Lesbian Pulp Novels and Us Cold War Culture." *Feminist Media Studies* 5, no. 2 (2005): 177–95.

Kennedy, Elizabeth Lapovsky, and Madeline D. Davis. *Boots of Leather, Slippers of Gold: The History of a Lesbian Community*. Penguin, 1993.

Kraft, Tom, and Ihsan Al-Issa. "Behavior Therapy and the Treatment of Frigidity." *American journal of psychotherapy* 21, no. 1 (1967): 116–20.

Lorde, Audre. *Zami: A New Spelling of My Name*. Crossing Press, 1982.

Love, Heather. "Lesbian Fiction 1900–1950." In *A Companion to the Modern American Novel 1900–1950*, edited by John T Matthews, 392–413. Wiley-Blackwell, 2009.

Makinen, Merja. *Feminist Popular Fiction*. Palgrave, 2001.

Morgan, Claire. *The Price of Salt*. Bantam, 1953.

Morse, Benjamin. *The Lesbian*. A Monarch Human Behavior Book. Monarch Books Inc, 1961.

"Midwood." Lynne Munroe Books, 2020, tinyurl.com/munbookwood.

Nestle, Joan. *A Restricted Country: Essays & Short Stories*. Sheba Feminist Publishers, 1987.

———. "The Will to Remember." *Journal of Homosexuality* 34, no. 3–4 (1998): 225–35.

Pourdes, M.D. *The Deviate Patterns*. Challenge Publications, 1966.

Reissner, Albert. *Female Perversions: Sex and the Lesbian*. Wee Hours, 1965.

Rich, Adrienne. "Compulsory Heterosexuality and Lesbian Existence." *Signs* 5, no. 4 (1980): 631–60.

Rubin, Gayle. "Of Catamites and Kings: Reflections on Butch, Gender, and Boundaries." In *Transgender Studies Reader*, edited by Susan Stryker & Stephen Whittle, 471–81. Routledge, 2006.

Salem, Randy. *Baby Face*. Softcover Library, 1964.

———. *Chris*. Naiad, 1989.

———. *The Sex Between*. Midwood, 1962.

Seeley, E.S. *Sorority Sin*. UPD Book Export Inc, 1965.

Sela, Lora. *I Am a Lesbian*. Saber, 1959.

Simmons, Christina. "Companionate Marriage and the Lesbian Threat." *Frontiers: A Journal of Women Studies* 4, no. 3 (1979): 54–59.

Sinclair-Palm, Julia. "'It's Non-Existent': Haunting in Trans Youth Narratives About Naming." *Bank Street Occasional Paper Series 2017*, no. 37 (2017): 1–13. tinyurl.com/Sinclair-Palm.

Smith, Elizabeth A. "Butches, Femmes, and Feminists: The Politics of Lesbian Sexuality." *NWSA Journal* 1, no. 3 (1989): 398–421.

Storms, Michael D. "Theories of Sexual Orientation." *Journal of Personality and Social Psychology* 38, no. 5 (1980): 783–92.

Taylor, Valerie. *Whisper Their Love*. Little Sister's Classics. Arsenal Pulp Press, 2006.

unattributed. "The Petit Maître, 1749." In *Homosexuality in Eighteenth-Century England: A Sourcebook*, edited by Rictor Norton. Rictor Norton (online), 2000.

Wade, Carlson. *Sexual Behavior of the Lesbian*. Imperial, 1964.

Weinstein, Jeff. "In Praise of Pulp." *Voice Literary Supplement* (October 1983): 8–9.

Weir, Angela, and Elizabeth Wilson. "The Greyhound Bus Station in the Evolution of Lesbian Popular Culture." In *New Lesbian Criticism*, edited by Sally Munt, 95–113. Harvester Wheatsheaf, 1992.

Weissman, Aerlyn, and Lynne Fernie. "Forbidden Love: The Unashamed Stories of Lesbian Lives." National Film Board of Canada, 1993.
Whitbread, Jane. "A Report on Current Attitudes to Chastity." *Mademoiselle*, no. 49 (1959): 37–40.
Woodward, L.T. *Twilight Women*. Lancer, 1963.
Yusba, Roberta. "Twilight Tales: Lesbian Pulps 1950–1960." *On Our Backs*, Summer 1985: 30–31, 43.

IV "Everybody gets married."[1]

Love and marriage, love and marriage,
Go together like a horse and carriage.
Dad was told by mother:
You can't have one.
You can't have none,
You can't have one without the other.[2]

A theme beyond the authors' intentions

Ann Bannon was styled by Cleis, her twenty-first century publisher, "Queen of Lesbian Pulp Fiction,"[3] but this, to cognoscenti of the paperback-collecting world, is a marketing ploy, a matter of "retro kewl" and a "hipness signifier" rather than a reflection of reality.[4] Bannon herself has no objection to being thought hip,[5] and can't be blamed for that if the hipness keeps the profile of her work high, giving her pre-eminence in the sub-genre. But that hyperbolic title on the book covers and the three labels it contains have an unfortunate totalising effect. "Pulp" is a dubious nomenclature, as I have shown before, bracketing all cheap, ephemeral literature regardless of genre, niche, or quality of composition. "Queen" claims pre-eminence for Bannon; I won't quarrel with that assessment, but having said that, Cleis were quick enough to recruit as worthy courtiers, or even pretenders, Vin Packer, March Hastings, Carol Caine, and Della Martin, and would, I am sure, pick any others they thought they could place amongst their current catalogue of erotica, or even challenge for Bannon's metaphorical crown. "Lesbian" is the label which, perhaps surprisingly, gives the most trouble, as it is the one which is most totalising. Judith Butler is scathing about "identity categories"

1 Ann Bannon, *Beebo Brinker* (Cleis, 2001). 22.
2 Sammy Cahn, "Love and Marriage,"(1955).
3 Bannon, *Beebo Brinker*. Rear cover.
4 This was a comment made to me within a Facebook thread, by private enthusiast Todd Mason, in 2018.
5 Personal email, 30th September 2018.

DOI: 10.4324/9781003422679-5

"Everybody gets married." 135

as "instruments of regulatory regimes,"[6] even when they are seized on by the (self-)categorised as rallying points. To give a modern-day contrast, broadcaster and writer Sue Perkins describes being gay as "maybe the 47th most interesting thing in my life;"[7] but the baldly stated "Lesbian" in "Lesbian pulp" attempts, as a marketing strategy, to fix sexuality as the overriding characteristic of the writer, the theme, and the identity of each protagonist along with that of several supporting characters. It may even have been Bannon's intention, under the market-savvy eye of editor Dick Carroll, to let that identity steer her novels.[8] Christopher Nealon states unequivocally that "the project of Bannon's books, of course, is to present homosexuality as an acceptable identity – and, more than that, as an acceptable *life*,"[9] stressing the very totalisation with which Judith Butler takes issue. However, when asked in 2018 whether she had been aware of having a specific project, Ann Bannon said:

> I was lucky, in that my book came along a few years after [Vin Packer's *Spring Fire*], and the social contumely and Congressional restrictions on LGBT literature were slowly fading. As other books followed *Odd Girl Out*, I was able to ponder, if only tangentially, the effect of my stories on my readers. I should have thought more deeply about this than I did.[10]

The intention of the author and the niche into which a publisher thrusts a novel, do not necessarily mean that that is what the novel deals with. People, and by extension characters in novels, "refuse, unhappily, to function in so neat and one-dimensional fashion," as James Baldwin says.[11] That is why I now take the opportunity to challenge one of the givens about this literary niche; I suggest that, whether intentionally on Bannon's part or not, the salient theme in her novels, and in those of her contemporaries, is that of the relationship, specifically the relationship between couples, and that this theme often overtakes the issue of the sexuality of any of the characters in a

---

6 Judith Butler, "Imitation and Gender insubordination," in *The Lesbian and Gay Studies Reader*, ed. Michèle Aina Barale Henry Abelove, & David M. Halpin (Routledge, 1993). 308.

7 "Being gay is the 47th most interesting thing about me," Chortle, 2013, tinyurl.com/Gay47th

8 Although when Dick Carroll accepted the cut-down second draft of Bannon's first novel, *Odd Girl Out*, he did so unaltered and without even inserting the word "lesbian" into the text. Ann Bannon, *Odd Girl Out* (Cleis, 2001). vii.

9 Christopher Nealon, "Invert-History: The Ambivalence of Lesbian Pulp Fiction," *New Literary History* vol.31, no.4 (2000). 757.

10 Personal email, 30th September 2018.

11 James Baldwin, "The Preservation of Innocence," in *Collected Essays* (The Library of America, 1998). 600. The full quotation runs "It is quite impossible to write a worth-while novel about a Jew or a Gentile or a Homosexual, for people refuse, unhappily, to function in so neat and one-dimensional fashion." This is equally true when applied to a lesbian protagonist.

136 *"Everybody gets married."*

relationship. I have already shown the importance and salience of the father-daughter relationship, and I do not intend to reintroduce it here. As broadly hinted at in the heading of this chapter, I shall focus on marriages and other *ménages à deux*, and on the family life built around them, in Bannon's work and in the work of some of her contemporaries. Throughout, it is not only the central characters who face perplexities, but most of the other characters, even relatively peripheral ones too. All relationships shown in her novels are fraught with problems, obliging us to ask, "what is 'normal'?"

In the hundred-and-thirty or so years in which the term "heterosexuality" has been in use, its meaning has morphed from indicating a sexual pathology[12] to describing the statistical norm of sexuality – essentially the means by which humankind reproduces. In the same period, that norm has accrued much beyond its simple definition. Especially it has inherited from earlier models and cultures, such as the monotheistic world religions, the structure of monogamous couplehood and the institution of marriage. Even if it is nothing more than a handy, structural, societal tool, marriage is now emblematic of heteronormativity, inextricable from the societal norms of male and female behaviours, and thus any *ménage* can be assumed to be somehow heteroemulative.[13] This assumption is reflected in Foucault's assertion that a norm brings with it a principle of both qualification and correction, being always linked to a positive technique of "intervention and transformation,"[14] and in the following observation by Karma Lochrie:

> One of the byproducts of our statistically realized experience of the world is the concept of the norm, both an average and a collective ideal, like the American Family and Family Values in American politics. One part the quantified creation of census bureaus and pollsters and one part cultural ideology, the norm is no longer just the most frequent segment of a distribution curve. It is also that which is the most desirable. Norms have become a way of life – have become normative – insofar as they structure our decisions and our values [...][15]

---

12 Bukk G. Carleton, *A Practical Treatise on the Sexual Disorders of Men* (Boericke, Runyon & Ernesty, 1898). 121.

13 My coining. If "heteronormative" expresses the normalising pressure of heterosexuality, then "heteroemulative" expresses the conforming responses to the pressure, including from within heterosexuality.

14 Michel Foucault, *Abnormal: lectures at the College de France, 1974–1975*, trans. Graham Burchell, ed. Valerio Marchetti and Antonella Salomoni (Verso, 2016). 50. This does not contradict Foucault's principle that assembling a group is a process of exclusion, not inclusion; rather it states that the "like" within a taxonomy is an internal product rather than a pre-requisite. See pages 43 and 44 in Chapter I.

15 Karma Lochrie, *Heterosyncrasies: Female Sexuality When Normal Wasn't* (U of Minnesota P, 2005). 9.

"Everybody gets married." 137

In 1950s America, in the new suburbs modelled on Levittown, the Depression of the 1930s and the disruption of World War II were all but forgotten under the "Exurbanite"[16] norm of the working father, the domestic mother, and the schoolkids of the cereal packet, the Christian leaflet,[17] and situation comedies such as *I Love Lucy*.[18] However, this chapter will show that the examples of couplehood in the texts under study, far from being ideal in any way, are unstable to the point of offering direct resistance to Foucault's internal intervention and transformation.[19] Even the most superficially conventional partnership within these novels has too many "radical inconsistencies"[20] to be considered stable, and therefore this is a good moment to reintroduce the issue of "disappearing heteronormativity." Bannon herself was writing from within a long-standing marriage which had its share of tensions. She considers it to have been an unbalanced and difficult relationship, her husband being older than she was, he having the expectations of "a Victorian *pater familias*,"[21] and her treatment of relationships in her writing shows the effect of her marriage.

In the following section of this chapter, **Marriages and *ménages*: incest**, I will start by looking at Bannon's novel *The Marriage* as a reversal of the conventions established by some of America's earliest Romantic writers, who presented sibling incest in their fiction as a symbol of all that was baleful and destructive in their nation's democratic experiment. As Bannon implied, her novel came at a time when America's obsession with the "Lavender scare"[22]

---

16 Auguste Comte Spectorsky, *The Exurbanites* (Lippincott, 1955).

17 I am thinking in particular of one postcard headed "Let's all go next Sunday," with a quotation from Psalm 122:1 at the bottom. It is a well-enough known image from the 1950s but seems to be unattributable.

18 *I Love Lucy* was probably the most popular American, family-based situation comedy of the 1950s. Even the fact that it featured, as the working father of the family, a Cuban bandleader, did not render it sufficiently unconventional to blunt its overall conventionality.

19 See page 43 in Chapter I.

20 I take this phrase from Edmund Leach's 1968 examination of the "cereal packet" family. The phrase comes from elsewhere in this paragraph: "The contemporary [...] stereotype of the monogamous, neolocal (i.e. two generation) elementary family has a marked "matrifocal" emphasis – the king-pin [sic] of the structure tends to be "mum" rather than "dad." From any historical or ethnographic point of view this is a very unusual form of domestic grouping and in all probability it is a transient form." Edmund Leach, "The cereal packet norm," *The Guardian*, January 29 1968. 8. Leach's article refers to British families, but I have taken that reference out, and could easily drop in the word "American" without invalidating the statement.

21 Personal email, 22nd September 2020.

22 This is not a 1950s term as such; rather it is the title of a more recent book about McCarthyism's persecution of gays, by David K. Johnson, in which he spoke of the "Red Scare" having "a tinge of lavender." David K. Johnson, *The Lavender Scare: The Cold War Persecution of Gays and Lesbians in the Federal Government* (U of Chicago P, 2004). 16. He drew that phrase from a remark by Senator Everett Dirksen to the effect that the US State Department was full of "lavender lads." Stephen J. Whitfield, *The Culture of the Cold War*, 2nd ed. (Johns Hopkins UP, 1996). 44.

138 *"Everybody gets married."*

and a perceived communist threat to US democracy appeared to have lost a little of its public urgency, though not to have been removed completely. Thus her shift from concentrating on lesbian characters to introducing the subject of sibling incest is not all that surprising. It could be that the slight relaxing of public attitudes had, for Bannon, also relaxed the urgency of examining that aspect of sexuality; it could equally have been that her publisher was expecting something more sensational and sensationalist from her. The Fawcett Gold Medal cover proclaims, "As weird, as shocking, as honest as any story you have ever read."[23] Whatever the case may be, looking at that novel leads on, in the section **Marriages and *ménages*: "gay marriage,"** to consideration of the marriage of convenience, in particular to that of Laura Landon and Jack Mann, to whom the story of *The Marriage* is narrated, and whose ostensibly stable *ménage* brackets the narrative. The study of Laura's and Jack's couplehood, from *Women in the Shadows* onward, will go into considerable depth, and will examine it in the light of Monique Wittig's theory of heterosexuality and compulsory reproduction as a political regime.[24] From there, in the section **Marriages and ménages: the real marriage of convenience**, I will go on to look at issues of marriages, of convenience and otherwise, and heteronormativity as viewed by another author, Valerie Taylor, in her novel *Whisper Their Love*.[25]

A different kind of marriage of convenience, as a façade for Hollywood glamour, forms an important part of the Landon-Brinkeriad prequel, *Beebo Brinker*, with which I open the final section, **Marriage and divorce**. *Beebo Brinker* examines the radical inconsistencies and tensions in the couplehood of a businessman and a film star with a history of serial divorce. Their marriage is complicated by issues of sexuality, affairs and age differences in those affairs, abrogated and appropriated motherhood, and celebrity culture in the public eye. The character Leo Bogardus is the driving force of the Hollywood family. The focus of this chapter puts him in the position of family manager, rather than *pater familias*. The Bogardus marriage introduces further consideration of divorce in the texts under study, and of the attitudes towards divorce that formed the social context of the novels.

Marriages and *ménages*: incest

Ann Bannon published two books in 1960: *Journey to a Woman*, generally acknowledged as the fourth in the Landon-Brinkeriad, and *The Marriage*,

---

23 Ann Bannon, *The Marriage* (Fawcett Gold Medal, 1960). Front cover paratext.
24 Monique Wittig, *The Straight Mind and other essays* (Beacon, 1992). xiii, 6.
25 I feel justified in speaking of the author's "view" as expressed in the novel, as the more recent republication includes an interview with her, which gives clear indications why certain elements of the novel were put in place.

"*Everybody gets married.*"   139

which is usually excluded from that corpus.[26] I include it here, and indeed start with it, because the very title proclaims the base from which and yard-stick by which couplehood is conventionally measured. The eponymous marriage is a love match between two beautiful and intelligent heterosexual people, that is "so normal:"

> They took a small furnished apartment in Chicago. It was cramped and plain, but they loved it. They went to the movies, bought modernistic ashtrays, soaped each other and made love in the shower. It was all wonderful and all so normal [...][27]

Theirs might not have been a chaste relationship prior to marriage, a period in which there are, according to the superficial view of an Ivy League fresh-man cited in the section on male agency, two kinds of women, the type you marry and "the type you go out with for sex,"[28] but the premarital aspect of the relationship between Sunny and Page is a good step away from that dichotomy.

> By the following spring Sunny Rotheli was no longer a virgin. But it had all been accomplished in a beautiful place, at a beautiful time; a starry evening, a rich, perfumed hotel room, a dime-store diamond. Sunny had felt a wistful nostalgia for the drafty auto and the cold October moon, but it couldn't be helped. She had enough sense to realise she was special to him, and that he would not take her there where he had made love to so many other girls.[29]

Jack Mann pronounced Sunny to be "the kind of girl you marry," and "the one woman a man has got to like as well as love."[30] The implication in the passage above is that, in his time, Page had had relationships that had led to the back seat of a car, and indeed that Sunny harbours a certain regret that they would not experience together that particular locus of conven-

---

26 Ann Bannon herself regards it as a stand-alone novel and would not wish to see it repub-lished. Personal email, 30th September 2018. Julian Carter notes that the novel was never republished because it was "not of interest to lesbians." Julian Carter, "Gay Marriage and Pulp Fiction: Homonormativity, Disidentification, and Affect in Ann Bannon's Lesbian Nov-els," *GLQ: A Journal of Lesbian and Gay Studies* vol.15, no.4 (2009). 585. She notes further that all criticism of Bannon's work has proceeded as if *The Marriage*'s disappearance is inconsequential, and that even Bannon's official Web site mentions the book only to say that it is "not part of the Beebo Brinker chronicles." Carter, "Gay Marriage and Pulp Fiction: Homonormativity, Disidentification, and Affect in Ann Bannon's Lesbian Novels." 607n8.

27 Bannon, *The Marriage*. 32.

28 Jane Whitbread, "A Report on Current Attitudes to Chastity," *Mademoiselle*, no.49 (1959). 39.

29 Bannon, *The Marriage*. 19.

30 Bannon, *The Marriage*. 20.

140 *"Everybody gets married."*

tional teenage promiscuity.[31] The novel implies that this was during Page's "champagne playtime before he settled down to the beans-and-gravy of earning a living."[32]If Sunny had had other lovers before Page, she keeps this to herself.[33] The couple, both blond and green-eyed, form the kind of bond in which partners start to adopt each other's gestures and expressions.[34] They are defined conventionally by Page's professional progress.[35] The next logical step in family conventionality would be children; Sunny almost complains that "He's been after me since our wedding day to [have a baby],"[36] and indeed Sunny becomes pregnant early in the marriage.

Bannon telegraphs in advance, however, that the marriage was "a horrifying mistake."[37] Sunny's pregnancy comes before the revelation that she and Page were brother and sister, separated at an early age and separately parented.[38] The couple have diametrically opposed reactions to the news. Sunny maintains that their marriage must be saved, and any issues of morality dealt with later; Page, on the other hand, is certain that morality demands their separation.[39] He states "You can't be moral on a part-time basis. It's a condition, like being alive," as though morality was a matter of essentialism rather than a set of socially acceptable behaviours of a particular time.[40] To him, incest is "a childish, immature, emotionally crippling sort of thing."[41] Jack attempts to help Page come to terms with the moral aspect of the situation by revealing that he is gay, but to Page gay men are "pretty boys cruising the streets in ridiculously tight pants,"[42] and, offended by an act in a club where a man dances in a hula skirt,[43] he refers to Jack disparagingly

31 At the time the two characters met, Sunny was seventeen and Page twenty-eight. The age difference would go a long way to accounting for the disparity in experience. Bannon, *The Marriage*. 14. The encounter in Page's car (14–17) is passionate, but both of them hold back, Sunny even hinting that Page would have to wait until after marriage. 17.

32 Bannon, *The Marriage*. 20.

33 Page's questioning about "Did you ever [...] do this with anyone else?" appears to refer to a period after they had met, but when he was still "roaming around." Bannon, *The Marriage*. 29. However, Sunny had previously admitted that she had "done everything else *but*" (15) and that she was a virgin (16).

34 Bannon, *The Marriage*. 14.

35 Bannon, *The Marriage*. 47.

36 Bannon, *The Marriage*. 45. Bannon regarded this opening section of *The Marriage* as being "rather dull," and wished for some editorial input for the book in general. Her mind was already engaged in planning *Beebo Brinker*. Personal email, 16th December 2019.

37 Bannon, *The Marriage*. 21.

38 Bannon, *The Marriage*. 52.

39 Bannon, *The Marriage*. 63.

40 Bannon, *The Marriage*. 77.

41 Bannon, *The Marriage*. 98. This recalls Charlie's declaration that lesbianism was "kid stuff." Bannon, *Odd Girl Out*. 206.

42 Bannon, *The Marriage*. 81.

43 Bannon, *The Marriage*. 43.

"Everybody gets married." 141

as "queer,"[44] a "fag," and a "pansy."[45] Jack recites to him from the poetry of Lord Byron:

> For thee, my own sweet sister, in thy heart
> I know myself secure, as thou in mine;
> We were and are—I am, even as thou art—
> Beings who ne'er each other can resign;
> It is the same, together or apart,
> From life's commencement to its slow decline
> We are entwin'd—let death come slow or fast,
> The tie which bound the first endures the last![46]

It is not surprising that Ann Bannon, a university graduate of no mean intellect, would quote a canonical poet. On the face of it, however, this is not appropriate to the situation in the novel. Throughout the series of Bannon's novels, Jack always has an apposite wisecrack ready, but Lord Byron was a person of great privilege, a voluptuary perhaps, who could afford to ignore most of the world's conventions, although in fact rumours of his incestuous affair with his half-sister Augusta were never satisfactorily substantiated. People elsewhere, whose positions in society did not isolate them from morality, could not allow themselves the behavioural luxuries that Byron realised. The milieu of 1950s to 1960s middle-class America in which Page, Sunny, Jack, and Laura are depicted, was one in which respectability could not be so easily overturned. The graduate author, fluent enough in French to have read de Beauvoir's *La Deuxième Sexe* in its original language,[47] and of sufficient acumen to go on eventually to obtain a doctorate and to become a Professor of Linguistics, had been in an academic environment where not only Byron but such classics as Chateaubriand's *René*, or William Hill Brown's *The Power of Sympathy* were in the discursive field. The latter is widely considered to be the first American novel,[48] and both deal with incest between brother and sister. Accessing Byron, Bannon could equally have accessed Shelley's preface to *Laon and Cythna*, in which he says that incest is "only a crime of convention," and that in including it in his poetic work he is breaking through "the

---

44 Bannon, *The Marriage*. 105. The comment is shouted, with emphasis on the word "queer," to Sunny.
45 Bannon, *The Marriage*. 44. These words, along with "lousy queer," are used by Page whilst drunk.
46 Bannon, *The Marriage*. 78–79. George Gordon, Lord Byron, "Epistle to Augusta," *Poetry Foundation*, accessed 21st March 2019, tinyurl.com/ByronAugusta.
47 Personal email, 22nd September 2020.
48 In 1933, Milton Ellis declared it "the first serious attempt" at such. Milton Ellis, "The Author of the First American Novel," *American Literature* vol.4, no.4 (1933). 359. Philip Young put this claim under scrutiny, but suggests that "majority vote" gave it that status. Philip Young, ""First American Novel": "The Power of Sympathy," in Place," *College Literature* vol.11, no.2 (1984). 116.

142 *"Everybody gets married."*

crust of outworn opinions on which established institutions depend."[49] By contrast, the novel *The Power of Sympathy* by Bannon's compatriot Brown is typical of American Romanticism in its stance against solipsism[50] and self-absorption, symbolised by sibling incest, considering such things to be the avenue to dementia and eventual destruction.[51] In *The Marriage* Bannon will eventually overturn this literary establishment and side more with the French and English writers.

Chateaubriand's eponymous René longs for a mirror image of himself as a companion. In declaring *"O Dieu! Si tu m'avais donné une femme selon mes desirs; si, comme à notre premier père, tu m'eusses amené par la main une Eve tirée de moi-même..."*[52] he longs for an Eve, wrenched out of his own body. Bannon introduces Page to us as an Edenic, naked Adam upon whom his as-yet-unknown sister stumbles by chance.[53] Page is an ideal American young man – good looking, over six feet tall, blond, clean cut, and intelligent[54] – and Sunny is his blonde, green-eyed counterpart.[55] The overturning of Brown and the "dark Romantics"[56] is not achieved without a struggle, however. According to James D. Wilson, Brown et al. were writing at a time when they saw a self-destructive element implicit in their nation's experiment in democracy, a form of government which is fine if the soul is inspired by reason and by the divine, as the man of the enlightenment or the optimistic Romantic conceived it; but if the self is a morass of psychological disorder too weak to bear scrutiny, then democracy becomes an experiment in terror.[57] In the mid-twentieth century the experiment of American democracy, still relatively young in historical terms,[58] had been obliged to meet head-on the autocracies of Japan, Italy, and Germany. The emergence of America from isolation after World War II had pitted it against one-party states such as its former ally the

---

49 Roger Igpen and Walter E. Peck, eds., *The Complete Works of Percy Bysshe Shelley* (Ernest Benn Ltd, 1965). 247.

50 "[A] philosophical doctrine that we create the world in the act of perceiving it." James D. Wilson, "Incest and American Romantic Fiction," *Studies in the Literary Imagination* vol.7, no.1 (1974). 31.

51 Wilson, "Incest and American Romantic Fiction." 31. Wilson groups together with W.H Brown the "dark Romantics" Charles Brockden Brown, Nathaniel Hawthorne, Herman Melville, and Edgar Allan Poe.

52 François-René de Chateaubriand, *Atala. René* (Garnier Flammarion, 1964). 160.

53 Bannon, *The Marriage.* 13.

54 Bannon, *The Marriage.* 11.

55 Bannon, *The Marriage.* 14.

56 For an explanation of this term see Gary Richard Thompson, *Gothic Imagination: Essays in Dark Romanticism* (Washington State U P, 1974). 6.

57 Wilson, "Incest and American Romantic Fiction." 32.

58 And still with a long way to go; since Bannon started writing, the United States has seen Civil Rights come to a head in the 1960s, the "Hanging Chad" controversy of 2000, and since 2020 not only "Black Lives Matter" but also the reinvigorating of overt racism, a Presidential election attacked with the legal equivalent of a scattergun, the real violence of an invasion of Congress, and a potential Presidential candidate vowing to become a dictator on election.

"Everybody gets married." 143

Soviet Union, and the People's Republic of China. The time in which Bannon wrote was an era of American economic success and exceptionalism on the one hand, but also of paranoia about the still-perceived threat of communism to the American vision of democracy on the other. Paranoia is hardly a state inspired by reason and by the divine.

The struggle in *The Marriage* is displayed in the heated exchanges between Page and Sunny over what they should do, having discovered the illegality of their marriage. Page misinterprets Jack's arguments and personal revelation entirely, as a claim that "abnormality can be fun."[59] Over two pages of text, Page and Sunny argue about what Jack had been trying to tell them. Sunny says that Jack's point was that one can live with abnormality, not "turn tail and run."[60] Bannon gives Sunny the harshest words she says to Page in the whole novel:

> "You're a damn coward, Page. You're afraid of Jack because he's more of a man than you are [...] He has guts. I mean that, Page. He had the courage to tell you a terrible secret, to risk losing your affection and respect – which by the way he did – because he had faith in you. He wanted to help. His mistake was that you weren't worth it [...] I know what Jack is, and he isn't degenerate. If you had his courage you'd be a better man."
>
> "*You're* the coward, Sunny, as long as we're pointing fingers. You're the one who's clinging to the rosy dream."[61]

Page compares their relationship to the hypothetical case of their father forcing himself upon Sunny, to which comparison she is vehemently opposed;[62] they quarrel about whether to abort Sunny's pregnancy, Page being initially for it as the only recourse, but later calling it "murder."[63] Whilst it is fairly obvious that Bannon inclines to Sunny's side in these confrontations, she gives Page his own stance, and allows him to point out weaknesses in her arguments, though Sunny says later, in a letter to Laura, "I don't think either of us really knew what courage meant that day."[64] An acknowledgement of courage comes later, when the couple are stranded in the desert and in danger of death.[65] Whilst this episode is a melodramatic interjection, almost seeming to be padding in an otherwise too short novel, a shared adversity does

---

59 Bannon, *The Marriage*. 105.
60 Ibid.
61 Bannon, *The Marriage*. 106.
62 Bannon, *The Marriage*. 101.
63 Bannon, *The Marriage*. 70, 72.
64 Bannon, *The Marriage*. 109.
65 Bannon, *The Marriage*. 161–176. One clearly heteronormative aspect of this episode is the way in which Page is cast as the strong, protective male, and Sunny as the weak, protected

144   *"Everybody gets married."*

reconcile the sibling lovers, and by the end of the novel also reconciles them to their parents and to their newly-born child.[66] The legal institution of marriage may not have been overturned, but Page and Sunny have, in the final analysis, not turned tail and run.

It is worth noting that, in dealing with incest, Bannon not only returned to a theme from Romantic literature, but also was neither alone amongst the paperback writers of the 1950s and 1960s in doing so, nor far removed from reality. In 1955 Berkley published the thirty-five-cent, lesbian-themed paperback *My Sister, My Beloved* by Edwina Mark.[67] In 1961 *One* magazine announced almost gleefully the *"cheap* thrill" to be had from books published under the related Fabian and Saber imprints. The magazine declared: "Happily for the publishers, some of their books are under attack as "unfit for public reading because they deal with sex too intimately." This should bolster sales considerably."[68] One of the 1961 Saber titles was Kip Madigan's *Incest for René*; banned unread by a court, it was republished simply as *René*.[69] 1963 saw the publication of Valerie Taylor's *A World Without Men*, the second in her "Erika Frohmann Series," in which protagonist Kate's and her brother Paul's first experience of sex is with each other.[70] In 1965, Edwin West's *Brother and Sister* was published by Monarch Books, proudly proclaiming itself "A Tender and Compassionate Novel of Incestuous Love,"[71] but in fact echoing the destructive theme of the early nineteenth century by ending in death and madness. Bannon's theme of unwitting love between two related people is echoed in real life; in *Pleasure and Danger*, Carole S. Vance notes:

> Prosecutions are rare, but two were reported recently. In 1979, a 19-year-old Marine met his 42-year-old mother, from whom he had been separated at birth. The two fell in love and got married. They were charged and found guilty of incest, which under Virginia law carries a maximum ten-year sentence. During their trial, the Marine testified, "I

---

female. However, as I point out, the episode is not the strongest aspect of the otherwise short plot.

66 Bannon, *The Marriage*. 184.

67 Republished in the UK as *My Sister, My Bride* by Corgi Books.

68 Dick Tyner, "Books," *One: The Homosexual Viewpoint*, no.1 (1961). 29.

69 Tyner, "Books." 29.

70 Paul and Kate, who were fourteen and twelve at the time, have severe problems later in their lives. Paul becomes a virtual hermit, and eventually is sentenced to life imprisonment for an apparently senseless murder. Kate struggles with alcoholism. Though the blame for this is probably the cruelty and beatings inflicted on them by their father, the novel depicts them both as carrying a lot of guilt, but Kate as willing to take up Paul's burden, to "to run to Paul and tell him it was all right – he could lay down the burden of his guilt and she would pick it up." Valerie Taylor, *A World Without Men* (Volute, 1982). 147.

71 Edwin West, *Brother and Sister* (Monarch Books, 1965). Front cover. Edwin West was one of the pen names of Donald E. Westlake.

"*Everybody gets married.*"   145

love her very much. I feel that two people who love each other should be able to live together." In another case, a brother and sister who had been raised separately met and decided to get married. They were arrested and pleaded guilty to felony incest in return for probation. A condition of probation was that they not live together as husband and wife. Had they not accepted, they would have faced twenty years in prison.[72]

Beyond Bannon's intellectual background, connecting any of the fiction under study directly to Romantic literature is tenuous. Considering that in its marketplace lesbian- and gay-themed fiction would sit with westerns, detective fiction, romances in the popular sense, and much else,[73] and within the lesbian niche would sit works diverse in theme, subject treatment, and indeed literary quality, all the cheap books of the paperback heyday could be said to align with the hostility of Romanticism itself to genre. Romanticism specialist David Duff states that this argument "has taken many forms, the most radical of which, dating from the period itself, equated Romanticism with an outright rejection of received literary categories."[74] It might have given some satisfaction, therefore, to those who rejected the idea of genre, to see cheap paperback versions of Hawthorne's *The Scarlet Letter*, Melville's *Moby Dick*, Poe's *The Fall of the House of Usher*, and Charles Brockden Brown's *Wieland* on the same newsstand racks as Ann Bannon, Mickey Spillane, and Zane Grey. The 1950s and 1960s saw a film version of *Moby Dick* and Roger Corman's series of films based on the Poe canon, including his adaptation *The House of Usher*. Therefore if there is an obvious link between my area of study and the early Romantic writers, particularly the Americans, it is their shared place in popular culture and in the popular imagination.[75] Other links, such as the outing of a woman for her sexual behaviour in *The*

---

72 Carole S. Vance, *Pleasure and Danger: Exploring Female Sexuality* (Pandora, 1992). 305. The cases were reported in the following: unattributed, "Marine and Mom Guilty of Incest," *San Francisco Chronicle*, November 16 1979. Clark Norton, "Sex in America," *Inquiry*, October 5 1981. 18. In the case of the brother and sister reported by Norton, however, the couple had sought each other out and knew they were related.

73 When I asked Frédéric Savard of the National Film Board of Canada whether a still shot of a bookstand with mixed genres, within the documentary *Forbidden Love* was an original, he replied that it was an archive picture (personal email, 29th October 2018). According to collectors *d'un certain age*, who recall how paperbacks were marketed, only larger outlets would segregate paperbacks by apparent genre or theme. A photo from the front cover of *Sunday Midwest*, the weekend magazine of the *Chicago Sun-Times* for December 6th, 1959, shows a similarly diverse selection of paperbacks on a newsstand at the Union Station.

74 David Duff, *Romanticism and the Uses of Genre* (Oxford U P, 2009). 1.

75 It has to be said, however, that both early Romantics and contemporaneous lesbian-themed fiction would, along with cheap paperbacks of, say, *Pride and Prejudice* and *Rebecca*, have been so many drops in a large bookstand ocean.

146   *"Everybody gets married."*

Scarlet Letter, the implied incest in Poe's Usher family whose stem "lay in the direct line of descent, and had always, with very trifling and very temporary variation, so lain"[76] and where only a brother and sister remain of that stem, and the relationship between brother and sister in *Wieland*,[77] are matters of speculation.

Marriages and *ménages*: the "gay marriage"

"Could their love tower above society's deepest taboos?" asked the main cover paratext of *The Marriage*.[78] The radical inconsistency of sibling love remaining uncrushed within the ambit of heteronormativity is a direct challenge to that normative pressure. The story of this inconsistency is bracketed by another marriage, that of Jack, the indirect storyteller, and Laura. Further paratext said:

> Laura and Jack Mann, featured in Ann Bannon's other bestselling books, tell the compelling story of a marriage made in hell ... the story of two golden people, in their love and their agony – living in a wild twilight world, carrying a dread and damning secret deep inside them.[79]

The rear cover paratext first lists all of Bannon's corpus – the Landon-Brinkeriad – doubtless to attract existing readers with trigger words such as "love," "agony," "wild," and "twilight," the latter most often being used in a lesbian context. At the nadir of Page's and Sunny's marriage, Laura and Jack ask each other, "How come two inverts like us can make a marriage work, and two normal people [...] can't?"[80] Bannon states that for them love and marriage were inviolate, therefore fully emulative of the heterosexual ideal, although Laura says to Jack "it hurts you to see me with a woman."[81] This tension within the "[making] a marriage work" and its supposed inviolability is exacerbated by the fact that, whilst Laura continues to enjoy sex, presumably without forming fixed partnerships, Jack has "renounced the painful homosexual adventures that used to fill his life before he got married," and

---

76 Edgar Allan Poe, *The Fall of the House of Usher and Other Writings* (Penguin Classics, 2003). 94.
77 Leslie Fielder is one critic who considers Theodore and Clara in *Wieland* to have an incestuous relationship. Leslie Fiedler, *Love and Death in the American Novel* (Stein and Day, 1966). 36.
78 Bannon, *The Marriage*. Front cover.
79 Bannon, *The Marriage*. Rear cover.
80 Bannon, *The Marriage*. 9. Jack replies "If I could explain that, I'd write a book." Julian Carter reminds us that "*The Marriage* is that book." Carter, "Gay Marriage and Pulp Fiction: Homonormativity, Disidentification, and Affect in Ann Bannon's Lesbian Novels." 600.
81 Ibid.

in his celibacy has become socially clumsy and anxious around any of his gay former acquaintances.[82]

Jack and Laura's marriage comes about from his persistence in asking her to marry him. At the beginning of *Women in the Shadows*, Laura confides to her notebook "*Jack asked me to marry him again ... but I could never marry a man, not even him. Never.*"[83] This note is made against the backdrop of the disintegration of her current relationship with Beebo Brinker, and is ironic given the outcome of the novel. At its opening, Beebo and Laura are celebrating a milestone in their relationship. Laura writes, "*Today was our second anniversary. If I have to go on living with her I'll go crazy. But if I leave her – ? I'm afraid to think what will happen.*"[84] The milestone has become a millstone, and the passion between the two is now "*the corpse of that romance.*"[85] Beebo fights tooth-and-nail against the demise of their relationship, by the desperate and despicable measures I described in Chapter II; but by the time of their final separation, which actually occurs after Jack and Laura have got married, it is Beebo who faces separation more realistically. Laura has returned to Beebo and has resolved to go and talk to her husband and be back at Beebo's apartment for good in two hours; Beebo says "I doubt it," and in response to Laura's plea not to talk as though nothing mattered any more, says, "Jack still matters, baby. Don't do it to him too."[86] If Laura would return to Jack, Beebo would equate it to a sign of maturity – "You're his wife. Either go home to him and grow up or don't go back"[87] – implying that fidelity to someone whom the law regards as a husband is somehow superior to the "child stuff" and "kid stuff" of lesbianism[88] and even the "immature, crippling" nature of incest.[89]

However, it is not simply the disintegration of the lesbian relationship that draws Laura and Jack into marriage. In a conversation with Beebo, Jack reveals the real reason why, contrary to his and Laura's individual sexualities, he wants to marry her:

"Jack, you don't want to get married."
"I know. It's ridiculous, isn't it?"
"What would you do if she said yes?"
"Marry her."

---

82 Bannon, *The Marriage*. 42.
83 Ann Bannon, *Women in the Shadows* (Cleis, 2002). 2. The suggestion is also made by Terry, Jack's boyfriend, in a section cut from *Women in the Shadows* and published separately. Ann Bannon, "The Nice Kid," *ONE Magazine* vol.9, no.1 (1961). 25.
84 Bannon, *Women in the Shadows*. 1.
85 Ibid.
86 Bannon, *Women in the Shadows*. 187.
87 Bannon, *Women in the Shadows*. 186.
88 Bannon, *Odd Girl Out*. 205, 206.
89 Bannon, *The Marriage*. 98.

148 *"Everybody gets married."*

"Why?"

"I love her."

"Drivel! You love me. Marry me."

"I could live with her, but not with you," he said. "I love her very much. I love her terribly."

"That's not the reason you want to marry her. You can love her unmarried as well as not. So what's the real reason? Come on."

If he had not been so drunk he would probably not have said it.

"I want a child," he admitted suddenly, quietly."[90]

Jack has referred to Laura by the nickname "Mother" since early in the previous novel *I am a Woman*.[91] He jokes that it is "in honor of my Oedipus complex,"[92] but by then the real reason has been revealed. In some way, Jack has always seen Laura as the mother of his child, and has held to the regime of heterosexuality in that particular heteroemulative way.[93] I use Monique Wittig's term "regime" rather than "institution" here,[94] as Jack's desire is, despite his genuine love for her, for her "submission and appropriation" in "the compulsory reproduction of the "species" by women [as] the system of exploitation on which heterosexuality is economically based."[95] His revelatory conversation with Beebo continues:

> Jack stood in front of her, the faintest sad smile on his face. "It would be a girl," he mused. "She'd have long pale hair, like Laura."
>
> "And horn-rimmed glasses like her old man."
> "And she'd be bright and sweet and loving
> "With *dames* anyway."
> "With me."
> "Oh, God! All this and incest, too!" And Beebo's laughter, cruel and helpless, silenced him suddenly. He couldn't be angry, she meant no harm. She was writhing in a net of misery and it eased the pain when she could tease. But the lovely child of his dreams went back to hide in the secret places of his heart.[96]

---

90 Bannon, *Women in the Shadows*. 16–17.

91 Ann Bannon, *I am a Woman* (Cleis, 2002). 30.

92 Bannon, *Women in the Shadows*. 166.

93 I do not claim that this is the only way that Jack sees Laura, and the only reason he gives her this nickname. He also says that "a boy's best friend is his mother," which implies that the nickname can be read as an expression of their friendship. Bannon, *I am a Woman*. 31.

94 Wittig, *The Straight Mind and other essays*. xiii.

95 Wittig, *The Straight Mind and other essays*. 6.

96 Bannon, *Women in the Shadows*. 17.

"Everybody gets married." 149

Beebo's gibe about incest is a reverberation from Laura's violent encounter with her father,[97] and reverberates in turn with Page's comparison of sex between himself and Sunny to the hypothetical case of her father forcing himself upon her.[98] If there can be no hint of sexual incest in Jack's longings, then neither is there any hint of Laura's involvement in parenthood in this exchange, beyond providing the daughter with her looks. The child will belong to Jack as surely as ever *"les enfants appartiennent au père."*[99]

It is Laura who makes the final proposal of marriage, and Jack of course accepts, as it is what he had wanted all along; they marry in a civil ceremony which seems to be a conveyor belt of "half a dozen other sweating, hand-clasping couples,"[100] and the next few pages describe their setting up what they hope will look like a "normal" marital partnership. In a gesture of what can only be described as respectability politics, Jack makes the following declaration:

> "Ours will be a happier marriage than any of these," he said with a contemptuous wave of his hand. He sat down suddenly beside her. "Ours could be damn near perfect, Laura, if we work at it a little. You know that? We won't have to face the usual pitfalls. Ours will be different ... better."[101]

This is Jack's vision of their bourgeois respectability, their both being gay stripping away the "usual pitfalls" that almost guarantee marital tension in a 'normal' relationship. There is a paradox in his emulation of respectability whilst holding it in contempt. Laura is content to be guided by him in all things, letting him do the thinking and the planning, letting him take her by the hand and lead.[102] Her compliance contrasts with her rebellion against Beebo, her refusal to be dressed like a "damned princess;"[103] she is at ease, her tension alleviated, living in a pretty apartment where she could be "as lazy as a cat" and feel "like a princess."[104] The irony is complete. They cleave to what is "normal" as their yardstick: "You'd think we were a couple of normal people [...]" says Laura, to which Jack replies, "They have no monopoly on happiness, Mother. We have a right to our share."[105] This right to a share of happiness is entirely justifiable, but the fact is that in order to

---

97 Bannon, *I am a Woman.* 208.
98 Bannon, *The Marriage.* 101.
99 Colette Guillaumin, "Practique du pouvoir et idee de Nature: (1) L'appropriation des femmes," *Nouvelles Questions Feministes*, no.2 (1978). 11.
100 Bannon, *Women in the Shadows.* 110.
101 Bannon, *Women in the Shadows.* 111.
102 Ibid.
103 Bannon, *Women in the Shadows.* 29.
104 Bannon, *Women in the Shadows.* 116.
105 Bannon, *Women in the Shadows.* 113.

150   *"Everybody gets married."*

have it Jack and Laura feel they have to live heteroemulative lives. Normality is "real" and "straight;" "Jack filled her with determination to make herself a part of what he called "the real world," the *straight* world. He made it seem very desirable to her for the first time."[106] Their marriage helps them think of each other as "normal."[107]

Jack himself becomes celibate,[108] but in conceding that Laura is not, he insists: "There'll be women in your life [...] But there's only one man, and there will only be one man and don't you ever forget it."[109] Thus he takes possession of his wife as surely as she takes his surname, even if that possession does not directly imply sex between them. There is a level of physicality to their bond – there always has been, ever since Laura became content for Jack to show her affection earlier in their friendship:

> "Poor Laura." He said it sympathetically. "Come here, honey." He put his arms around her and held her, stroking her back. When he did it, she didn't mind. She'd have resented any other man ... except maybe Merrill Landon. But Merrill Landon never showed affection to anyone.[110]

> When she was frightened or depressed he held her and stroked her hair and talked to her the way she had always prayed her father would.[111]

At the end of *Women in the Shadows* this affection is amplified. Jack kisses Laura on the mouth,[112] and she nestles "against his warm body and relax[es] in the circle of his strength, a real strength, a man's strength" which feels very good to her.[113] The implication here is that Beebo's strength, even her courage in finally giving up Laura, is of an inferior sort.[114] This, then, is the closest that Bannon comes, after the genre-conventional *Odd Girl Out*, to

---

106 Bannon, *Women in the Shadows*. 114.
107 Bannon, *Women in the Shadows*. 119.
108 Bannon, *The Marriage*. 42.
109 Bannon, *Women in the Shadows*. 115.
110 Bannon, *I am a Woman*. 105.
111 Bannon, *Women in the Shadows*. 116.
112 Bannon, *Women in the Shadows*. 194.
113 Bannon, *Women in the Shadows*. 195.
114 Even though Laura says of her, "I respect and admire her. She's amazing. And much stronger than I gave her credit for." Bannon, *Women in the Shadows*. 195. An initial reaction to this is that it is rather over-the-top for the late maturing of a person who has killed two dogs, faked a rape, and half-strangled her lover – not to mention the contemptuous behaviour in *I am a Woman*. But on the other hand, perhaps Beebo was the "woman" in *I am a Woman*, inasmuch as her masculinity is what led to the subtitle *Must Society Reject Me?* and she has been involved in an uphill struggle since then, to emerge with her 'self' intact.

"*Everybody gets married.*"   151

making an ending where a male character succeeds in capturing an assumed lesbian principal.

It would be just so but for two important factors. Firstly, that it is specifically a pregnancy that cements the relationship and makes Laura believe that her future lies in conjugality with a man. I want to look at the following short passages together:

"I'm going to have a child [...] I'm going to be a woman."[115]

Here [Page] was, a man and a father, with the living proof of his virility in that bassinet [...][116]

"I've made a female of you!"[117]

On ne naît pas femme: on le devient.[118]

The first two, from Bannon's novels, serve to define "woman" and "man" in terms of their part in reproduction, and reproduction can be said to be "the system of exploitation on which heterosexuality is economically based."[119] Monique Wittig says that we have been compelled in our bodies and in our minds to correspond, feature by feature, with the *idea* of nature that has been established for us.[120] By "we" and "us" she is referring to women, but it can be seen from the first two lines above, by the frankly performative nature of each character's part in reproduction, that both a woman and a man here are defining themselves, declaring themselves to be either sex. Not that either of them may be conscious of this, certainly not Page if we are to take on board Wittig's statement that men do not need to express the fact that they dominate women all the time, for one can scarcely talk of domination over what one owns.[121]

But men are not a default, are not a neutral condition, and are as much produced by and maintained by the concepts of the heterosexual society as

---

115 Bannon, *Women in the Shadows.* 190.

116 Bannon, *The Marriage.* 184.

117 Lora Sela, *I am a Lesbian* (Saber, 1959). 184.

118 Simone de Beauvoir, *Le Deuxième Sexe*, vol.2 (Éditions Gallimard, 1976). 13.

119 Wittig, *The Straight Mind and other essays.* 6.

120 Wittig, *The Straight Mind and other essays.* 9.

121 Wittig, *The Straight Mind and other essays.* 4. Earlier in *The Marriage*, Bannon had said of Jack Mann that the news of Laura's pregnancy had given him "a soaring feeling that a normal man, sure of his virility, would never know," as though she is ascribing to Jack the achievement of a kind of hyper-virility by virtue of his part in reproduction. Bannon, *The Marriage.* 45. Julian Carter, however, reminds us that Laura's pregnancy is not the result of any conventional sex act, but that Laura is "the mother of the first test-tube baby in lesbian fiction." Carter, "Gay Marriage and Pulp Fiction: Homonormativity, Disidentification, and Affect in Ann Bannon's Lesbian Novels." 600. In fact, Laura's pregnancy is by artificial insemination, not *in vitro* fertilisation, which was not a scientific fact at the time that Bannon was an active author.

152 *"Everybody gets married."*

anyone else is. We lose sight of this because of their dominance, because of their defining, hegemonic role, and we ignore that they are just as trapped in it as women are by it. This is difficult to realise when considering the third quotation above; it is spoken by the rapist Bob in *I am a Lesbian*, as though his act of violence, along with his triumphant statement, not only confers femaleness on his victim but also, by implication, maleness on himself. It is falsely performative, but wholly indicative of a captive mindset.[122] It is in fact a prime example of the *non*-performative, because in this case "to name is not to bring into effect,"[123] unless we regard rape by a man to be the major agency how one "*devient femme.*" Bob certainly does.

The final quotation, perhaps Simone de Beauvoir's most famous words, seem on the face of it to support precisely what is being enacted or claimed in the previous three quotations, as though it is also possible to say "*on ne naît pas* homme, *on le devient.*" Gill Plain makes this point, when she says that in the conventionally gendered landscape of the twentieth century, masculinity is seen as a "mode of becoming – a separation from and, ultimately, a triumph over the feminine and the domestic."[124] The alternative to femininity and masculinity being matters of becoming, no matter how that becoming is effected, is that everything is decided at birth, when the midwife looks at the baby's genitals and an entry is made on a birth certificate. What follows may seem inevitable, a product of nature, but as Monique Wittig says, the masters (men) "explain and justify the established divisions as a result of natural differences," whereas "[it] is oppression that creates sex and not the contrary."[125] The baby in the bassinet and the baby that Laura is carrying are therefore *tabulae rasae*, with their future to be decided by what influences them from this point in the narratives onward; Jack's statement of intent – that his daughter would have long hair, and would be sweet and loving with him[126] – shows what he intends to write upon that particular *tabula*. It may not have been Ann Bannon's intention to make this particular challenge to heteronormativity, but in effect what she has done is laid bare how it is all a matter of power, even in her most favoured principals.

---

122 The rape itself does lead to a pregnancy, but the ensuing miscarriage serves to emphasise the false performativity of his declaration. Sela, *I am a Lesbian.* 76.
123 Sara Ahmed, *On Being Included: Racism and Diversity in Institutional Life* (Duke U P, 2012). 117.
124 Gill Plain, *Prosthetic Agency: Literature, Culture and Masculinity after World War II* (Cambridge U P, 2023). 3–4. Plain's book mostly concerns masculinity in post-war Britain rather than the United States, but this principle is relevant. She cites Arthur Flannigan Saint-Aubin's description of masculinity as "something to be achieved and experienced as a triumph over nature." Arthur Flannigan Saint-Aubin, "The Male Body and Literary Metaphors for Masculinity," in *Theorising Masculinities*, ed. Harry Brod and Michael Kaufmann (Sage, 1994). 241.
125 Wittig, *The Straight Mind and other essays.* 2.
126 Bannon, *Women in the Shadows.* 17.

"Everybody gets married." 153

The second important factor is that Laura's and Jack's is a marriage of convenience. Jack may have claimed that he and Laura won't have to face the "usual pitfalls" that affect heterosexual marriages, but the tensions in their marriage are, for all that they are unusual, just as real. Jack maintains celibacy and has given up his lifestyle (though not necessarily his love for Terry, with whom he was planning to go away until Laura came back to him).[127] He has also given up a substantial part of his social life, the residual elements of which are now an embarrassment to him.[128] Laura is not celibate although she cannot form a steady relationship with a woman, but she does realise that Jack harbours a kind of jealousy – "it hurts you to see me with a woman"[129] – although that doesn't stop her from taking advantage of even a married friend.[130] Their marriage is therefore only a triumph of heteronormativity in as far as it is wholly and deliberately heteroemulative, aligning to what Lisa Duggan calls "heterosexist institutions and values."[131] Duggan, and Julian Carter amongst others, refer to this mode of emulation as "homonormative."[132] Carter says that

> it is significant that the single instance of a happy marriage in these stories is what Bannon calls "gay marriage." That marriage is between a gay man and a lesbian woman [...] Bannon paints gay marriage in highly idealistic terms. Her lesbian wife and gay husband flourish together: their marriage provides them with emotional stability, material comfort, domestic calm, and access to social respect, all without requiring them to submit to the heterosexual mandate. For her, the fact that most observers read this couple as straight negates neither its partners' homosexuality nor the sincerity of their commitment to one another.[133]

What I have highlighted in the texts involving Jack and Laura, however, shows a different picture. Just because it has fewer superficial problems than most of Bannon's other couplehoods and is marked by a kind of general contentment, that makes it neither ideal nor idealistic. It is, in effect, an arrangement between a broody, newly celibate, gay man, whose celibacy now seems

---

127 Bannon, *Women in the Shadows*. 192.
128 Bannon, *The Marriage*. 42.
129 Bannon, *The Marriage*. 9.
130 Bannon, *The Marriage*. 45. Laura gets a frisson from holding and briefly kissing Sunny.
131 Lisa Duggan, "The New Homonormativity: The Sexual Politics of Neoliberalism," in *Materializing Democracy: Toward a Revitalized Cultural Politics*, ed. Russ Castronovo and Dana Nelson (Duke U P, 2002). 179.
132 Carter, "Gay Marriage and Pulp Fiction: Homonormativity, Disidentification, and Affect in Ann Bannon's Lesbian Novels." 583 *et seq.*
133 Carter, "Gay Marriage and Pulp Fiction: Homonormativity, Disidentification, and Affect in Ann Bannon's Lesbian Novels." 586.

154   *"Everybody gets married."*

almost akin to asexuality, and an aromantic, allosexual gay woman. Carter claims that their marriage is "sexless,"[134] but in fact it is only *mutually* and one-sidedly sexless. When Carter says that "In Bannon's books gay marriage is a haven for respectable gays whose erotic deviance is not clearly marked by signs of inversion or trans identification, and whose sexuality is not signaled as excessive by their class or racial marking,"[135] she is simply making an apologia for respectability politics, and papering over the difficulties in the relationship between Jack and Laura. Homonormativity, according to Carter, is how Bannon's characters

> mesh widely accepted signifiers of social normality with denigrated and deviant emotional impulses and erotic expressions. That combination is a source of considerable dramatic and affective tension, providing much of the sensational appeal of Bannon's novels.[136]

That very tension, however, illustrates my viewpoint, as does Carter's statement that "gay marriage" has "a history as the homonormative fantasy of a safe white space between a queer rock and a heterosexual hard place."[137] It is a fantasy of safety, not a reality where tensions, pitfalls, and problems do not exist. Any stability in Jack's and Laura's marriage is provided by their affectionate but platonic feelings for each other, which, as Beebo pointed out, did not need to be expressed by marriage.[138] It has been necessary to trace this marriage extensively from the texts, in order to show, apart from anything else, that there is much more to Jack Mann – much more that can be read in him – than simply the "good guy" of the narrative(s). If he cannot be considered a principal of the novels, in five out of six of which he appears, then he is certainly more than just a supporting character, as can be seen from what I have brought out in this chapter – his role in trying to shape others and to determine what will become of them.

---

134 Carter, "Gay Marriage and Pulp Fiction: Homonormativity, Disidentification, and Affect in Ann Bannon's Lesbian Novels." 595.

135 Carter, "Gay Marriage and Pulp Fiction: Homonormativity, Disidentification, and Affect in Ann Bannon's Lesbian Novels." 586.

136 Carter, "Gay Marriage and Pulp Fiction: Homonormativity, Disidentification, and Affect in Ann Bannon's Lesbian Novels." 587.

137 Carter, "Gay Marriage and Pulp Fiction: Homonormativity, Disidentification, and Affect in Ann Bannon's Lesbian Novels." 587–588. Carter quotes Warner, Somerville, and Jakobsen, all of which I have to hand.

　　Michael Warner, *The Trouble with Normal: Sex, Politics, and the Ethics of Queer Life* (Harvard U P, 1999).

　　Siobhan B. Somerville, "Queer *Loving*," *GLQ: A Journal of Lesbian and Gay Studies* vol.11, no.3 (2005).

　　Janet R Jakobsen, "Sex + Freedom = Regulation: WHY?," *Social Text* vol.23, no. 3–4 (2005).

138 Bannon, *Women in the Shadows*. 16–17.

"Everybody gets married." 155

Marriages and *ménages*: the real marriage of convenience

The marriage of convenience is an important theme not just in Bannon's work, but more generally within lesbian paperbacks of this period, where it enables writers to explore the social dominance of heterosexuality. In Valerie Taylor's *Whisper Their Love*, which was courageous enough to deal frankly with issues such as abortion and suicide, and which became one of the paperbacks of the period to attract the attention of a later publisher,[139] a marriage of convenience comes under brief but intense scrutiny. I have referred to this novel in an earlier chapter, specifically to comment on the "male prestige"[140] of the older lesbian character. The marriage of convenience opens the way for a study of the heterosexual regime in general in the novel, and for comparison with what has been seen so far in her contemporary Bannon's writing.[141] In what follows I shall quote at length from a few pages in a single chapter, as this marriage of convenience and its social environment is dealt with in quite a densely packed episode. Fritzi and Anitra Schultz live in a house that appears to be "sleek and expensive, but not quite real,"[142] and "one of those self-consciously informal suburban houses built by people living beyond their means."[143] Joyce, the protagonist of *Whisper Their Love* takes to Fritzi but not to Anitra, whom she considers to be "a fake."[144] Their marriage differs from that of Jack and Laura in two major respects. Firstly it is not based on as deep an emotional connection, nor apparently on the same level of affection. Edith, Joyce's lover, calls it "one of the few sensible marriages I've known,"[145] and states that it is companionship that cements the relationship: "You can have a very fine companionship with a man as long as

---

139 *Whisper Their Love* was republished in 2006 by Arsenal Pulp Press in Canada. Many of Taylor's other books were republished by The Feminist Press in the 2010s. Bradley and Damon call *Whisper Their Love* "unsympathetic" and "over-written." Marion Zimmer Bradley and Gene Damon, *Checklist 1960: A Complete, Cumulative Checklist of Lesbian, Variant, and Homosexual Fiction, in English, or Available in English Translation, with Supplements of Related Material, for the Use of Collectors, Students, and Librarians* (Self-published by Marion Zimmer Bradley, 1960). Unnumbered. Mark Macdonald, in a puff for the book, calls it " a beacon of emerging lesbian consciousness," even though Taylor herself denies that it is at all a pro-lesbian novel. Valerie Taylor, *Whisper Their Love*, Little Sister's Classics, (Arsenal Pulp Press, 2006). 7, 238.
140 Simone de Beauvoir, *The Second Sex*, trans. Howard Madison Parshley (Picador, 1988). 367.
141 Though Taylor and Ann Bannon were active at the same time, and their times at Fawcett Gold Medal overlapped, Bannon has never given any indication of having read Taylor's work, nor of having met her. Bannon's work was overseen by editor Dick Carroll, whilst Taylor's, according to her 1998 interview, was under the aegis of Leona Hedler; in the same interview she says she did not have much contact with other writers at all. Taylor, *Whisper Their Love*. 232, 244. I can find no information at all about Leona Hedler.
142 Taylor, *Whisper Their Love*. 156. The description is also applied to Anitra herself.
143 Taylor, *Whisper Their Love*. 155.
144 Taylor, *Whisper Their Love*. 171.
145 Taylor, *Whisper Their Love*. 153.

156　*"Everybody gets married."*

he doesn't get any silly ideas. You'll discover that for yourself when you have a chance to get acquainted with a more mature type of man."[146] Fritzi and Anitra are trumpeted as "Really civilised people" in the opening words of the relevant chapter.[147] Secondly it has not induced either partner to be celibate. Fritzi often has a man friend staying with him because he "knows they're welcome."[148] Anitra's extra-marital activities are not mentioned, but in the course of a party at her house she leans her breasts against Joyce's back.[149]

One parallel with Laura and Jack can be seen in the couple's attitude to reproduction, expressed in Edith's words "They've even talked about having a child, to make the picture complete."[150] Of course this is only an assessment by one character, with her own overview of things, but it is the only assessment given in the novel. Here the child is not even contemplated as a figure of love, but only as a heteroemulative device to make the picture of a socially normal marriage complete. The inconsistency in Anitra's and Fritzi's marriage has much to do with the question of honesty, which is something Taylor comes back to frequently in the novel. Edith says, "People hate us because we're free of their petty restrictions, because we dare to love honestly, without a lot of little social conventions to back us up."[151] But earlier she has said "We can't be honest [...] We have to be careful," when referring to the lack of openness in the lives of gay people, and specifically to her liking "an evening out now and then" with men.[152] To Joyce this was "old stuff:"

> She'd heard it a hundred times before, and the first few renditions had made quite an impression on her. Nobody loves us, everybody hates us. The only thing that could get Edith worked up, besides making love, was the idea that everybody had it in for sex deviates, including God. Joyce was beginning to wonder if people were that much interested.[153]

Moreover, she cannot see why Anitra and Fritzi are married at all:

> "I don't see what they get out of it," she said.
> "Don't be dense," Edith said coldly. "Nobody questions them, don't you see? They're part of the conventional design, the pattern society wants to mold everybody into."

146　Taylor, *Whisper Their Love.* 154.
147　Taylor, *Whisper Their Love.* 153.
148　Ibid.
149　Taylor, *Whisper Their Love.* 161.
150　Taylor, *Whisper Their Love.* 54.
151　Ibid. The mention of "conventions" almost has an echo of Shelley's apologia for sibling incest in *Laon and Cythna*, already mentioned.
152　Taylor, *Whisper Their Love.* 84.
153　Taylor, *Whisper Their Love.* 154–155.

"Everybody gets married." 157

Yes, then where's the wonderful honesty? She didn't ask it.[154]

When, later, Joyce actually voices Edith's opinion that "[e]veryone's down on people like that" as her own, her eventual partner John says:

> "Not half as much as they're down on normal people," John said. "That's a lot of hooey, that propaganda they give you, how persecuted they are. Most people simply feel sorry for queers. They're sort of handicapped, like somebody with an artificial leg." He pondered. "More. An artificial leg doesn't have to handicap a person."[155]

The lack of interest and the pity make an interesting critique of 1950s gay existence, which contrasts with the statements given in the various introductions to Cleis republications; Ann Bannon, for example speaks of "the arrogant ignorance of the authorities" and "the contempt of conventional society"[156] of the police raids on bars,[157] and of being "an illegal social category [...] with no right to exist."[158] It also contrasts with the violence and discrimination during the same period that Leslie Feinberg writes about in *Stone Butch Blues*; the dichotomy here is one of class attitudes.

The unsympathetic portrayal of the marriage of convenience comes immediately before the chapter devoted to the visit to the tacky club, and the entrance and exit of the peripheral butch lesbian character Bobbie. Both episodes serve to mark Joyce's disenchantment if not with Edith, then certainly with the milieu she inhabits. It is worth remembering that *Whisper Their Love* is the first novel of Taylor's productive period,[159] and that it does not appear to have been intended as a "pro-lesbian" novel in any way. When asked if she had been pressured into giving her later novel *Stranger on Lesbos* a "sad ending" she said no, and also stated "People felt *Whisper Their Love* had a sad ending. The girl ends up with a nice young man and she is really not a lesbian she's a young girl looking for a mother figure."[160] The "mother figure" echoes, *in parvo*, Simone de Beauvoir's unmarried, professional, and by implication both virile and divine woman.[161] Ending up with a "nice young man" appears to vindicate de Beauvoir's view of a younger woman's

---

154 Taylor, *Whisper Their Love*. 155.
155 Taylor, *Whisper Their Love*. 175–176.
156 Bannon, *Odd Girl Out*. xi.
157 Bannon, *Odd Girl Out*. xiii.
158 Bannon, *Odd Girl Out*. xiv.
159 Though not her first novel per se. That had been *Hired Girl* four years previously in 1953.
160 Taylor, *Whisper Their Love*. 237. This appendix to the novel is a transcript of an interview Taylor gave to Irene Wolt, and which was featured in *Lesbian Review of Books* in 1998. On page 201 of the narrative text, Joyce says to Edith, "I don't need a mother any more [...] I've grown up."
161 de Beauvoir, *The Second Sex*. 367, 368, 369.

158 *"Everybody gets married."*

infatuation with an older woman as a transition, a temporary state: *"Elle est vouée à l'homme, elle le sait, et elle veut une destinée de femme normale et complete."*[162] Taylor goes on to say that ending up with the nice young man was "the way I intended it from the start. I didn't think of it at the time as a lesbian story because the lesbian [Edith] was something of a villain," and that even at the time the book came out "people thought [Joyce] should have remained a lesbian."[163]

For all that, *Whisper Their Love* is not an unsubtly anti-lesbian or pro-heterosexual novel. Taylor is much too astute a novelist to create a simply formulaic narrative, although "formulaic" is the word used by Barbara Grier, in her foreword to the Arsenal Pulp Press edition, to describe both the ending and the setting in a women's college.[164] There was little financial motive for Taylor to write what Grier calls "male masturbation fantasies,"[165] as "[w] riting lesbian novels doesn't pay much, anyway," and she never made more than a thousand dollars a year from her writing.[166] If there is a formulaic element to the novel, it does not lie so much in that admittedly familiar plot structure, with "a necessary façade of heterosexuality,"[167] but more that it follows de Beauvoir's description of a younger woman's infatuation with an older before developing the desire for a male partner. Before her relationship with Edith, Joyce is at the very least heterocurious. The first object of her curiosity is her mother's fiancé Irv Kaufman, a stocky, handsome *bon viveur*. Irv takes Joyce's virginity while her mother sleeps in the next room. To Grier, Joyce is "violated," and her commentary uses the word "rape" in an adjacent sentence.[168] Certainly Irv has cynically and selfishly violated the conventional code of monogamy, but in an expertly-phrased piece of writing, Taylor makes it absolutely clear that Joyce is the co-initiator of consensual sex.[169] The passage is neither romantic nor sordid, but nor is it devoid of eroticism; if anything it is slightly bathetic, with Joyce thinking Irv looks rather silly half-dressed and wishing she could see him fully naked. What it does, however, is signal Joyce's heterosexuality and foreshadows the exchange with John at the end of the narrative.

The aftermath of the encounter is less positive. Irv's vocabulary – "baby," "kid," "girl"[170] – is irritatingly infantilising; memory of the "quick brief

---

162 de Beauvoir, *Le Deuxième Sexe*, 2. 112. I cite the French version here because I am dissatisfied with the translation by Parshley at this point. My translation, if a little awkwardly phrased, is: "She is promised to man – she knows it – and wants a woman's destiny, normal and whole."
163 Taylor, *Whisper Their Love.* 238.
164 Taylor, *Whisper Their Love.* 14.
165 Grier in Taylor, *Whisper Their Love.* 11.
166 Taylor, *Whisper Their Love.* 235.
167 Grier again, in Taylor, *Whisper Their Love.* 16.
168 Grier, again, in Taylor, *Whisper Their Love.* 15.
169 Taylor, *Whisper Their Love.* 67–68.
170 Taylor, *Whisper Their Love.* 69–70.

"*Everybody gets married.*" 159

pain" presumably of the rupture of her hymen,[171] along with the "dull knife stabbing where you were tender, how sore and achey you were the next day, pains across your lower back and down the insides of your legs," though some of that could be due to sleeping on a Davenport sofa.[172] Irv's not unkindly-meant advice to "try and forget it"[173] is nonetheless crass; Joyce's internal, angry retort is, "Forget it, he says. Like hell I'll forget it. Who does he think he is?"[174] and she recalls the materteral opinion of "the dirtiness and meanness of men and women and what lay between them […] as if hot water and French soap could wash away the touch of a man's hot hands, the pressure of a man's body."[175] Having set up the later exchange between John and Joyce, Taylor quickly offers it a severe challenge. Joyce's resentment builds. "If a man put his hand on me I'd kill him," she thinks, and more specifically:

> She remembered, against her will, Irv Kaufman. That was one thing she really wanted to forget. What it was like – and then the kindness and regret in his voice. If he had come into the room at that moment she would have probably killed him.[176]

Having vowed not to forget Irv's attitude, here Joyce is tormented by not being able to forget him and, paradoxically, it is his "kindness and regret" that she most resents. She feels a sense of outrage.[177] It is ironic that Edith commends a relationship with "a more mature type of man"[178] when Joyce has already had and bitterly resents an encounter with a mature man. However, it is during the exchange with John, in the final two or three pages in the book, that her encounter with Irv is reappraised. John, who already knows about Joyce's affair with Edith, has been waiting patiently for her to tell him that she has also had sex with a man. She says, "It was horrible," and to his pressing with "Really horrible? You didn't like it at all?" she reacts with an "Oh!" of self-realisation.[179] John is unperturbed by her revelation that it was her "mother's husband,"[180] but instead goes to the apparent heart of the matter that has been troubling Joyce:

> "And of course you didn't encourage him or anything like that."

---

171 Taylor, *Whisper Their Love*. 70. This rupture is, admittedly, a simplistic way of looking at loss of virginity.
172 Taylor, *Whisper Their Love*. 71.
173 Taylor, *Whisper Their Love*. 70.
174 Taylor, *Whisper Their Love*. 73.
175 Taylor, *Whisper Their Love*. 72.
176 Taylor, *Whisper Their Love*. 117.
177 Taylor, *Whisper Their Love*. 136.
178 Taylor, *Whisper Their Love*. 154.
179 Taylor, *Whisper Their Love*. 224.
180 Ibid. This isn't strictly true. At the time Irv was her mother's fiancé. She does not, however, say "my stepfather."

160 *"Everybody gets married."*

If she could have laid her hand on something heavy, she'd have thrown it at him. She'd dragged out her darkest and most terrible secret – betrayed herself, she thought furiously – and he acted as if it were a thing that could have happened to anybody. As if he'd listened to millions of case histories. She was damned if she was going to be a case history. "If you knew how I hate you!" she said.[181]

It is difficult to read with equanimity an accusation of encouragement, but the actual episode with Joyce and Irv has no hint of coercion or non-consent. When her mother, whom she only calls "Mimi," encourages her to lean forward when putting on her bra so that she can produce a definite cleavage, it seems almost as though there has been collusion in making her alluring to the older man.[182] Irv excuses his predatory behaviour by citing Mimi's lack of interest in sex, saying he is determined to marry her anyway.[183] Joyce does not understand what he means, until she realises that Mimi is actually pregnant.[184] The wedding ceremony is banal, the clerk mumbling "words that should have been poetry."[185] When Joyce reacts with anger to John's challenge – anger that is more likely self-directed – he leaves, she pursues him, and within two pages they agree on an immediate marriage.[186]

This sudden and apparently romantic heterosexual ending almost comes as a surprise. Barbara Grier reads into it an intentional irony, wondering if Taylor was "sticking it to the man," and trying to circumvent postal regulations.[187] Taylor herself brushes this off with a single sentence in her interview.[188] In fact citing the US mail system is somewhat of a straw man argument, as the 1957 Annual Report of the US Postal Service states: "Most obscene material sold at newsstands is not sent through the mails."[189] I offer another possible explanation, and that is that Taylor, disapproving of the predatory nature of older exploiters of younger people's emerging sexuality – of which exploiters there are clearly two in *Whisper Their Love* – is using the whole book to advise young (heterosexual) women who are tempted to "visit" lesbianism, for whatever reason, to make a commitment or leave well alone. Whatever may be the case, the hasty marriage planned by John and Joyce – of which John says "This is only the beginning"[190] – carries with it

---

181 Taylor, *Whisper Their Love.* 224–225.
182 Taylor, *Whisper Their Love.* 61–62.
183 Taylor, *Whisper Their Love.* 69–70.
184 Taylor, *Whisper Their Love.* 70.
185 Taylor, *Whisper Their Love.* 73.
186 Taylor, *Whisper Their Love.* 225–227.
187 Grier's introduction in Taylor, *Whisper Their Love.* 19.
188 Taylor, *Whisper Their Love.* 238.
189 unattributed, *Annual Report of the United States Postal Service*, US Postal Service (1957). 88.
190 Taylor, *Whisper Their Love.* 227.

"Everybody gets married." 161

no more guarantee of success than does Irv's and Mimi's shotgun wedding or Fritzi's and Anitra's marriage of convenience. John's and Joyce's marriage may well turn out to be as destined to fail as that of Charlie's and Beth's at the end of Ann Bannon's *Odd Girl Out* was by the time of the setting of *Journey to a Woman*;[191] as Taylor did not write a sequel to this novel, that will have to rest as a speculation. The fact that the convention of marriage, whether supposedly heteronormative or heteroemulative, can be manipulated in the way that *Whisper Their Love* depicts, shows that its social strength is illusory.

Marriage and divorce

In 1946, screenwriter John Howard Lawson wrote about the illusion and reality of Hollywood, asserting that the Hollywood stereotype had not been manufactured accidentally, and calling it "a significant social phenomenon."[192] Whilst his purpose in writing was to draw attention to the political and economic interests that he believed threatened freedom of expression in the movie industry, he knew well enough about "the expensive foolishness about the stars that fills the fan magazines."[193] In *Beebo Brinker*, Ann Bannon introduces us to her idea of that expensive foolishness, in the part of the novel which begins with its protagonist delivering a pizza to the New York *pied-à-terre* of film star Venus Bogardus and her current husband Leo. The way Bannon uses word-play to name this couple seems more than the simple selection of fictitious names; there is something here that Lawson might consider manufactured to fulfil the Hollywood stereotype, to produce its glamour, its delusive or alluring charm. Both have given names with celestial connotations. Venus is a planet and a goddess. Leo is a constellation and correlates to the macho image of the King of the Beasts (to Venus, "Leo is my courage"[194]). The "Bogard" component of their name is a contraction of the French-American name "Beauregard," meaning "of beautiful features;"[195] however, once three letters are removed from the full name it spells "bogus," indicating a sham. Taking this further, there is also the vernacular word "bogart," which means to keep for oneself,[196] i.e. Leo keeps Venus. Leo is

---

191 See later in this section.
192 John Howard Lawson, "Hollywood: Illusion and Reality," *Hollywood Quarterly* one, no. two (1946). 232.
193 Lawson, "Hollywood: Illusion and Reality." 231.
194 Bannon, *Beebo Brinker*. 215,
195 This is certainly pertinent to Venus's continued beauty, if not to Leo's being "attractive without being handsome." Bannon, *Beebo Brinker*. 174. Against acting convention, Bannon appears to show Venus adopting her current husband's family name. Her original name is Jeanie Jacoby. Bannon, *Beebo Brinker*. 184.
196 The OED's earliest reference is to the film *Easy Rider, 1968*. The reference was to a song by The Fraternity of Man, which indicates that the word was in use before then. It is supposed to refer to the way movie actor Humphrey Bogart was often pictured with a cigarette hang-

162 *"Everybody gets married."*

her business manager and director as well as her husband, and he recognises that the appearances of a happy Hollywood marriage must be kept up, even though Venus has affairs with men and women.[197] Thus it is also a marriage of convenience, bolstering a public image for star-struck movie enthusiasts. Venus's son Toby – Leo's stepson – has grown up to his young teens "conversant with sophisticated sex beyond his years,"[198] having had a childhood "with men climbing in and out of Mom's bed while I played on the floor with my blocks."[199] Toby would have preferred

> a mother comfortably middle-aged and unpretentious, like other people's mothers. Instead, he had what other people thought he wanted, a glittering courtesan who couldn't kiss him at night for fear of smudging her mouth, who took him on vacation trips with her lovers while her husband [...] stayed behind in Hollywood.[200]

She is "terrible to men," to the extent that they "make fools of themselves for her," but at the time of Beebo's arrival has "sworn off men forever."[201] Toby's being conversant with sophisticated sex does not extend to sexual relationships between women; when he and Beebo have a conversation at cross-purposes about Venus's possible interest in her, Toby says "Not *that* way [...] she's not *sick*."[202]

Toby is an integral part of the Bogardus cereal packet image and provides us with a picture of the family from the inside. Bannon never tells us the surname of his actual father; all we learn of his background is that when Beebo talks of her own father in Wisconsin, Venus says frankly "How primitive [...] Just one father? [...] Toby has six,"[203] and that he was raised not by Venus but by "the old bag" – Mrs. Sack – who has "been around so long, she's part of the family, even if I am too old for her now."[204] The only thing Toby appears to have acquired from his procession of "fathers" is a love of guns.[205] He loves Venus, even though she is a disappointment as a mother,[206] and he appears to respect Leo for being "the only man in her life who won't go

---

ing from his lips, and was mainly current in the drug sub-culture. Therefore it may not be very relevant here, but I note it in passing.

197 Leo tells Beebo, "She's tried this Lesbian stuff before." Bannon, *Beebo Brinker*. 183.
198 Bannon, *Beebo Brinker*. 120.
199 Bannon, *Beebo Brinker*. 147.
200 Bannon, *Beebo Brinker*. 100.
201 Bannon, *Beebo Brinker*. 120.
202 Bannon, *Beebo Brinker*. 121. Obviously, the fact that Venus has had female lovers is something that has escaped Toby's attention.
203 Bannon, *Beebo Brinker*. 100.
204 Bannon, *Beebo Brinker*. 121.
205 Bannon, *Beebo Brinker*. 119.
206 Bannon, *Beebo Brinker*. 120.

"*Everybody gets married.*"   163

down on his knees to her,"[207] and for being a director who "can get a performance out of her nobody else can."[208] The Bogardus family appears to be, at
this point, in a more stable state than it has been for some time. Beebo enters
as something of a wild card, becoming a friend to Toby, who is approaching a stage in life not removed by many years or by growing maturity from
Beebo's own, and a lover to Venus, who is about twice her age. The age
mismatch differs somewhat from that between Joyce and Edith in *Whisper
Their Love*. There is no institutional relationship – Beebo is, initially, Venus's
pizza delivery "boy," before becoming a kind of kept companion. The fact
of a marriage does not prevent their relationship's being met with a degree
of toleration, so long as the appearance of that marriage is not disturbed –
Leo warns Beebo, "[i]f it gets out she's sleeping with a girl, we're dead. All
of us,"[209] and Venus, "do you want me to sit by and watch that kid wreck
the career I've spent twenty years of my life to build? Yours, my dear – all
yours!"[210] He issues a more pointed warning about the mismatch of ages:

> "By the time Beebo's twenty-eight you'll be nudging fifty. Probably a
> grandmother with a face full of charming crow's feet. Every night you
> and Beebo will sit by the TV and watch old Bogardus movies on the
> late late show."[211]

He imagines a domestic scene ten years further on, by which time Toby
would be into his twenties and could even be a father, Venus's career would
be over because of her association with Beebo and would be experienced
only as nostalgia and, in a heteroemulative parody of settled married life, sex
replaced by television.

The tension between Venus's love life and the public image of Bogardus
family life is brought to a head when Toby has a fit and is injured. His mother
and his stepfather are absent, at a party following the launch of her TV series.
Their absence allows Mrs Sack to reveal how maternal duties were thrust
upon her, by Venus's lack of care for him, and how much she has convinced
herself that Toby is her own child. This is certainly her emotional position,
even if she is only half a step away from an actual delusion:

207 Bannon, *Beebo Brinker*. 121.
208 Bannon, *Beebo Brinker*. 147.
209 Bannon, *Beebo Brinker*. 182.
210 Bannon, *Beebo Brinker*. 209.
211 Bannon, *Beebo Brinker*. 210. The "late late show" is a vernacular expression from the
    1950s to refer to any television broadcasts, normally old films, that occur well after normal
    bedtime. It never referred to an actual TV show. An early reference is in a song composed
    by Roy Alfred and Murray Berlin, and recorded in 1957 by Dakota Staton, which indicates
    that the expression pre-dates the recording. Later twentieth and twenty-first century TV
    shows have taken on the name.

164   *"Everybody gets married."*

To Beebo, staring at [Mrs Sack], it became clear that Venus didn't just give Toby up. Toby was deftly taken from her by this plump, kind-hearted woman who never had a child of her own, but was obviously made to mother one. She believed Toby was truly her child because Venus had forfeited her right to him, even the right to comfort him and patch his wounds.[212]

Motherhood is seen – by Mrs. Sack herself, and by Beebo observing her – as a right, as a "natural" and "biological" process, both being oblivious to society's "programming" women to produce children,[213] a right she has been denied except by the proxy position she has assumed. Both Mrs. Sack and Beebo are, in effect, invisible, "kept" members of an extended Bogardus family, each with a function to fulfil that clearly does not feature within the actual, public family. Mrs. Sack's insistence, that Beebo should go and deliver the news of Toby's hospitalisation in person to Venus and Leo, precipitates the violent confrontation between Leo and Beebo, and the resulting newspaper scandal about Venus having a lesbian lover. The ready glee with which the newspapers seize on the story is matched by their instant acceptance of Leo's cover story – that Beebo was a member of staff who had a crush on Venus, and that, far from being over, the Bogardus marriage was stronger than ever[214] – and although this is a rather facile plot element it underlines society's relief at having heterosexuality confirmed.

Toby features in the cover story only peripherally, Beebo's proximity to the family being a product of her becoming "a close friend" of the boy,[215] almost as though that was a ploy on her part to reach Venus. In fact, he has been more pivotal than any other offspring or stepchild seen so far in the books under study. Joyce in Valerie Taylor's *Whisper Their Love* of course becomes the stepdaughter of Irv Kaufman, and his having sex with her has a profound effect on her *Bildung*, but the rest of that process takes place remote from family life. Toby's character, on the other hand, is the product of divorce and re-marriage several times. The shining example of stability that Venus and Leo display and that the media are only too willing to accept is a sham, and all concerned know it is and partake in the conspiracy.

This superficiality that Bannon puts in front of the reader, in the last book she wrote in the Landon-Brinkeriad, along with the instability of monogamy, was hinted at in the first book in the series, *Odd Girl Out*. Laura Landon, newly arrived in college considers that "[h]er divorced parents were a faraway sorrow she tried to pretend out of existence."[216] She speaks of the "fresh

---

212 Bannon, *Beebo Brinker*. 196–197.
213 Wittig, *The Straight Mind and other essays*. 11.
214 Bannon, *Beebo Brinker*. 223–224.
215 Bannon, *Beebo Brinker*. 224.
216 Bannon, *Odd Girl Out*. 17. In her subsequent novels, of course, Bannon made Merrill Landon a widower as the result of a tragic accident. See Chapter I.

"*Everybody gets married.*" 165

wounds" of that divorce, declares herself "ashamed, even afraid to mention it to anyone,"[217] and feels that her family is "falling apart."[218] Beth notices that she won't talk about her parents and appears scared if anyone asks about them.[219] While she doesn't speak about them, she does remain in touch with them; her father is a better correspondent than her mother,[220] and they both speak to her by phone, though their exchanges hardly seem affectionate. Eventually she is goaded into speaking of them with contempt: "My family doesn't care what happens to me, just so they have something to tell their friends."[221] Between Laura's arrival at college, encumbered by her sorrow at the state of her parents' marriage, and Beth's walking optimistically out of the railroad station into the sunshine[222] – presumably to marry Charlie – very little happens to commend marriage. The love between Beth and Laura might have been dismissed, but the picture that the novel builds up of the college as a marriage factory where someone vows to make it a "special project" to have Beth "married off" within the year,[223] and study hardly merits a mention, is not an appealing one. The only other significant couple is Bud and Emily. He is a feckless jazz musician and a permanent student, and it is often music that comes between them, so much so that Beth's Uncle John refers to Emily as a "trombone widow."[224] It is Emily who proposes marriage, and although Bud says he would make "a lousy husband," he agrees.[225] Later he appears to have forgotten his promise and vacillates,[226] eventually becoming incommunicado while Emily reveals to Beth that she is pregnant.[227]

Whether Emily and Bud marry is not revealed in the narrative, and in fact there is no satisfactory heteronormative model in *Odd Girl Out*. In the sequel, *I am a Woman*, the most prominent heterosexual couple, Burr and Marcie, have been married, are divorced, continue to have sexual relations, and one of them is pressing for re-marriage. "Burr" is yet another Cratylic name, like those of Venus and Leo Bogardus; it recalls the well-built actor Raymond Burr, famous for his portrayal of Perry Mason – Burr is described as "powerfully built,"[228] not unlike the actor himself – but also the seed-husk that sticks fast to hair or clothing. Burr sticks fast to Marcie his ex-wife,

217 Bannon, *Odd Girl Out*. 34.
218 Bannon, *Odd Girl Out*. 40.
219 Bannon, *Odd Girl Out*. 36.
220 Bannon, *Odd Girl Out*. 34.
221 Bannon, *Odd Girl Out*. 186.
222 Bannon, *Odd Girl Out*. 212.
223 Bannon, *Odd Girl Out*. 67.
224 Bannon, *Odd Girl Out*. 51. Note that Uncle John defines Emily not by any quality of her own, but by her relation to a man and to his major interest.
225 Bannon, *Odd Girl Out*. 176.
226 Bannon, *Odd Girl Out*. 183.
227 Bannon, *Odd Girl Out*. 201–202.
228 Bannon, *I am a Woman*. 15.

166 *"Everybody gets married."*

to his forthright suggestion of re-marriage,[229] and to their continuing sex life,[230] claiming most of her free time.[231] Her apartment is full of his books, as though that somehow adheres him to it.[232] Marcie puts it strangely: "He's divorced [...]" almost as though she has no connection with their former marriage.[233] She describes him as "very nice to know [...] But hell to live with."[234] This exchange is a vivid summary of their relationship:

> "You'll get along fine with Burr," Marcie said, [...] "He's always read-ing something. Those are his books in there." She waved a hand toward the living room. "He brings them over in the hopes that I'll improve my mind." [...]
>
> "Does he come over a lot?" Laura asked.
> "Yes, but don't worry. He's harmless. He talks like Hamlet some-times – gloomy, I mean – but he's nice to dogs and children. He has a parakeet, too. I always think a man who has a parakeet can't be very vicious. Besides, I lived with him for two years, and the worst he ever did to me was spank me one time. We shouted at each other constantly, but we didn't hit each other."
> "Sounds restful," Laura said.[235]

Laura's sarcasm highlights the strange almost subversive nature of Burr's and Marcie's relationship.[236] Marcie confesses that "[w]e see each other [...] because we can't keep our hands off each other. We fight because we're ashamed of what we want from each other."[237] It is subversive inasmuch as it depends upon only one positive factor – sexual attraction – upon Marcie's appreciation of Burr's "big broad shoulders."[238] The coy, coded message of the popular song quoted at the beginning of this chapter, suggesting "Dad was told by mother" that a man's insistence on sex is dependent on a wom-an's insistence on marriage,[239] is reversed by Burr's use of sex to reinforce constant proposals of marriage. It is this relationship of on-off love-hate that

---

229 Bannon, *I am a Woman*. 10–11.
230 Bannon, *I am a Woman*. 18. Marcie puts on a less than convincing show of resistance.
231 Bannon, *I am a Woman*. 14.
232 Bannon, *I am a Woman*. 12.
233 Bannon, *I am a Woman*. 9. In fact, Marcie is reacting to Laura's "almost sympathetic" response to her announcement that Burr "was" her husband. The full phrase is "He's divorced, not dead."
234 Ibid.
235 Bannon, *I am a Woman*. 12.
236 To a twenty-first century reader, the distinction between "spank" and "hit" will seem ques-tionable.
237 Bannon, *I am a Woman*. 21.
238 Ibid.
239 Cahn, "Love and Marriage."

"Everybody gets married." 167

Bannon uses as a template for Laura and Beebo; after Laura has revealed to Beebo her feelings for Marcie, there is this exchange:

"I've never made a secret of mine for you, baby."
"We'd never do anything but fight, Beebo."
"Fight and make love. I could live forever on such a diet."[240]

This is precisely what she and Laura eventually do, all the way through *Women in the Shadows*. Beebo and Laura only fulfil Christopher Nealon's claim on Bannon's behalf, that her project is "to present homosexuality [...] as an acceptable *life*"[241] if we accept that the partnership it emulates is acceptable too. I do not claim that either is *un*acceptable, but I do put both forward as examples that challenge both the heteronormative and the heteroemulative. If anything, the parallels between the two partnerships establish that in these novels, despite their being set in the world where the sitcom, the cereal packet, the church flyer, and the popular song deliver propaganda of conformity, both homosexual *and* heterosexual couples are heteroemulative. Rather than an irresistible force of "intervention and transformation"[242] in society, there is a sense of striving to achieve a supposed norm that goes against nature.

It is, of course, dangerous to take a fictional text as representing historical fact. In her treatment of divorce, in particular the excessive divorce record of Venus Bogardus, Ann Bannon plays along with the stereotype of the Hollywood marriages that "Soon Strike Rocks."[243] Press coverage such as was attracted to twenty-one-year-old Angela Lansbury's divorce from Richard Cromwell after one year of marriage in fact,[244] and the Bogardus family story in fiction, was more likely to feed off sensation than stability.[245] In 1950 twenty percent of marriages in the United States ended in divorce,[246] and prior to the late nineteen-sixties,

Americans were more likely to look at marriage and family through the prisms of duty, obligation, and sacrifice. A successful, happy home was one in which intimacy was an important good, but by no means

---

240 Bannon, *I am a Woman*. 150.
241 Nealon, "Invert-History: The Ambivalence of Lesbian Pulp Fiction." 757.
242 Foucault, *Abnormal: lectures at the College de France, 1974–1975*. 50.
243 Shelagh Graham, "Soon Strike Rocks," *The St Joseph News-Press*, July 31 1938. 11.
244 unattributed, "Angela Lansbury awarded divorce," *The Spokane Daily Chronicle*, September 12 1946. 12.
245 The fact that Angela Lansbury's second marriage lasted fifty-three years would hardly merit a mention while it was ongoing.
246 William Bradford Wilcox, "The Evolution of Divorce," *National Affairs*, no.45 (2009). 81. That appears to be an estimate, as figures in an official survey indicate 23.1%. unattributed, 100 Years of Marriage and Divorce Statistics, United States, 1867–1967, (U.S. Department of Health, Education, and Welfare; Public Health Service, 1973). 22.

168 *"Everybody gets married."*

the only one in view. A decent job, a well-maintained home, mutual spousal aid, child-rearing, and shared religious faith were seen almost universally as the goods that marriage and family life were intended to advance.[247]

Such was the pressure upon couples to conform to the regime. Remaining single was considered to be deviant, irresponsible, and immature, even though marriage could be considered emasculating.[248] A divorce rate of twenty percent is therefore a not inconsiderable proportion. That rate more than doubled after 1969, when US state after state followed Governor Ronald Reagan's no-fault divorce bill in California, to the extent that the rate in 1970 was fifty percent.[249] Allowing that stability does not make good fiction, Ann Bannon's use of divorce as a plot device seems to have tapped into an unrecognised social undercurrent.

The fall of the couple?

It is not necessary for fiction such as that of Bannon's and her contemporaries to reflect real life, and therefore tapping into the undercurrent of disaffected life-partners waiting for a chance to divorce is serendipitous. Other social realities are not reflected so readily or indeed consistently. Sandra Dijkstra, arguing against Betty Friedan's idea that post-war women had retreated into domesticity, that full-time motherhood was lauded as a woman's true profession, and that having a career was regarded as deviant or evil,[250] says

> Although the fifties bore witness to a revitalization of family life and to a baby boom, it was also marked by a doubling of women's employment outside the home. The most striking feature of the period was the degree to which women continued to enter the job market.[251]

---

247 Wilcox, "The Evolution of Divorce." 83.
248 Kathrina Glitre, *Hollywood Romantic Comedy: States of the Union, 1934–65* (Manchester University Press, 2006). 141.Writing in *Playboy* magazine in 1958, novelist Philip Wylie, author of the 1951 novel *The Disappearance* which shores up every conceivable stereotype of gender, sexuality, race, and religion, opined that women "had said they wanted to be partners with their males, and to "share everything." That turned out to mean that the ladies wanted to invade everything masculine, emasculate it, cover it with dimity, occupy it forever – and police it." Philip Wylie, "The Womanization of America," *Playboy*, no.9 (1958). 52 and 77.
249 Wilcox, "The Evolution of Divorce." 81.
250 Betty Friedan, *The Feminine Mystique* (Dell, 1972). 40.
251 Sandra Dijkstra, "Simone de Beauvoir and Betty Friedan: The Politics of Omission," *Feminist Studies* vol.6, no.2 (1980). 291. Dijkstra is actually citing William Chafe here. William Chafe, *The American Woman: Her Changing Social, Economic, and Political Roles, 1920–1970* (Oxford UP, 1972). 218.

"Everybody gets married." 169

Canadian archive film footage of the 1950s shows middle-class women both with the latest domestic gadgets, and trooping off to work dressed smartly for the office, implying that they can have "careers, or cradle, or both."[252] The fictional world under study defies all this at two extremes, however. On the one hand, throughout *I am a Woman* Laura Landon fails to hold down any job and Beebo Brinker has to hide behind transmasculinity to occupy the most menial position, or rather to take that position in order to maintain transmasculinity. On the other hand, in Randy Salem's imagination, the eponymous *Chris* breaks the glass ceiling as an adventurer and top marine biologist, and Lee van Tassel in *The Sex Between* becomes a CEO with enough influence to forbid an arranged marriage.[253] Although Laura ends up a mother,[254] neither Chris nor Lee show the slightest inclination in that direction. The issue of incest is also seen in several lights. In *The Marriage* love and secrecy defy "the crust of outworn opinions on which established institutions depend,"[255] but in *Journey to a Woman* an Usheresque hint brings about self-destruction and death:

> "It just makes you wonder if Cleve and Vega wouldn't have been better off to stay with each other and tell the world to go to hell."

> "You know it wouldn't," he said, and though his voice was even she could feel the sudden rise in his emotional temperature.
> "At least Vega wouldn't have ended up horribly dead on the floor of a hotel room."
> "I wouldn't count on it. It's never better to prolong a sick relationship. She might have ended up dead even sooner."
> "If prolonging a sick relationship will keep you alive, it's worth it."
> "Things would have been much worse for them if they lived together," he said positively. Anything abnormal he automatically loathed, without understanding it, without questioning himself.[256]

There's a similar hint in Salem's *The Sex Between* about brother and sister Pieter and Trudel,[257] she having been portrayed throughout that novel as being dull and slow-witted. Again we see two extremes against which to balance real-life cases.

What is germane to this study, however, is what is presented in the novels, rather than whether they reflect actuality. If novels contained nothing but

---

252 Aerlyn Weissman and Lynne Fernie, "Forbidden Love: The Unashamed Stories of Lesbian Lives," (National Film Board of Canada, 1993).
253 Randy Salem, *The Sex Between* (Midwood, 1962). 176.
254 In name, as Jack is the more maternal towards their daughter.
255 Igpen and Peck, *The Complete Works of Percy Bysshe Shelley*. 247.
256 Ann Bannon, *Journey to a Woman* (Cleis, 2003). 237.
257 Salem, *The Sex Between*. 180.

170 *"Everybody gets married."*

stories from everyday life, they would merely catalogue boredom. Where boredom is found in them, it is shown as a spur to a radical change of life. When Beth and Charlie fell into a dull and empty routine[258] where she had "an overdose of children"[259] and her only "friend" is the wife of Charlie's business partner, with whom she goes bowling,[260] she leaves him and their children to look for her former lover Laura. This is Bannon's first portrayal in depth of the fall of a heteroemulative partnership between a man and a woman. In *Women in the Shadows*, a heteroemulative partnership between two women disintegrates, despite an attempt to shore it up by the convention of an anniversary party. A similar *ménage* in *Chris* fails because of the imbalance between two partners, one of whom is conventionally uxorious yet possibly asexual, and the other allosexual, if not hypersexual, and oriented towards career and adventure. Where *ménages* appear most stable, where they adhere to "heterosexist institutions and values,"[261] there are other pressures at work, such as in the marriages of convenience of one sort or another – Jack and Laura, Fritzi and Anitra, Leo and Venus for example. About the Mann's marriage, that Julian Carter holds up as Bannon's only happy one,[262] he nonetheless says that "gay marriage" has "a history as the homonormative fantasy of a safe white space between a queer rock and a heterosexual hard place."[263] Even he concedes the tension that this creates.[264]

The only real optimism for a couple comes at the end of the worst-written book, Lora Sela's *I am a Lesbian*, where nature finally "strikes a balance"[265] between the supposedly masculine and feminine lesbian couple. However, even the most partisan bibliographers found the idea of that book's "Happy Well-Adjusted Noble Lesbian" ludicrous.[266] In all these texts the regime is acknowledged equally by revolution against it and capitulation to it. To paraphrase and expand on de Beauvoir, then, one is born neither woman nor man, but becomes such by reference to the regime, and in particular in the attempt at couplehood.

---

258 Bannon, *Journey to a Woman.* 14.
259 Bannon, *Journey to a Woman.* 10.
260 Bannon, *Journey to a Woman.* 6.
261 Duggan, "The New Homonormativity: The Sexual Politics of Neoliberalism." 179.
262 Carter, "Gay Marriage and Pulp Fiction: Homonormativity, Disidentification, and Affect in Ann Bannon's Lesbian Novels." 586.
263 Carter, "Gay Marriage and Pulp Fiction: Homonormativity, Disidentification, and Affect in Ann Bannon's Lesbian Novels." 588.
264 Carter, "Gay Marriage and Pulp Fiction: Homonormativity, Disidentification, and Affect in Ann Bannon's Lesbian Novels." 587.
265 Sela, *I am a Lesbian.* 10.
266 Bradley and Damon, *Checklist 1960: A Complete, Cumulative Checklist of Lesbian, Variant, and Homosexual Fiction, in English, or Available in English Translation, with Supplements of Related Material, for the Use of Collectors, Students, and Librarians.* No page numbers.

"Everybody gets married." 171

Bibliography

Ahmed, Sara. *On Being Included: Racism and Diversity in Institutional Life.* Duke University Press, 2012.

Baldwin, James. "The Preservation of Innocence." In *Collected Essays*, 594–600. The Library of America, 1998.

Bannon, Ann. *Beebo Brinker.* Cleis, 2001.

———. *I am a Woman.* Cleis, 2002.

———. *Journey to a Woman.* Cleis, 2003.

———. *The Marriage.* Fawcett Gold Medal, 1960.

———. "The Nice Kid." *ONE Magazine* 9, no. 1 (1961): 23–28.

———. *Odd Girl Out.* Cleis, 2001.

———. *Women in the Shadows.* Cleis, 2002.

Perkins, Sue. Being Gay Is the 47th Most Interesting Thing About Me." Chortle, 2013. tinyurl.com/Gay47th.

Bradley, Marion Zimmer, and Gene Damon. *Checklist 1960: A Complete, Cumulative Checklist of Lesbian, Variant, and Homosexual Fiction, in English, or Available in English Translation, with Supplements of Related Material, for the Use of Collectors, Students, and Librarians.* Self-published by Marion Zimmer Bradley, 1960.

Butler, Judith. "Imitation and Gender Insubordination." Chap. 20 In *The Lesbian and Gay Studies Reader*, edited by Michèle Aina Barale Henry Abelove and David M. Halpin, 307–20. Routledge, 1993.

Cahn, Sammy. "Love and Marriage." (1955).

Carleton, Bukk G. *A Practical Treatise on the Sexual Disorders of Men.* Boericke, Runyon & Ernesty, 1898.

Carter, Julian. "Gay Marriage and Pulp Fiction: Homonormativity, Disidentification, and Affect in Ann Bannon's Lesbian Novels." *GLQ: A Journal of Lesbian and Gay Studies* 15, no. 4 (2009): 583–609.

Chafe, William. *The American Woman: Her Changing Social, Economic, and Political Roles, 1920–1970.* Oxford University Press, 1972.

de Beauvoir, Simone. *Le Deuxième Sexe*, Vol. 2: Éditions Gallimard, 1976.

———. *The Second Sex.* Translated by Howard Madison Parshley. Picador, 1988.

de Chateaubriand, François-René. *Atala. René.* Garnier Flammarion, 1964.

Dijkstra, Sandra. "Simone De Beauvoir and Betty Friedan: The Politics of Omission." *Feminist Studies* 6, no. 2 (1980): 290–303.

Duff, David. *Romanticism and the Uses of Genre.* Oxford University Press, 2009.

Duggan, Lisa. "The New Homonormativity: The Sexual Politics of Neoliberalism." In *Materializing Democracy: Toward a Revitalized Cultural Politics*, edited by Russ Castronovo and Dana Nelson, 175–94. Duke University Press, 2002.

Ellis, Milton. "The Author of the First American Novel." *American Literature* 4, no. 4 (1933): 359–68.

Fiedler, Leslie. *Love and Death in the American Novel.* Stein and Day, 1966.

Foucault, Michel. *Abnormal: Lectures at the College De France, 1974–1975.* Translated by Graham Burchell. Edited by Valerio Marchetti and Antonella Salomoni. Verso, 2016.

Friedan, Betty. *The Feminine Mystique.* Dell, 1972.

Glitre, Kathrina. *Hollywood Romantic Comedy: States of the Union, 1934–65.* Manchester University Press, 2006.

Gordon, George, and Lord Byron, "Epistle to Augusta." Poetry Foundation, accessed 21st March 2019, tinyurl.com/ByronAugusta.

Graham, Shelagh. "Soon Strike Rocks." *The St Joseph News-Press*, 31 July 1938, 11.

Guillaumin, Colette. "Practique Du Pouvoir Et Idee De Nature: (1) L'appropriation Des Femmes." *Nouvelles Questions Feministes*, no. 2 (1978): 5–30.

172 *"Everybody gets married."*

Igpen, Roger, and Walter E. Peck, eds. *The Complete Works of Percy Bysshe Shelley*: Ernest Benn Ltd, 1965.

Jakobsen, Janet R. "Sex + Freedom = Regulation: Why?". *Social Text* 23, no. 3–4 (2005): 285–308.

Johnson, David K. *The Lavender Scare: The Cold War Persecution of Gays and Lesbians in the Federal Government*. University of Chicago Press, 2004.

Lawson, John Howard. "Hollywood: Illusion and Reality." *Hollywood Quarterly* 1, no. 2 (1946): 231–33.

Leach, Edmund. "The Cereal Packet Norm." *The Guardian*, 29 January 1968, 8.

Lochrie, Karma. *Heterosyncrasies: Female Sexuality When Normal Wasn't*. University of Minnesota Press, 2005.

Nealon, Christopher. "Invert-History: The Ambivalence of Lesbian Pulp Fiction." *New Literary History* 31, no. 4 (2000): 745–64.

Norton, Clark. "Sex in America." *Inquiry*, 5 October 1981, 18.

Plain, Gill. *Prosthetic Agency: Literature, Culture and Masculinity after World War Ii*. Cambridge University Press, 2023.

Poe, Edgar Allan. *The Fall of the House of Usher and Other Writings*. Penguin Classics, 2003.

Saint-Aubin, Arthur Flannigan. "The Male Body and Literary Metaphors for Masculinity." In *Theorising Masculinities*, edited by Harry Brod and Michael Kaufmann, 239–58. Sage, 1994.

Salem, Randy. *The Sex Between*. Midwood, 1962.

Sela, Lora. *I Am a Lesbian*. Saber, 1959.

Somerville, Siobhan B. "Queer *Loving*." *GLQ: A Journal of Lesbian and Gay Studies* 11, no. 3 (2005): 335–70.

Spectorsky, Auguste Comte. *The Exurbanites*. Lippincott, 1955.

Taylor, Valerie. *Whisper Their Love*. Little Sister's Classics. Arsenal Pulp Press, 2006.

———. *A World Without Men*. Volute, 1982.

Thompson, Gary Richard. *Gothic Imagination: Essays in Dark Romanticism*. Washington State University Press, 1974.

Tyner, Dick. "Books." *One: The Homosexual Viewpoint*, no. 1 (1961): 28–29.

unattributed. *100 Years of Marriage and Divorce Statistics, United States, 1867–1967*. U.S. Department of Health, Education, and Welfare; Public Health Service, 1973.

———. "Angela Lansbury Awarded Divorce." *The Spokane Daily Chronicle*, 12 September 1946.

———. *Annual Report of the United States Postal Service*. US Postal Service, 1957.

———. "Marine and Mom Guilty of Incest." *San Francisco Chronicle*, 16 November 1979, 16.

Vance, Carole S. *Pleasure and Danger: Exploring Female Sexuality*. Pandora, 1992.

Warner, Michael. *The Trouble with Normal: Sex, Politics, and the Ethics of Queer Life*. Harvard University Press, 1999.

Weissman, Aerlyn, and Lynne Fernie. "Forbidden Love: The Unashamed Stories of Lesbian Lives." National Film Board of Canada, 1993.

West, Edwin. *Brother and Sister*. Monarch Books, 1965.

Whitbread, Jane. "A Report on Current Attitudes to Chastity." *Mademoiselle*, no. 49 (1959): 37–40.

Whitfield, Stephen J. *The Culture of the Cold War*. 2nd ed. Johns Hopkins University Press, 1996.

Wilcox, William Bradford. "The Evolution of Divorce." *National Affairs*, no. 45 (2009): 81–94.

Wilson, James D. "Incest and American Romantic Fiction." *Studies in the Literary Imagination* 7, no. 1 (1974): 31–50.

Wittig, Monique. *The Straight Mind and Other Essays*. Beacon, 1992.

Wylie, Philip. "The Womanization of America." *Playboy*, no. 9 (1958): 51–52, 77–81.

Young, Philip. "'First American Novel': 'The Power of Sympathy,' in Place." *College Literature* 11, no. 2 (1984): 115–24.

V Conclusion
Failure and another normality

> From the street, I looked up into the apartment
> buildings, into the naked windows of the tiny
> cubicle rooms. More haggard faces peering
> blankly; skinny, maimed bodies of uncaring
> women in slips; men without shirts. All have
> the same look: the look of nolonger-
> questioning, resigned doom.[1]

The failure of masculinity

The serious research for this book was begun fifty years after the Stonewall
Riots, considered a watershed event in the recent history of individuals and
societal groups who do not accede to heteronormativity. Work on it continued through the fiftieth anniversary of Del Martin's essay "If That's All
There Is," which accused gay rights organisations of being sexist, and the fiftieth anniversary of the first lesbian separatist movement. Such overt actions,
along with the developments and tensions within the sexuality- and gender-
divergent movement(s) since then, have tended to mask the view that the
envelope of divergence was being pushed, in many powerful ways, in the
period before Stonewall,[2] and that the popularity of cheap paperback novels
on a lesbian theme – even the salacious and badly-written ones – was one

---

1 John Rechy, *City of Night* (Grove Press, 1964). 296. Rechy was present at Cooper's, see next
footnote.
2 In fact, the Stonewall riots were not the first mid-twentieth-century street reactions to arbitrary
oppression. My research began *sixty* years after the riot that occurred at Cooper's Doughnuts,
Main Street Los Angeles, between two of the area's older gay bars, the Waldorf and Harold's,
in answer to police harassment. Lillian Faderman and Stuart Timmons, *Gay L.A.: A History of Sexual Outlaws, Power Politics, and Lipstick Lesbians* (Basic Books, 2006). 1-2. Eric
A. Stanley, "Introduction: Fugitive Flesh: Gender Self-Determination, Queer Abolition, and
Trans Resistance," in *Captive Genders: Trans Embodiment and the Prison Industrial Complex*, ed. Eric A. Stanley and Nat Smith (AK Press, 2011). 3. Ann Aldrich was confident enough
in 1955 to write, albeit of "sophisticated society," that it was "no longer considered to react
with belligerence, distaste, or complete ignorance towards the abnormality." Ann Aldrich, *We
Walk Alone* (The Feminist Press, 2006). 9.

DOI: 10.4324/9781003422679-6

Conclusion   175

factor in that push. Valerie Taylor said of them, "I think it's been one of the best things [to happen to lesbians]. Reading helped to form our viewpoints. For a while when a lesbian book came out, you would buy it no matter how bad it was."[3] Critic and archivist Lisa K. Speer, on the other hand, maintains that paperback novels reflected rather than affected a society already in the throes of change.[4]

In considering masculinity as imagined in a group of these novels, I have explored whether the male characters signify some kind of 'authentic' masculinity in comparison to the butch women in the novels, or whether the latter undermine the hegemonic triumph of the "Big Handsome Hero,"[5] and thereby destabilise essentialised and monolithic gender. If the female characters are just as effective, or even more effective, in their masculinity, does this further the argument that 'gender' should not be attached to particular bodies, and does it also suggest that Packer's, Bannon's, and Salem's texts, and those of their contemporaries, present a radical view on gender identity? I have interrogated these novels as a space of masculine negotiation, where not only women but also men can read about 'manly' or 'mannish' women, and where the male readers thereby find their exclusive claims to masculinity under close question. This is not to say that "masculinity" has proved easy to define. As cited at the end of Chapter I, the Oxford English Dictionary's definition of "the assemblage of qualities regarded as characteristic of men,"[6] offers little help, as it does not list those "qualities," leaving them as matters to be decided within the culture of the reader. The critics cited at the beginning of Chapter II, such as Halberstam, Rubin, and Sedgwick, do not settle on an adequate definition, and even though Jeffreys is adamant that it can be expressed simply as "the behaviour of male dominance,"[7] the tenor of

---

3 Valerie Taylor, *Whisper Their Love*, Little Sister's Classics, (Arsenal Pulp Press, 2006). 239. As to "no matter how bad," Yvonne Keller reminds us that "[u]nlike post-Stonewall lesbian fiction or literary fiction at the time, pro-lesbian pulps [were] fully immersed within, and indeed obligated to attend to, the discourse of voyeurism because of the constraints of their mass-market cultural form." Yvonne Keller, "Pulp Politics: Strategies of Vision in Pro-Lesbian Pulp Novels 1955-1965," in *The Queer Sixties*, ed. Patricia Juliana Smith (Routledge, 1999). 5. I take this view seriously, even though I have challenged it as a simplistic division of the readership, in the Introduction.

4 Lisa K Speer, "Paperback Pornography: Mass Market Novels and Censorship in Post-War America," *Journal of American & Comparative Cultures*, no. 24 (2001). 158. Joel Foreman characterised the 1950s in general as an era of "the emergence of oppositional forces that, in subsequent decades, achieve[d] either dominance or general acceptance." Joel Foreman, ed., *The Other Fifties: Interrogating Mid-century American Icons* (U of Illinois P, 1997). 5.

5 Marion Zimmer Bradley and Gene Damon, *Checklist 1960: A Complete, Cumulative Checklist of Lesbian, Variant, and Homosexual Fiction, in English, or Available in English Translation, with Supplements of Related Material, for the Use of Collectors, Students, and Librarians* (Self-published by Marion Zimmer Bradley, 1960).

6 "masculinity," in *Oxford English Dictionary* (3rd: Oxford U P, 2021).

7 Sheila Jeffreys, *Unpacking queer politics: a lesbian feminist perspective* (Polity Press in association with Blackwell, 2003). 7.

176   *Conclusion*

her *Unpacking Queer Politics* is to apply it to anything she personally disapproves of, in particular "butch/femme role-playing," which she stigmatises as "aping the most exaggerated versions of femininity and masculinity available in heterosexual culture."[8] However, the fact that she uses the word "dominance" in her definition has legitimised my consideration of any dominant behaviour as an arguably masculine aspect.

The views of Sheila Jeffreys are not dissimilar from those of lesbian feminists and lesbian separatists of the 1970s, inasmuch as her politics are a product of and development of her involvement with the feminism of that era. Though encounters with this trend in feminism feature in Feinberg's *Stone Butch Blues*,[9] earlier fiction pre-dates it. A defence of the butch-femme dynamic was put up in 1981 by Joan Nestle:

> [...] although I have been a lesbian for over 20 years and I embrace feminism as a world view, I can spot a butch 50 feet away and still feel the thrill of her power. Contrary to belief, this power is not bought at the expense of the fem's identity. Butch-fem relationships as I experienced them, were complex erotic statements, not phony heterosexual replicas [...] None of the butch women I was with [...] ever presented themselves to me as men [...] Butch-fem was an erotic partnership, serving both as a conspicuous flag of rebellion and as an intimate exploration of women's sexuality.[10]

For Nestle, the dynamic was not an imitation of binary heterosexuality, it was a conspicuous cultural statement. This view is, however, not much less sweeping and narrow than that of Jeffreys, as each tends to adopt the orthodoxy of her own cosm and ignore the wider, individual nuances of the human experience.

I have shown in this book that most of the authors of the highlighted books could appreciate nuance, and could show cracks in male dominance, to the extent that readers must have been left with the impression that what was commonly believed to be masculinity was little more than a façade. Even the "virile adventures,"[11] being based as much on a winning formula – that of *Spring Fire* – as on a need to shore up a cultural norm during a period of

---

8 Jeffreys, *Unpacking queer politics: a lesbian feminist perspective*. 127. This opinion is despite the obvious fundamental difference between stone butches and men that I proposed earlier in this book.

9 "It seemed like everyone in the bar was wearing flannel shirts, jeans, and boots [...] One of the women at the dance made fun of the butch I was with because she helped me off with my coat." An example from Leslie Feinberg, *Stone Butch Blues* (self-published, 2014). tinyurl.com /StoneButchB. 232

10 Joan Nestle, "Butch-fem Relationships: Sexual Courage in the 1950s," *Heresies 12: Sex Issue* 3, no. 4 (1981). 213.

11 Keller, "Pulp Politics: Strategies of Vision in Pro-Lesbian Pulp Novels 1955-1965." 2.

masculinity crisis and male panic,[12] must have seemed outworn by the time that the novels of Bannon, Salem, Taylor, and their contemporaries began to present different narratives. Apart from John in Taylor's *Whisper Their Love* and Charlie in Bannon's *Odd Girl Out*, male characters are by and large unattractive, unsuccessful in their masculinity, and identifying with them would have been difficult. It is a matter of speculation whether the thousands of casual, male readers did try on different identities, as Allyson Miller argues specifically for Bannon's *I am a Woman*,[13] imagining themselves carrying masculinity as, for example, Beebo Brinker, Christopher Hamilton, or even Beth Cullison, or cast opposite them in a more feminine role, with a masculine partner less threatening to their heterosexual self-image than one in a gay romance.[14] However, the likes of Beebo and Chris, as fictional characters, also find difficulty in carrying masculinity. In the case of Beebo, it is not simply to do with society's incomprehension and disapproval; in most of the narratives in which she is involved she struggles to find a place for her masculinity in the balance of a relationship. Chris's story happens in a mesocosm where there is no disapproval of lesbian couples, but her masculinity is conjoined with hypersexuality and indecision. If anything, I have not simply shown that these novels destabilise monolithic gender, but rather that they have put nothing stable in its place.

Along with the cracks in the façade of masculinity, as imagined in these novels, come similar cracks in heteronormativity. Chapter IV, dealing with couples, introduced the concept of heteroemulativity, being a response to that normativity, suggesting that even the novels' heterosexual couples tried – with varying degrees of failure – to fill a pattern that was as much cultural as biological, if not more so. Whilst it is important to remember that these failures and this overall instability in genders and sexualities are narrative devices to maintain tension, without which the novels would be shorn of their drama, it seems that the novels question normality in general.

"Life is so queer" – "normal" in the novels

"Damn. It's queer. Life is so queer," says Beth in Bannon's *Journey to a Woman*.[15] That begs the question, if life is queer how can anything about it be normal? The instability of gender in the examined novels leads to the

---

12 See James Gilbert, *Men in the Middle: Searching for Masculinity in the 1950s* (U of Chicago P, 2005). 3, 16.

13 Allyson Miller, "Postwar Masculine Identity in Ann Bannon's *I am A Woman*" (MA University of Missouri-Columbia, 2009). v.

14 It should be noted, however, that these possibilities still depend, as Yvonne Keller said, to the female characters in the novels being "still sexually available to men" (although not necessarily as potential heterosexual conquests). Keller, "Pulp Politics: Strategies of Vision in Pro-Lesbian Pulp Novels 1955-1965." 3.

15 Ann Bannon, *Journey to a Woman* (Cleis, 2003). 197.

178   *Conclusion*

conclusion that it can't. Further on in *Journey to a Woman*, there is a short passage of free indirect discourse which focalises on the thoughts and feelings of Beth as she struggles with the consequences of leaving her husband and family:

> [...] lost between those two worlds, one renounced, the other closed to her. One was normal, ordinary, reassuring, with a home and a husband and children. And it had failed her. The other was gay and strange, exotic and dangerous, painful and, possibly, wonderful. But it was still untried, inaccessible somehow [...] caught dead center between the two [...] in limbo. [...][16]

This short extract is replete with rhetorical antitheses, as Beth finds herself isolated equally from the "renounced" world and the "closed" one. It is possible to tabulate these antitheses along with their fulcral words:

normal	limbo	gay
ordinary	dead center	strange
reassuring	caught	exotic
home	lost [both]	dangerous
husband		painful
children		possibly wonderful
failed		untried
		inaccessible

The prominence of "normal" in the passage is typical of Bannon's work; the word itself and the concept of normality are to be found throughout her novels. There is a precedent for this in Packer's *Spring Fire*, in which the protagonist Mitch finds a thick volume on psychology, which describes a Lesbian as "abnormal, a female who could not have satisfactory relations with a male"[17] and contains following passage:

> The female homosexual, the Lesbian, often preys on girls who are not true homosexuals. Such girls may enjoy men, and be capable of normal heterosexual life if they do not become involved with a genuine Lesbian type, whose technique is often more skilful than that of many of her young men suitors [...] A normal man finds sex with this type of woman extremely difficult, if not impossible [...] Many times, under the proper circumstances, a female homosexual may learn to control, if not eliminate, her active homosexual tendencies once she is removed

16 Bannon, *Journey to a Woman*. 199.
17 Vin Packer, *Spring Fire* (Cleis, 2004). 83. I had wondered if this was from an actual book of the era, but Marijane Meaker told me she had written from her own imagination the passage which follows. Personal email, 28th April 2019.

Conclusion 179

from an environment where the temptation is great. But on the other hand, a change in environment may only lead to new conquests. [...][18]

This picture of normality and abnormality is part of the edifice of misunderstanding that Packer makes Mitch build, that leads to the tragic outcomes of the novel. As Mitch tries to fit herself into this picture, she worries that she has been predatory in her attitude to Leda, and would predate on other girls if she moved to an independent dormitory. A move from one microcosm to another would only be a further confusion, and the imposed 'rules' of the sexology book are like the rules of the sorority – compulsory on pain of punishment, so apparently easy for others to follow and to understand, yet so arcane to Mitch. Mitch's world is Kafkaesque, almost as much as Kafka's own, as described in his letter to his father.[19] Normality, even though the world has been labelled "queer," is that cliff face on which the characters in the novels keep banging their heads.

It is invoked elsewhere in the world of the cheap paperback, in works of faux sexology and pop-psychology, and in pseudo-science. L.T. Woodward,[20] in his ostensibly non-fiction paperback *Twilight Women*, acknowledges at least that normality is defined from within the culture that considers itself normal:

On the borders of what we rather smugly call the "Normal World" – because it is our world – of sex, there impinges the twilight world of the homosexual. There, in shadows and dim light, millions of human beings fulfil their sexual desires, happily or otherwise. Choosing to ignore the biological commandment to be fruitful and multiply, they intertwine in love forbidden by law, forbidden by custom, forbidden by popular opinion.[21]

Woodward acknowledges society's smugness in defining its own cosm as normal, but nevertheless sees reproduction as a biological commandment. Another science-fiction writer, L. Ron Hubbard, whilst attempting to change the way humanity sees its thought-process and physical drives, refers to a set

---

18 Packer, *Spring Fire*. 103-104.

19 "[...] the world was for me divided into three parts: one in which I, the slave, lived under laws that had been invented only for me and which I could, I did not know why, never completely comply with; then a second world, which was infinitely remote from mine, in which you lived, concerned with government, with the issuing of orders and with the annoyance about their not being obeyed; and finally a third world where everybody else lived happily and free from orders and from having to obey." Franz Kafka, *Letter to the Father / Brief an den Vater*, trans. Philip Boehm, The Schocken Kafka Library, (Schocken, 2013). 25.

20 One of the pen names of Robert Silverberg. Sixty years on, give or take a year, Silverberg is reluctant to discuss early potboilers like *Twilight Women*, given current controversies about gender. Fair enough. Personal email, 6th of October 2018.

21 L. T. Woodward, *Twilight Women* (Lancer, 1963). 7.

180   *Conclusion*

of "Dynamics" of survival which a person must obey, the second of which is "[t]he urge of the individual to reach the highest potential of survival in terms of *sex*, the act and the creation of children."[22] "The sexual pervert" – in which term Hubbard brackets together "all kinds of deviation in Dynamic Two"[23] – "is actually quite ill physically,"[24] adding that he[25] is "very far from culpable, but he is also far from normal and so extremely dangerous to society."[26] The queerness of the world as imagined in the novels sits uncomfortably with what the outside world sees as monolithic normality. Karma Lochrie, whom I have quoted in Chapters II and IV, points out that the term "normal," borrowed from the relatively young discipline of statistics, only began to be used metaphorically to mean "constituting, conforming to, not deviating from the common type or standard" and "regular or usual" barely one hundred years before the novels were published.[27] These early applications of normality "were not simply old theological and moral ideals dressed in new lexicons. The element of numerical calculation differentiated norms from their predecessors."[28] But words such as "common," "standard," "regular," and "usual" imply that there was a phenomenon to observe and to describe *avant la lettre*, and not simply that our mode of description was affected by an innovation in observation, which in turn altered our understanding. In the case of the lifestyles depicted in the novels, the old ideas and ideals were grafted back into supposed normality and normativity; writing in 2004, Vin Packer said, "The church and synagogues called us sinners, they still do [...]"[29] The old ideas and ideals were intact, and to someone under censure, the effect of the censure is severe no matter how it is defined or devised. The pressures of internal conformity existed long before Foucault defined them. I would be surprised to find anyone who would argue that there were no societal and cultural expectations before the authority of numbers became a discipline within the study of society, or that those expectations had no bearing to what was common at any time in history. Still, it is necessary to be aware of the "entirely new epistemological paradigm" which came to "[dominate] the late twentieth century."[30] Ian Hacking says:

---

22 Lafayette Ronald Hubbard, *Dianetics: The Modern Science of Mental Health* (New Era, 2007). iii.
23 Hubbard, *Dianetics: The Modern Science of Mental Health*. 125.
24 ibid.
25 Hubbard uses the inclusive "he" when generalising.
26 Hubbard, *Dianetics: The Modern Science of Mental Health*. 126.
27 Karma Lochrie, *Heterosyncrasies: Female Sexuality When Normal Wasn't* (U of Minnesota P, 2005). 3.
28 Lochrie, *Heterosyncrasies: Female Sexuality When Normal Wasn't*. 3.
29 Packer, *Spring Fire*. viii.
30 Mary Poovey, *A History of the Modern Fact: Problems of Knowledge in the Sciences and Society* (U of Chicago P, 1998). 317.

Words have profound memories that oil our shrill and squeaky rhetoric. The normal stands indifferently for what is typical, the unenthusiastic objective average, but it also stands for what has been, good health, and for what shall be, our chosen destiny. This is why the benign and sterile-sounding word "normal" has become one of the most powerful ideological tools of the twentieth century.[31]

The world imagined in the novels, where the "healthy" normal is indeed a "fiction,"[32] and behaviour corralled by the societal norm is in fact an impotent attempt at emulation, blunts that powerful ideological tool.

That imagined world has an alternative normativity. "And oh, the drinking!" notes Ann Bannon in her foreword to *I am a Woman*, describing the lifestyle of the denizens of the real lesbian bars she visited during her short sojourns in New York City, adding "Where else were we to go?"[33] This alconormativity was not confined to the bars, however. In Chapter I, I showed that hard drinking was one of the ostensibly masculine behaviours of the "frat men," and indeed the rape episode in Vin Packer's *Spring Fire* occurs when both Bud and Mitch are drunk.[34] Beer is touted as a kind of social and sexual anaesthetic, when Leda advises Mitch, "I used to get sick on beer myself. You'll get used to it,"[35] the inference being that if she can get used to beer she can get used to sex with men. The same fraternity culture and its sorority acquiescence features in Bannon's *Odd Girl Out*, with its habitual beer parties,[36] its portrayal of drink loosening social and sexual inhibitions – "Fortunately it was not very hard to be friendly at beer parties, and the more beer you drank the easier it was"[37] – and its use of drunkenness to blot out problems.[38] In *I am a Woman*, beer stops Laura Landon from thinking too hard about her implacable father.[39] Alcohol fuels Burr's ebullience,[40] and Jack's bonhomie.[41] It gives Laura the nerve to criticise Beebo's donning pants and at the same time serves as a stick to beat Beebo with – "You work all day at a lousy job [...] and then you drink all night [...] All for a pair of pants."[42] In *Women in the Shadows*, Bannon's darkest novel, both Beebo and Jack suffer from alcoholism; Beebo is in the habit of early-morning drink-

---

31 Ian Hacking, *The Taming of Chance* (Cambridge UP, 2004). 169.
32 Lochrie says "*Though a fiction*, the average man is the center of gravity for society" (my emphasis). Lochrie, *Heterosyncrasies: Female Sexuality When Normal Wasn't*. 8.
33 Ann Bannon, *I am a Woman* (Cleis, 2002). xiii.
34 Packer, *Spring Fire*. 52-55.
35 Packer, *Spring Fire*. 22.
36 Ann Bannon, *Odd Girl Out* (Cleis, 2001). 48.
37 Bannon, *Odd Girl Out*. 29.
38 Bannon, *Odd Girl Out*. 140.
39 Bannon, *I am a Woman*. 49.
40 Bannon, *I am a Woman*. 17-18.
41 Bannon, *I am a Woman*. 36.
42 Bannon, *I am a Woman*. 180.

182 Conclusion

ing and sucking mints to disguise it,[43] and Jack confesses to having "nearly drunk [himself] to extinction."[44] In the section excised from that novel and published separately in *ONE Magazine*, drink brings out extreme violence in Jack.[45] Jack even calls Laura an "alcoholic" for confessing that she has "a cocktail now and then."[46] In *Journey to a Woman*, everyone seems to be prey to alconormativity. Cleve is a heavy drinker,[47] and the rest of Vega's family is disintegrating under the influence of drinking:

> "All right, Hester, get the hell in the bathroom before you lose it," Gramp snapped impatiently, and Beth saw Vega's temper rising too. Beth didn't know whether she was amused or repelled by the whole scene: the ugly crumbling old woman, the way Vega lived, the wise-cracking with a hint of violence under the humor. She didn't understand why she said yes when Vega fixed her another drink, then another. And Vega drank two for her every one.[48]

At one point, Beth says very pointedly to Cleve, "*you're* normal and *you* drink."[49] In Randy Salem's *Chris*, drunkenness empowers the protagonist's weekly promiscuity,[50] and makes her "[...] a disagreeable bitch [...] snide and sarcastic and sometimes cruel [a] lecher and a drunkard to boot."[51] This is Chris's own self-description; she attributes her alcoholism to the staleness of her conjugal situation, but that could well be the fallacy of *post hoc ergo propter hoc*. Alcohol also fuels an episode of gender-based violence in *Chris*. Throughout the novels, the commonest social and individual factor is drink. But no matter how normative it seems to be, it is as much a false friend as any other supposed normativity in the novels. As heteronormativity breaks down, so does alconormativity, and normativity as a whole is brought into question. If the reader can see any salvation for the idea of normality at all, it is in the fact that these breakings down occur in specific microcosms – the college, the bar, etc.[52] – and thus the reader can assume that there is a slender hope for normativity outside fiction, within the broader, less specific macro-cosm of society at large.

---

43 Ann Bannon, *Women in the Shadows* (Cleis, 2002). 26, 29.
44 Bannon, *Women in the Shadows*. 62. Bannon gives Jack a history of alcohol abuse in the prequel *Beebo Brinker*, saying that he was prone to "hit the bottle." Ann Bannon, *Beebo Brinker* (Cleis, 2001). 2.
45 Ann Bannon, "The Nice Kid," *ONE Magazine* 9, no. 1 (1961). 26.
46 Bannon, *Women in the Shadows*. 14.
47 Bannon, *Journey to a Woman*. 7.
48 Bannon, *Journey to a Woman*. 44.
49 Bannon, *Journey to a Woman*. 55. Author's emphasis.
50 Randy Salem, *Chris* (Naiad, 1989). 2.
51 Salem, *Chris*. 7.
52 This is the case across the sub-genre, with so many novels being set in microcosms.

Conclusion 183

Further research

The research I have started in this book opens the door to further study in three specific areas. Firstly an expansion of the consideration of imagined masculinity to include not only the works of other writers of "pro-lesbian" fiction of that era, but also the more supposedly voyeuristic novels; secondly the issues of race in the sub-genre as a whole; and thirdly an augmentation of the study of these novels as part of transgender history.

Apart from Vin Packer, Ann Bannon, Randy Salem, and Valerie Taylor, who have been my main focus of, the list of notable women authors of ephemeral pocket-sized novels includes Artemis Smith (Annselm L.N.V. Morpurgo), Sloane Britain (Elaine Williams), Paula Christian (Yvonne MacManus), Joan Ellis (Julie Ellis), March Hastings (Sally Singer), Della Martin, and Rea Michaels.[53] This gives ample scope for further research. Yvonne Keller's definition of the "pro-lesbian" mode states that the authors "implemented three strategies in reaction to the conventional voyeurism of the genre: refusal to acknowledge its existence in their writing, appropriation, and subversion." This definition would appear to exclude a novel like Lora Sela's *I am a Lesbian* which, despite its lack of literary merit, and its inclusion of explicit sex scenes,[54] has a central message that lesbian couplehood is or should be legitimate. However, exceptions are always interesting to consider, and as much as Sela's novel may be stylistically bad, it may prove possible to find both literary merit and serious questioning of what masculinity is in the "virile adventures." As the collections in the hands of private collectors and in academic libraries contain lesbian-themed paperbacks of all kinds and qualities, they all remain objects of popular culture which should be studied rather than neglected.

The novels that have been my subject all privilege white society. The only significant character who is other than European-American is Ann Bannon's Tris Robischon, in *Women in the Shadows*. Tris has "jade green eyes" and skin "the color of three parts cream and one part coffee," and has a *bindi* on her forehead.[55] She is a character "full of contradictions,"[56] presents as Indian to give herself a kind of exoticism in society but is in fact African-American. Her ability to "pass" as South Asian has parallels with Audre Lorde's mother being able to pass as "spanish [sic]" in *Zami*.[57] Racial stereotyping is not

---

53 See Keller, "Pulp Politics: Strategies of Vision in Pro-Lesbian Pulp Novels 1955-1965." 20-21n4. Keller's list only includes the pen names; I have supplied the authors' given names from other sources. Valerie Taylor is included along with Packer, Bannon, and Salem, even though I have concluded, earlier in this book, that *Whisper Their Love* is not a "pro-lesbian" oeuvre; her Erika Frohmann novels set the rest of her corpus apart.

54 unattributed, "*I am a Lesbian*," Review, *The Ladder* (January 1959). 17.

55 Bannon, *Women in the Shadows*. 30.

56 Bannon, *Women in the Shadows*. 72.

57 Audre Lorde, *Zami: a new spelling of my name* (Pandora, 2003). 1. The lower case "s" in "spanish" is typical of Lorde's usage, and the word may in fact refer to "Hispanic" as in

184   *Conclusion*

uncommon throughout the sub-genre; in Randy Salem's *Man among Women* for example, there is a scene in a bar in the Bahamas where black musicians and a dancer perform, and to Yvonne Keller, the scene "animalizes and primitivizes the Bahamians with stereotyped racist, sexist, and colonialist images."[58] To find anything within the sub-genre in which a person of colour is a principal one has to look to the novels of Rea Michaels, such as *Duet in Darkness* or *How Dark My Love,* with the coded shame-word "dark" in their titles,[59] or to Arthur Adlon's *A Special Passion* and Dale Greggsen's *Sisterhood of the Flesh.* All of the foregoing open up the possibility of examining "Euronormativity" within the sub-genre.

In the introduction, I briefly mentioned Melina Alice Moore's 2019 article in which she posited Beebo Brinker as a mid-twentieth-century figure and "an integral part of the history of trans storytelling."[60] In doing so, Moore refers back to the familiar "inversion" rhetoric of *The Well of Loneliness,* noting that a cheap paperback version of Radclyffe Hall's novel meant that Stephen Gordon "circulate[d] alongside Beebo as a contemporary representative masculine figure" in the 1950s and 60s.[61] Moore proposes that "Bannon's Beebo, inspired by Hall, shaped by inversion plots, and published alongside explicitly trans 'pulp' texts that shared a similar lineage, becomes an important bridge between inversion discourse and twentieth-century transmasculinity."[62] A late twentieth-century comment from Jay Prosser notes that "being trapped in the wrong body has become the crux of an authenticating transsexual 'rhetoric'" and that misembodiment "continues to be evoked in transsexual accounts […]."[63] To Prosser, this rhetoric still has "discursive power" and he states that "transsexuals continue to deploy the image of wrong embodiment because being trapped in the wrong body is simply what transsexuality feels like."[64] This introduces the possibility of studying, as trans texts, not simply the "dozens" of trans-themed novels that, according to Moore, cashed in on the fame of Christine Jorgensen[65] but also the even greater number of lesbian-themed novels, to see if the latter's masculine characters similarly support the bridge between inversion discourse and twenty-*first*-century transmasculinity.

Central- or South-American, rather than Iberian.

58 Keller, "Pulp Politics: Strategies of Vision in Pro-Lesbian Pulp Novels 1955-1965." 11.

59 C.f. titles containing "Shadows," "Twilight," etc.

60 Melina Alice Moore, "'A Boy Inside It': Beebo Brinker and the Transmasculine Narratives of Ann Bannon's Lesbian Pulp," *GLQ: A Journal of Lesbian and Gay Studies* 25, no. 4 (2019). 571.

61 Moore, "'A Boy Inside It': Beebo Brinker and the Transmasculine Narratives of Ann Bannon's Lesbian Pulp." 575.

62 Moore, "'A Boy Inside It': Beebo Brinker and the Transmasculine Narratives of Ann Bannon's Lesbian Pulp." 583.

63 Jay Prosser, *Second Skins: The Body Narratives of Transsexuality* (Columbia UP, 1998). 69.

64 Prosser, *Second Skins: The Body Narratives of Transsexuality.* 69.

65 Moore, "'A Boy Inside It': Beebo Brinker and the Transmasculine Narratives of Ann Bannon's Lesbian Pulp." 571.

Conclusion 185

It would also raise the question of whether considering these books to be trans texts would effectively erase their relevance to lesbianism – an issue which gender critical commenters would be bound to raise.

However, this point of view, which essentially looks back to an older model of homosexuality as transgender, is not the only contending theory for the attention of a student. Misembodiment is challenged by the likes of Jason Cromwell, who asks the rhetorical question, "If I have the wrong body, whose body do I have and where is my body?"[66] The tendency amongst the queer community of the twenty-twenties is to downplay dysphoria and emphasise joy, even when looking back a century. Jessica Taylor's recent study of E.M. Hull's 1919 novel *The Sheik* focuses on the "trans joy" of its protagonist Diana.[67] This sits a little more comfortably not only with Jack Mann's admonition to Beebo that there is "nothing wrong" with her body,[68] but also with the female masculinity of, say, Christopher Hamilton, for whom her body is the least of her problems, than it does with dysphoria narratives.

Most of the novels selected during research for this book have had second and third lives, and several are still in print. I have shown how they could serve as a space of masculine negotiation within the era and culture in which they originated. However, their continued life as texts that are read for pleasure and studied academically places them in relation to current considerations of gender and sexuality. Their narrative tension(s) fit them for the arena where dysphoria and joy contend for attention. It is possible to look at the conclusion of this book – that masculinity can neither be adequately defined, nor appropriated by a single type of body, being equally unsuccessful in any body – as a rather nihilistic one. This very lack of success, though impelled by the necessity of narrative tension, is sufficient to bring these mid-twentieth-century novels into contemporary reappraisals of gender and character traits. The masculinity crisis of the 1950s, and its manifestation in cheap novels, bears comparison with modern right-wing taunts of "#SoyBoy" and "cuck" on social media, and the right's obsession with effeminacy.[69] The social media explosion is as significant an ongoing mass literacy event as the paperback boom, if not more so, given its active rather than passive involvement. The inversion model of homosexuality may be called into question as archaic; but given the way that trans people, which in its broadest sense means anyone who does not accede to society's view on (their) gender,[70] are

---

66 Jason Cromwell, *Transmen and FTMs: Identities, Bodies, Genders, and Sexualities* (U of Illinois P, 1999). 25.
67 Jessica Taylor, "*Garçon manqué*: A Queer Rereading (of) The Sheik," *Journal of Popular Romance Studies*, no. 9 (2020). 3, 13.
68 Bannon, *Beebo Brinker*. 51.
69 Iselin Gambert and Tobias Linné, "From Rice Eaters to Soy Boys: Race, Gender, and Tropes of 'Plant Food Masculinity'," *Animal Studies Journal* 7, no. 2 (2018). 131-132.
70 Jason Cromwell, for example, uses the term "trans" to "encompass all manifestations of transness." Jason Cromwell, "Skin Memories," in *Thinking through the skin*, ed. Sara Ahmed and Jackie Stacey (Routledge, 2001). 263.

186 *Conclusion*

developing the vocabulary to express gender-divergence,[71] while their critics vehemently decry this vocabulary as propaganda, the novels dealt with in this book still have a clear role in the interrogation of gender. I coined the term "heteroemulative" to balance "heteronormative," and to propose that what was perceived or promoted as a "norm" was a cultural imposition which did not necessarily harmonise with nature, and that emulation can be ruinous.[72] Bearing that in mind, the novels under study here not only suggest that masculinity – no matter how you define it – cannot be confined to male bodies, but also suggest that gender is and genders are insufficiently understood overall and are due for a radical reappraisal. The nihilistic conclusion that masculinity and heteronormativity, no matter who emulates them, are failures is not necessarily a bad thing. As Jack Halberstam points out, it is the folly of "positive thinking" that attributes failure to bad attitude rather than structural conditions, and that failure preserves some of the wondrous anarchy of childhood and disturbs the supposedly clean boundaries between winners and losers.[73] This anarchy, where gender is stirred up, is where the reappraisal begins.

---

71 Cromwell, *Transmen and FTMs: Identities, Bodies, Genders, and Sexualities.* 25.

72 That emulation can be ruinous is not a new concept. Writing in 1828, Isaac D'Israeli said of bourgeois life in the reign of Charles I of England, that "the people were invited [by the repeal of laws against excess in apparel] to ruin their families in *emulative costliness.*" Isaac D'Israeli, *Commentaries on the Life and Reign of Charles the First, King of England*, vol. 1 (London: Henry Colburn, 1828). 65, my emphasis.

73 Jack Halberstam, *The Queer Art of Failure* (Duke UP, 2011). 3.

Bibliography

Aldrich, Ann. *We Walk Alone*. The Feminist Press, 2006.

Bannon, Ann. *Beebo Brinker*. Cleis, 2001.

———. *I am a Woman*. Cleis, 2002.

———. *Journey to a Woman*. Cleis, 2003.

———. "The Nice Kid." *ONE Magazine* 9, no. 1 (1961): 23–28.

———. *Odd Girl Out*. Cleis, 2001.

———. *Women in the Shadows*. Cleis, 2002.

Bradley, Marion Zimmer, and Gene Damon. *Checklist 1960: A Complete, Cumulative Checklist of Lesbian, Variant, and Homosexual Fiction, in English, or Available in English Translation, with Supplements of Related Material, for the Use of Collectors, Students, and Librarians*. Self-published by Marion Zimmer Bradley, 1960.

Cromwell, Jason. "Skin Memories." In *Thinking through the Skin*, edited by Sara Ahmed and Jackie Stacey, 52–68. Routledge, 2001.

———. *Transmen and Ftms: Identities, Bodies, Genders, and Sexualities*. University of Illinois Press, 1999.

D'Israeli, Isaac. *Commentaries on the Life and Reign of Charles the First, King of England*. Vol. 1. Henry Colburn, 1828.

Faderman, Lillian, and Stuart Timmons. *Gay L.A.: A History of Sexual Outlaws, Power Politics, and Lipstick Lesbians*. Basic Books, 2006.

Feinberg, Leslie. *Stone Butch Blues*. self-published, 2014. tinyurl.com/StoneButchB.

Foreman, Joel, ed. *The Other Fifties: Interrogating Mid-Century American Icons*. University of Illinois Press, 1997.

Gambert, Iselin, and Tobias Linné. "From Rice Eaters to Soy Boys: Race, Gender, and Tropes of 'Plant Food Masculinity'." *Animal Studies Journal* 7, no. 2 (2018): 129–79.

Gilbert, James. *Men in the Middle: Searching for Masculinity in the 1950s*. University of Chicago Press, 2005.

Hacking, Ian. *The Taming of Chance*. Cambridge University Press, 2004.

Halberstam, Jack. *The Queer Art of Failure*. Duke University Press, 2011.

Hubbard, Lafayette Ronald. *Dianetics: The Modern Science of Mental Health*. New Era, 2007.

Jeffreys, Sheila. *Unpacking Queer Politics: A Lesbian Feminist Perspective*. Polity Press in association with Blackwell, 2003.

Kafka, Franz. *Letter to the Father / Brief an Den Vater*. Translated by Philip Boehm. The Schocken Kafka Library. Schocken, 2013.

Keller, Yvonne. "Pulp Politics: Strategies of Vision in Pro-Lesbian Pulp Novels 1955–1965." In *The Queer Sixties*, edited by Patricia Juliana Smith, 1–25. Routledge, 1999.

Lochrie, Karma. *Heterosyncrasies: Female Sexuality When Normal Wasn't*. University of Minnesota Press, 2005.

Lorde, Audre. *Zami: A New Spelling of My Name*. Pandora, 2003.

Oxford English Dictionary. 3rd ed. Oxford University Press, 2021.

Miller, Allyson. "Postwar Masculine Identity in Ann Bannon's *I am a Woman*." University of Missouri-Columbia, 2009.

Moore, Melina Alice. "'A Boy inside It': Beebo Brinker and the Transmasculine Narratives of Ann Bannon's Lesbian Pulp." *GLQ: A Journal of Lesbian and Gay Studies* 25, no. 4 (2019): 569–98.

Nestle, Joan. "Butch-Fem Relationships: Sexual Courage in the 1950s." *Heresies 12: Sex Issue* 3, no. 4 (1981): 21–24.

Packer, Vin. *Spring Fire*. Cleis, 2004.

188 *Conclusion*

Poovey, Mary. *A History of the Modern Fact: Problems of Knowledge in the Sciences and Society*. University of Chicago Press, 1998.

Prosser, Jay. *Second Skins: The Body Narratives of Transsexuality*. Columbia University Press, 1998.

Rechy, John. *City of Night*. Grove Press, 1964.

Salem, Randy. *Chris*. Naiad, 1989.

Speer, Lisa K. "Paperback Pornography: Mass Market Novels and Censorship in Post-War America." *Journal of American & Comparative Cultures*, no. 24 (2001): 153–60.

Stanley, Eric A. "Introduction: Fugitive Flesh: Gender Self-Determination, Queer Abolition, and Trans Resistance." In *Captive Genders: Trans Embodiment and the Prison Industrial Complex*, edited by Eric A. Stanley and Nat Smith, 1–14. AK Press, 2011.

Taylor, Jessica. "Garçon Manqué: A Queer Rereading (of) the Sheik." *Journal of Popular Romance Studies*, no. 9 (2020): 1–20.

Taylor, Valerie. *Whisper Their Love*. Little Sister's Classics. Arsenal Pulp Press, 2006.

unattributed. "I Am a Lesbian." Review. *The Ladder* (January 1959): 17.

Woodward, L.T. *Twilight Women*. Lancer, 1963.

Index

Abate, Michelle Ann 77, 84, 87
Achmuty, Rosemary 118n65
Adlon, Arthur 58
Adventures of Ozzie and Harriet, The 129–130
Ahmed, Sara 152
Alcott, Louisa May 12
Aldrich, Ann 14n73, 27, 92, 174n2; *see also* Marijane Meaker
Al-Issa, Ihsan 124, 124n107
American Book Publishers Council 18n100, 23
American Journal of Psychotherapy, The 124, 124n107
American Library Association 18n100
American Scholar, The 24
Antioch Review, The 14
Artists and Models see Tashlin, Frank
Artists' Model see Bligh, Norman
Atlantic Coast Independent Distributors Association 8

Baldwin, James 135
Bannon, Ann, xi–xv, xviii, 2–4, 4n18, 6, 7, 10, 14n73, 25, 27, 28, 36–37, 39n28, 41n41, 52, 57, 66, 70, 76, 77n17, 79, 80, 84, 86, 87, 94, 94n139, 95, 97, 98n167, 114n40, 116, 129n139, 130n145, 134–137, 140n36, 141, 153–154, 155n141, 157; *Beebo Brinker* xiii, 30, 31, 36, 68, 78, 81, 96, 98–103, 138, 140n36, 161–164, 182n44; *I am a Woman* 2–3, 29, 30, 36, 41, 55, 77, 83–86, 88, 94, 98n165, 148–150, 165–167, 169, 177; *Journey to a Woman* 29, 30, 36, 56–68, 77, 81, 85–90, 94–96, 102–103, 169, 170, 177–178, 181, 182; *Marriage, The* 30–31, 76, 93, 137–144, 146–147, 149–151, 153,
169; "Nice Kid, The" 69n253, 147n83, 182; *Odd Girl Out* 6, 7, 17, 21, 25, 29, 36, 40–41, 52, 55, 57, 76, 89–90, 94n139, 96, 107, 108, 135, 140, 147, 150–151, 164–165, 177, 181; "Secrets of the Gay Novel" 76n15; *Women in the Shadows* 30, 57, 65, 68, 77, 83, 86–90, 93, 96, 97, 102, 103, 122, 138, 147–154, 167, 170, 181–183
Bantam Books 8n42, 14
Banyard, Kat 84n69
Barnes, Djuna 8, 79–80
Barthes, Roland 10
Beacon-Signal Books 24, 118
Beebo Brinker see Bannon, Ann
Ben, Lisa *see* Eyde, Edith
Bergler, Edmund 124
"Big Handsome Hero" 22n121, 37, 51, 69, 95, 175
Black, Bruce 11
Black, Samuel 8
Blank, Paula 80
Bligh, Norman: *Artists' Model* 19
bluff *see* ki-ki lesbian
Bogaert, Anthony F. 123
Bonn, Thomas L. 9n43
Bookscans (website) 11–12
Bradbury-Rance, Clara 117n61
Bradley, Marion Zimmer 27, 37, 40, 95, 111, 119n67, 122, 125, 155n139
Brinker, Beebo (character) xii, xvi, 3, 4n17, 30, 56n157, 58, 65, 68, 74–78, 80–81, 83–90, 94–103, 107, 110, 120–122, 147–150, 154, 162–164, 166–167, 169, 177, 181–182, 184, 185
Britain, Sloane 183
Brooks, Peter 96
Brown, Charles Brockden 142n51, 145

190   Index

Brown, Susan Love 45n72, 48, 127
Brown, William Hill 141
Browning, Elizabeth Barrett 12
Burr, Raymond 165
butch 15, 16, 30, 39, 40, 73–95, 98–99,
    101–102, 107–114, 120, 130, 157,
    175, 176; butch-femme xi, xvi, 3,
    5, 15, 80, 84, 91, 113, 176; butch-
    fluff 78, 80, 91; stone 85, 101n197,
    120, 122
Butler, Judith 4n20, 51, 134–135
Byron, George Gordon (6th Baron
    Byron) 141

Cahn, Sammy 134, 166
Caine, Carol 135
Caldwell, Greg 52
Canguilhem, Georges 100
Capote, Truman 12
Carlton, Bukk G. 136
Carroll, Dick 21, 23, 24, 41, 93n133,
    135, 155n141
Carter, Julian 83n58, 90n114, 139n26,
    146n80, 151n121, 153–154, 170
Cartier, Marie 91
Cassill, R. V. 52, 53
Chandler, Daniel 89
Chateaubriand, François-René de
    141, 142
Chesterton, G. K. 12
Chris see Salem, Randy
Christian, Paula 8, 21, 25, 79, 183
Cleis Press 21, 29, 41, 67n236, 76, 95,
    118n66, 134, 157
Cohen, Jack 13n65
Collins, Susan (U.S. Senator) 17
"Comstock laws" 21
Cooper, Pauline 52n114
Cooper's Doughnuts 174nn1–2
Corman, Roger 145
Coulter, Adam 16
Coward-McCann 14
Cromwell, Jason 185

Daigh, Ralph Foster 20, 21
Damon, Gene 29, 37, 40, 111, 119n67,
    122, 125, 128n129, 155n139
Davis, Madeline D. 15n74, 78n24,
    92n122
deadname 113, 118
de Beauvoir, Simone 54n136, 108–109,
    114–116, 141, 152, 157–158, 170
de Graff, Robert 11

de Grazia, Edward 20, 22
Dexter, John 52
diabazophilia 27
diavazophilia 27n165
Dijkstra, Sandra 168
Dirksen, Everett (U.S. Senator) 137n22
dominance 15, 16, 45, 74n8, 85, 97,
    108, 129–131, 152, 155, 175, 176
Dorr, Lisa Lindquist 44–45, 47nn80–81,
    50, 85n75, 115n46
Duff, David 145
Duggan, Lisa 153, 170
du Maurier, Daphne 58
Dworkin, Andrea 21–22

Echols, Alice 113
Editions for The Armed Services Inc. 11
Eisenhower, Dwight D. 12
Elder, Joe (literary agent) 21
Eliot, George 12
Ellis, Joan 31, 52, 115, 183; Girls
    Dormitory 31, 115–116, 130–131
Ellis, Milton 141n48
ephebophilia 52
Ermayne, Laurajean 78–79
"Exurbanite" 46, 64n217, 137
Exurbanites, The see Spectorsky,
    Auguste C.
Eyde, Edith 78, 79

Faderman, Lillian 84nn63–64, 85, 93,
    120n77
Farber, Gary xvii, 9
Fawcett Gold Medal see Fawcett
    Publications
Fawcett Publications 11, 12, 20, 21;
    Fawcett Gold Medal 6, 10, 12, 20–
    23, 41n41, 54–56, 76, 79, 93n133,
    118, 138, 155n141
Feinberg, Leslie 75, 77, 78n22,
    80, 83n57, 85n78, 102, 157;
    Stone Butch Blues 30, 75–77, 80,
    83n57, 85n78, 90, 95, 102, 120,
    157, 176
female masculinity 30, 73–133, 185
Feminist Press 29, 155n139
Fernie, Lynne 14n73, 130n144
fetishisation 16, 113; of lesbians 25,
    27–28, 68
Fielder, Leslie 146n77
Finch, Janet 129
Foote, Stephanie 27
Forrest, Katherine V. 25–26, 75n12

Index 191

Foucault, Michel 43–44, 83n56, 94, 136, 137, 167, 180
Fountainhead, The see Rand, Ayn
fraternities 35, 41–52, 54, 181
Fried, Richard M. 17
Frieden, Betty 114n40, 168
frigidity 108, 122–125
Frohmann, Erika *see* Taylor, Valerie

Gardner, Erle Stanley xv
Gathings, Ezekiel Chandler (Member of U.S. Congress) 18; "Gathings Committee" (*Investigation of Literature allegedly containing Objectionable Material: Hearings before the Select Committee on Current Pornographic Materials*) 8, 12, 13, 18–21, 51–52
"Gathings Committee" *see* Gathings, Ezekiel Chandler
gender iii, xii, xvi, 1, 3–6, 17, 18, 25n141, 27, 31, 51, 57, 68, 73, 75, 76, 80n38, 81–83, 86–89, 91–93, 96–98, 100–101, 103, 104, 111, 112, 123, 127, 152, 168n248, 174, 175, 179n20, 182, 185–186
gender critical 74, 185
Gilbert, James: *Men in the Middle* 17, 36, 37, 46, 64, 97, 130
Ginsberg, Allen 18n101
Girls Dormitory see Ellis, Joan
Goldberg, Jess (character) 30, 76–78, 102
Gold Medal Books *see* Fawcett Publications
Goodwin, Doris Kearns 10
Gordon, Stephen (character) 30, 76, 77, 79–82, 92, 101, 118, 119n73, 121, 184
Granahan, Kathryn E. (Member of U.S. Congress) 23; *see also* Subcommittee on Postal Operations of the Committee on Post Office and Civil Service.
Greenwich Village 55–56, 81, 84, 89, 93–94, 125
Greggsen, Dale 184
Grey, Zane 145
Grier, Barbara 1, 2, 25, 112, 158, 160
Guillaumin, Collette 61n197, 116, 149
Gutterman, Lauren Jae 117, 124

Hacker, Helen Mayer 115
Halberstam, Jack 4n20, 5, 35, 74, 75, 98, 175; *Female Masculinity*

35, 35n1, 69, 73, 98; *Queer Art of Failure, The* 5, 186; *Trans** 3, 5, 87n90, 101n190
Half see Kornbluth, Cyril
Hall, Radclyffe 76, 77, 79, 92, 118; *Well of Loneliness, The* 80, 81, 126, 184
Hall, Stuart 4n19
Hamer Diane 57n163
Hamilton, Christopher (character) xvi, 117, 119–123, 125–128, 131, 169, 177, 182, 185
Hastings, March 117n62, 134, 183
Hawthorne, Nathaniel 142n51, 145
Hector, Alley 90, 90n115
Hedler, Leona 93n133, 155n141
Hermes, Joke 6
heterocuriosity 110, 158
heteroemulativity iii, xii, 136, 148, 150, 153, 156, 161, 163, 167, 170, 177, 186
heteronormativity iii, xi, xii, xvi, 4, 29, 96, 119, 136–138, 143n65, 146, 152, 153, 161, 165, 167, 174, 177, 182, 186
Highsmith, Patricia xv, 14, 15n76, 27, 84; *see also* Morgan, Claire
Hitt, Orrie 52
Holk, Agnete 16
Holliday, Don 52
homophobia 25, 50, 86
House Committee on Un-American Activities 17
Housman, A. E. 12
Hubbard, L. Ron 179–180
Hull, E. M. 185

I am a Woman see Bannon, Ann
incest 64, 137–138, 140–149, 156n151, 169
intersex xii, 4
Isherwood, Christopher 12–13
Ivy League 45, 46, 69, 139

Jack Woodford Press, The 19
James, Henry 12
Jameson Frederic 28, 29
Jamieson, John 11n56
Jeffreys, Sheila 5, 74, 175, 176; *Unpacking Queer Politics* 5, 175
Johnson, David K. 137n22
Jorgensen, Christine 4n21, 184
Josselyn Irene 46
Journey to a Woman see Bannon, Ann

192 Index

Keller, Yvonne 2, 10, 25, 37, 177n15, 183
Kennedy, Elizabeth Lapovsky 15n74, 78n24, 92n122
Kent, Harrison 16
Khazan, Olga 26–27
ki-ki lesbians 75, 91–93; bluff 91
Kipling, Rudyard 12
Kornbluth, Cyril: *Half* 4n21
Koski, Fran 6, 25
Krafft-Ebing, Richard von 82
Kramer, Gerald: *Penthouse Party* 16
ky-ky *see* ki-ki lesbians

Lacy, Dan 23, 24
Ladder, The 2, 38, 79, 109n10
"Landon-Brinkeriad" 76, 80n38, 86, 88, 90, 96, 102, 104, 138, 146, 164
Landon, Laura (character) 31, 36, 55–69, 76–78, 83–91, 93, 94n139, 97, 102–104, 108, 122, 138, 141, 143, 146–156, 164–167, 169, 170, 181, 182
Landon, Merrill (character) 29, 36, 54–68, 69n253, 70, 150
Lansbury, Angela 167
Larrabee, Eric 20–21
Lawrence, D. H. 12
Lawson, John Howard 161
Leach, Edmund 65n216, 137n20
Lesbian in Literature, The 29, 115, 128
Levi, Rene 52
Levin, Carl (U.S. Senator) 17
Lochrie, Karma 40n34, 100, 136, 180, 181n32
Lorde, Audre 5, 92, 94, 103; *Zami: A New Spelling of my Name* 5, 92, 103, 129, 183
Love, Heather 117
Lucerne, Bob 52
Luksic, Nicola 76
Lynch, Jennifer M. xviii, 22, 23

McCarrick, Malia 2, 3
McCarthy, Joseph (U.S. Senator) 10, 17–18
McCarthyism 10, 17, 137n22
McHale, Brian 1n4
MacManus, Yvonne 183
MacNeil, Kerry 92
Madigan, Kip 144
Makinen, Marja 28, 29, 118n64
Malenkov, Georgi 82
"male panic" 37n7, 46, 70, 97, 130, 177

Mann, Jack (character) xiii, 31, 69, 75, 83–84, 86–87, 97, 98n165, 100, 103, 138–141, 143, 146–151, 151n121, 152–156, 169n254, 170, 181–182, 185
Mann, Laura (character) *see* Landon, Laura
Mann, Peter H. 28–29
Marie Claire 26
Markham, Clancy 16
Marriage, The see Bannon, Ann
Marshall, Edward 16
Martin, Della 134, 183
"masculinity crisis" 29, 36, 37n7, 46, 47, 64, 70, 130, 177, 185
Mason, Todd xvii, 10, 134
Matelski, Elizabeth M. 3
Maugham, W. Somerset 12
Meaker, Marijane xviii, 8, 27, 84, 92, 178n17; *see also* Packer, Vin
melodrama 39, 40, 57, 102, 143
Melville, Hermann 142n51, 145
Mentor Books 11
Michaels, Rea 183, 184
Midwood Books 24, 115n47, 118
Miller, Allyson 2, 3, 177
Miller, Meredith 93n133, 96
Moll, Keely 26n154
Monarch Books 24, 144
Montefiore, Simon Sebag 82
Moore, Melina Alice 3, 4, 75n12, 101n190, 184–185
Morgan, Claire 14; *Price of Salt, The* xvii, 14, 30, 41n42, 108, 116–117, 130
Morgan, Helen 16
Morpurgo, Annselm L. N. V. 183
Morro, Don 16
Morse, Benjamin 124
Moskin, J. Robert 46n74

Naiad Press 29, 41, 118n66, 128
NAL *see* New American Library
Nealon, Christopher 2, 10, 17, 39n28, 57, 68, 69, 83n58, 85–86, 88, 135, 167
Nestle, Joan 5, 95, 113, 176; "Butch-Fem Relationships: Sexual Courage in the 1950s" 5, 176; "Fem Question, The" 95; *Restricted Country, A* 113–114; "Will to Remember, A" 114
New American Library 10–12
New York 15n76, 24, 55, 58, 60–61, 66, 76, 78, 84, 99, 116, 161, 181

Index   193

New York Times 19
Noble, Jean Bobby 75, 78n22, 94, 101
Norday, Michael 52
Norton, Clark 145n72

Ogas, Ogi 26
Orwell, George xv, 12, 82
Ozard, Stephanie 14, 26

Packer, Vin xviii, 8, 19, 21, 25, 41,
  54, 79, 80, 134, 175, 180, 183;
  Spring Fire 8, 21, 25, 29, 41–44,
  45n69, 47–53, 70, 80, 118n64, 135,
  178–181
Page, Bettie 28
paperback original 12, 14, 21, 118,
  124, 128
Park, Jordan 52
Pasquini, Pete (character) 68, 99
Pasternak, Boris 13
Penelope, Julia 91
Penguin Books 11
Perkins, Sue 135
Permanent Subcommittee on
  Investigations on Government
  Operations 17
Phi Beta Kappa Society 24
Phillips, Baryé 14, 51
Plain, Gill 152
Pocket Books 10, 11, 13–14
Poe, Edgar Allan 142n51, 145–146
pop-Freudianism 15, 42n45, 63, 65
Pornhub 26
Pornography 20, 23–26
Pourdes, M. D. 124
Pratt, Theodore 19; *Tormented, The* 18
Price of Salt, The see Morgan, Claire
"pro-lesbian" 10, 25, 30, 41, 85,
  111–112, 155n139, 157, 175n3, 183
Prorokova, Tatiana 86
Prosser, Jay 184
pulp xi–xv, 1, 2, 4n21, 6–10,
  12–14, 25–26, 76, 115, 134–135,
  175n3, 184
"Pulp Fiction" (movie) 6

Rabinowitz, Paula 9, 10, 12; *American
  Pulp* 7, 11, 12, 17
Rand, Ayn 36, 47, 70; *Fountainhead,
  The* 36, 48, 70
rape 39, 42, 44, 45, 47, 48, 54,
  83n57, 85, 86, 127, 150n114, 152,
  158, 181

Reagan, Ronald (State Governor) 168
Rechy, John 174
Reissner, Albert 123n98, 124
Rich, Adrienne 123
Roark, Howard (character) 48, 64, 70
Rogers & Hammerstein 35, 37
Romanticism 137, 142, 144–146
Rubin, Gayle 4n20, 73–75, 77n21,
  92–93, 95, 102, 108, 114, 175

Saber Books 24, 38, 144
Saint-Aubin, Arthur Flannigan 152n124
Salem, Randy xv, xvi, 30, 117n62, 121,
  175, 177, 183; *Baby Face* 129n139;
  Chris 30, 31, 68–69, 108, 117–122,
  125–129, 182; *Man among Women*
  184; *Sex Between, The* 118nn63,
  65, 169
Salisbury, Harrison E. 13
Savard, Frédéric 145n73
Scott Meredith (literary agency) 21
"scv" *see* "short course in voyeurism"
Sedgwick, Eve Kosovsky 4n20, 73–
  74, 175
Seeley, E. S. 52, 113n32, 114; *Sorority
  Sin* 30, 108, 112–113, 130
Sela, Lora 38, 70, 114n40; *I am a
  Lesbian* 16, 29, 35, 37–41, 108–109,
  130, 152, 170, 183
Select Committee on Current
  Pornographic Materials *see*
  "Gathings Committee"
Senn, Kathleen 15n76
Sex and Censorship 38
Shelley, Percy Bysshe 141–142
Shield, Frank 52
Shklovsky, Viktor 2n4
"short course in voyeurism" 37
Signet Books 11, 48n89
Silverberg, Robert 15n75, 80n33,
  179n20
Simon and Schuster 11
Simon, Richard L. 11
Sinclair-Palm, Julia 113n33
Singer, Sally 117n62, 183
Sky, Melissa 2, 25, 88n95, 98n167
Smith, Artemis 183
Smyth, Cherry 87
sororities 41–44, 47–48, 51–53,
  94n139, 179, 181
Sorority Sin see Seeley, E. S.
Spectorsky, Auguste C. 46, 64n217;
  Exurbanites, The 46

194   *Index*

Speer, Lisa K. 175
Spillane, Mickey 145
Spring Fire see Packer, Vin
Steinbeck, John 19; *Wayward Bus, The*
   18, 19
Stekel, Wilhelm 125
Stevenson, Robert Louis 12
Stone Butch Blues see Feinberg, Leslie
Stonewall riots 91, 174
"stop order" 22
Storms, Michael D. 123
Stratton, S. Lou 2, 83n58, 92
Stryker, Susan 4n20
Subcommittee on Postal Operations of the
   Committee on Post Office and Civil
   Service 18, 23–24
Summerfield, Arthur E. (Member of U.S.
   Congress) 23–24
Summerfield, Penny 129
Swenson, Peggy 52

Tabet, Paola 94
Taft, Robert A. (U.S. Senator) 17
Tarantino, Quentin 6
Tashlin, Frank 7; *Artists and Models*
   (movie) 1, 7
Taylor, Valerie xv, 8, 79, 111, 114n40,
   175,183; "ErikaFrohmannseries" 144,
   183n53; *Journey to Fulfillment* 91;
   *WhisperTheirLove*1,44,53,108–112,
   120n77, 155–161, 163, 164; *World
   without Men, A* 144
Thorn, Abigail 84n69
Tilchen, Maida 6, 25
Tóibin, Colm 5
Tormented, The see Pratt, Theodore
Torrès, Tereska: *Women's Barracks* 19,
   51–52, 79
transgender xvi, 4, 27, 30n178, 87n90,
   113n33, 183, 185
transmasculinity 75, 101n190, 103, 109,
   113n33, 169, 184
transsexualism 96–97, 102n202, 104
transvestite 110
Tyner, Dick 144
Tynyanov, Yury 1n4, 3n13

Unmoral see Woodford, Jack
U.S. Post Office xviii, 18, 20–24

Vance, Carole S. 144–145
Vice Versa 78–80, 91–92
Village Voice, The 6, 54, 121
Villarejo, Amy 5, 14
violence6,44,47,56,69,126–128,142n58,
   152, 157, 166, 182
"virile adventure" 37, 70, 112,
   176, 183
voyeurism 25, 27–28, 37, 79n26, 127,
   129n139, 175n3, 183

Wade, Carlson 125
Walker v. Popenoe (legal case) 22
Walters, Suzanna Danuta 87
Wayward Bus, The see Steinbeck, John
Weinstein, Jeff 6, 54n142, 62, 121n88
Weir, Angela 119, 120, 122, 125–128
Weissman, Aerlyn 14n73, 130n144
Well of Loneliness, The see Hall,
   Radclyffe
West, Edwin 144
Whitbread, Jane 45, 47n80, 127
Whitfield, Stephen J. 137n22
Wilcox, William Bradford 167n246
Wilhelm, Gale 8; *We Too Are
   Drifting* 126
Williams, A. P. 16
Williams, Elaine 183
Willis, A. M. 16
Willow, Peter 16
Wilson,Elizabeth119,120,122,125–128
Wilson, James D. 142
Wittig,Monique44,52,81–82,94,97,99,
   138, 148, 151, 152, 164
Women's Barracks see Torrès, Tereska
Woodford, Jack 19; *Unmoral* 18, 19
Woodward, L. T. *see* Silverberg, Robert

Yusba, Roberta 17n95, 25, 129–130

Zeig, Sande 51, 81–83
Zhdanov, Andrei 82